METHODOLOGY IN THE STUDY OF INTERNATIONAL RELATIONS

METHODOLOGY IN THE STUDY OF INTERNATIONAL RELATIONS

By

TRYGVE MATHISEN

FELLOW, THE NORWEGIAN RESEARCH COUNCIL FOR
SCIENCE AND THE HUMANITIES

GREENWOOD PRESS, PUBLISHERS
WESTPORT, CONNECTICUT

076387

Library of Congress Cataloging in Publication Data

Mathisen, Trygve.
 Methodology in the study of international relations.

 Reprint of the 1959 ed. published by Oslo University
Press, Oslo.
 Bibliography: p.
 1. International relations—Study and teaching.
I. Title.
JX1291.M39 1974   327'.01'8   74-3753
ISBN 0-8371-7472-4

FOREWORD

The increasing impact of world affairs upon the everyday life of people could not fail to entail greater attention being paid to international politics. Moreover, the present state of affairs in the academic study of interstate relations has necessarily stimulated interest in problems of methodology. How are international affairs in general to be studied? Should one select a single discipline, and in that case which one? Should one rather try to extract from several subjects what seems relevant, and if so which subjects, what subject matter, and what pedagogic technique should be chosen? Is there perhaps a subject of one kind or another offering a general approach to the field within a framework suitable for a realistic study? What tools and techniques are available to the research scholar? These are some of the questions with which we are confronted.

During the past thirty years a considerable amount of work has been done in answering this kind of question. It may suffice to mention the activity of major institutions like The International Studies Conference, The Royal Institute of International Affairs in London, the Council on Foreign Relations in New York, the Carnegie Endowment for International Peace, and particularly UNESCO. But on the whole the literature on the subject is still very inadequate.

The purpose of this study is by no means to give a conclusive answer to all the questions mentioned above. What needs to be said in this respect is merely that I have devoted attention to methodological problems in this field for some years, and the present volume is the outcome of this activity.

In the first part of the book the so-called multidisciplinary method has been briefly discussed, and then the development of international relations as a special subject has been described. Textbooks are the main source material examined.

Part II is devoted to elements of international relations as conceived by the author. It was considered necessary to do more than to provide a list of topics. On the other hand, the aim was not to write a textbook, but merely to discuss methodological problems. The solution chosen was, therefore, to outline as briefly as possible the various topics, and to indicate from what point of view they may best be analyzed. Endeavors have been made to construct a model of analysis which has unity, gives a reasonably good over-all view, and can make use of the findings of the more specialized studies of international affairs. Some of the chapters are so concise that they resemble a theoretical study. The intention is, however, to deal in greater detail with some of these subjects in a later work.

In the third part some aspects of research have been dealt with. It is supposed that the solution of basic problems in this field is a prerequisite to sound progress, since research should provide the findings upon which teaching is based, although it is realized that the two sides are interdependent and interacting. The aim is not to repeat details which are well described in several textbooks, but rather to find out whether the kind of study outlined in part II is likely to meet with any impassable obstacles, and to discuss the merits and shortcomings of the various devices. The suggestions made should be looked upon merely as starting points for further improvement of the research process.

I have no illusions that my views are not vulnerable to criticism; that would seem impossible in a new and wide field like international relations. In fact, I hope that scholars interested in the subject may find my work worthy of attention and subject it to due and constructive criticism, which may enable me to elaborate it.

Reference to literature has been made in footnotes, and the alphabetical list of books appended contains only works directly concerned with methodology.

The study was started in 1951, when I received a Norwegian state grant for that purpose. The following year I was fortunate to get a Smith-Mundt research grant and a Fulbright travel grant, which enabled me to spend a year at Princeton University and to pay short visits to some other leading American centers of learning as well. I want to thank the respective authorities for recommending me for these generous grants. I am grateful also to the faculty of the Woodrow Wilson School of Public and International Affairs. I do not know whether any of these gentlemen will agree with the points of view expounded in this study. But it was most useful to me to observe in conversations and faculty seminars the way in which they looked at the problems. In particular I want to thank Professor Harold Sprout and Mrs. Margaret Sprout, who have read the entire manuscript and made numerous suggestions for improvement.

With interruptions in 1953 and 1954 I have been in a position to carry on the work as a research scholar at the Norwegian Research Council for Science and the Humanities, which also provided me with travel grants for short visits to Great Britain and Germany. I want to thank this institution as well as the Norwegian Ministry of Education for the economic support I have received.

I am much indebted to Mr. Gunnar Jahn, Chairman of the Joint Committee of the Norwegian Research Councils, for encouraging support. Professors Gutorm Gjessing and Arne Næss of the University of Oslo have been kind enough to comment on some chapters; and Fulbright Teacher David E. Mortimore and others have corrected many linguistic mistakes in the manuscript. Special thanks are due also to the library staffs of the Norwegian Foreign Ministry and the Nobel Institute in Oslo for their constant readiness to render me assistance.

Oslo, May, 1957.

Trygve Mathisen

TABLE OF CONTENTS

Some definitions. Importance and objectives. The inevitable antagonism between specialization and generalization. The search for better techniques.

PART I. THE DEVELOPMENT OF THE STUDY OF INTERNATIONAL AFFAIRS

Educational arrangements. Methodological implications of specialization.
The unitary approach in education.
The framework of the study. Basic assumptions about political behavior. The major topics.

PART II. ELEMENTS OF INTERNATIONAL RELATIONS: A PROPOSAL FOR A MODEL OF ANALYSIS

Changes in the natural environment. Physiographic factors in world affairs. Climatic factors. The political importance of resources.
Spatial variations in the pattern of culture. Implications of the accelerating dynamics.
The State System. Interstate groups. Regional variations in social structure.
Integration. Disintegration. Increasing homogeneity.
The development of world politics. The new political pattern.
Function and efficiency of law. Morality.

PART III. NOTES ON RESEARCH

INTRODUCTORY CHAPTER

Some Definitions

The development of any social science[1] seems to include an initial phase marked by considerable ambiguity of terms. The studies of international affairs share this fate with analogous branches of learning. It may, therefore, be necessary at the outset of this work to explain a few basic terms which are frequently used in the following chapters.

It may be appropriate to begin with the fundamental concept which is expressed by the term *international affairs*. It is used in this study to denote all kinds of relations traversing state boundaries, no matter whether they are of an economic, legal, political, or any other character, whether they be private or official. But the term *international* is not quite exact, since there are states which have several nationalities within their borders, and dealings *inter* such ethnic groups are naturally very different from international affairs as defined above. However, to retain the term *international* in this context may be to envisage the gradual decline of state boundaries in their present sense, while national peculiarities still remain.

The term *international politics* is used to denote only official relations, that is, relations between states as such,[2] not relations between private institutions or individuals in different

---

[1] The social sciences are conceived of in a broad sense and "may be defined as those mental and cultural sciences which deal with the activities of the individual as member of a group."- E. R. A. Seligman, "What Are the Social Sciences?" *Encyclopedia of the Social Sciences*, New York, 1930, Vol. I, p. 3.

[2] Bodies like the Catholic Church, which conduct an independent foreign policy, may be looked upon as equal to states in this respect.

states. The term *politics* implies a more restricted meaning than does *affairs* since it seems to exclude non-political aspects, whatever they may be.[3] It should, however, be added that the term is apparently far from always used in this restricted sense in the international literature.

In recent years the term *international relations* has become a semantic stumbling block which hardly any student of international affairs can manage to escape. It is being used with an increasing number of poorly defined meanings. To avoid any undue confusion, it is applied in this volume merely to denote a distinct discipline, although that is hardly the most common way of using it.[4] However, when we speak of international relations as a distinct subject, we obviously do not think of it as on a par with the older ones,[5] but rather as a sub-discipline under one or the other of the relevant major disciplines, history or political science, in a somewhat similar way as demography is dealt with as a sub-discipline under economics. But international relations may be capable of aspiring to a higher status.

---

[3] For a similar standpoint see G. Schwarzenberger, *Power Politics*, London, 1951, p. 5.

It is, of course, a moot point as to what is meant by the term *politics*. An authority regards international politics as dealing with "those forces which mold the foreign policies of national states, the manner in which they are exercised, and the influences which limit their effectiveness . . ." Grayson Kirk, *The Study of International Relations in American Colleges and Universities*, New York, 1947, p. 10.

[4] The most common meanings are: 1) A field of specialization, including the international aspects of several disciplines. 2) The history of recent international politics. 3) All international aspects of human social life: that is, the term designates all human behavior which originates on one side of a state boundary and affects human behavior on the other side of that boundary. (See C. A. Manning, *International Relations*, p. 10, for the definition given by Professor Harold H. Sprout.) It will be noted that this is exactly the same as we, in this study, mean by the term *international affairs*. 4) A distinct academic discipline. Cf. Manning, *International Relations*, Paris, 1954, p. 96.

[5] As far as the author of this volume has been able to ascertain, the only European institution which can claim to have a department of international relations is the London School of Economics, but a rapidly increasing number of chairs have been established. Several institutions in the United States give degrees in international relations, although they have no department in that subject.

Perhaps the most fundamental of all the concepts with which we are concerned is the notion of a *world society*.[6] It is conceived of as a social body integrated to such an extent that a major political event or disruption in one part of it is likely to have repercussions of varying strength in practically every other part. It is naturally a very heterogeneous body, and it is anarchical in the sense that it lacks a central authority for the maintenance of law and order. This fact influences fundamentally the patterns of behavior, and even moods, feelings, and ways of thinking. However, efforts of increasing strength —when viewed over a period of time—are devoted to the establishment of some sort of authority. The old legal notion of a society of states, somewhat ambiguously called *international society*, appears to convey a more narrow idea than does the world society, since the latter includes not merely states, but also other groups and even individuals. As for the state, we are inclined to conceive of it as one of many categories of social groups within the wider context of the world society, although we realize that it can be looked at from other points of view as well.

The necessity of introducing the world society concept is stressed by the fact that the great powers are operating on a world-wide scale, and their behavior and foreign policy strategies can hardly be properly understood except when analyzed within a world-wide context. Many authorities emphasize rightly the great spiritual dismemberment of this social body, which seems to render the use of the term *society* meaningless. It is argued that there is no common allegiance uniting the peoples of the world. However, there seems to be a small, and possibly increasing, number of people who have a sense of duty to humanity. The commonplace assertion that humanity

---

[6] There is, at present, disagreement as to whether the term *world society* or *world community* should be used.

For a rather lengthy discussion of this matter by a sociologist, see Louis Wirth, "World Community, World Society, and World Government: An Attempt at Clarification of Terms," *The World Community*, edited by Quincy Wright, Chicago, 1948.

See also the opinion of an authority on international law, P. E. Corbett, *Law and Society in the Relations of States*, New York, 1951, pp. 36—90.

lacks common goals and values needs further examination. In spite of the great variety of human social life, it may appear that the peoples of the world have many more goals and values in common than is generally realized. And it is important to remember that the world society is a social body in rather rapid transformation.[7]

When the subject of our study is given a global scope, it becomes natural to use the terms *world affairs* and *world politics* synonymously with international affairs and international politics respectively.

Importance and Objectives

The importance accorded to a set of social phenomena may not necessarily be equal to its actual importance, and it is the former which is most likely to determine the amount of energy devoted to its scientific examination. Particularly in states which for centuries have been involved in far-flung foreign policy commitments, there have long been a fair number of individuals who have studied international affairs, emphasized their importance to the nation, and occasionally even pointed out their impact upon the everyday life of the ordinary citizen. Especially in periods of war and destruction, the miseries of international anarchy have caused grave concern and engaged the best brains of the day.

Until recently the management of foreign affairs has, however, in nearly every country been entrusted to relatively few persons. Even after a high degree of political democracy had been achieved in domestic affairs, interest in this part of government remained remarkably limited. Only during the last fifty years has a far-reaching change in this state of affairs taken place. Secret diplomacy by a corps of more or less aristocratic specialists was severely denounced by liberal leaders as a major cause of war,[8] and to achieve democratic control of foreign

---

[7] This matter will be further examined in Part II.

[8] This attitude is well expressed by Frederic C. Howe in the book *Why War?*, New York, 1915.

policy became one of the major aims of the liberal parties in many countries. This aim was actually achieved by increasing the competence of the national assembly. A gradual democratization of the management of foreign affairs took place, which entailed less secrecy about international problems. And political parties began to devote more attention to foreign policy also in their activity outside the national assemblies.

This development could not fail to stimulate substantially a popular interest in international affairs. Increasing space was allotted to foreign policy issues by nearly every newspaper. Considerable reaction was bound to be felt in academic circles as well, although, initially, mainly a few time-honored disciplines benefited by it.

Gradually, people also became aware of the relative shrinking of distance. Many far-sighted persons began to realize that the technological integration of the world had proceeded to such a degree that their lives and fortunes might be jeopardized by the turn of events in the most remote parts of the globe.[9] And the last decades have revealed with increasing clarity the global nature of international affairs. Actually, this is one of the most significant social facts of our day, that the life and fortune of practically any citizen, no matter how secluded he lives and how disinterested he is in politics, may be affected by political events in any part of the globe. It is a phenomenon with both dismal and encouraging aspects, and its social and political consequences can not yet be properly assessed.

The physical and biological sciences have added new impact to the problems of international affairs. It has rightly been stressed that they have become monsters which are threatening

---

[9] An authority writing in 1930 states that: "It is an idea familiar now to everybody that the astonishing improvement in means of communications during the last hundred years has brought peoples more closely together. In old days frontiers were really frontiers. States, even neighbouring states, were far away from each other, separated by tracts of practically roadless plains, mountains, deserts or swamps. Today there are almost no frontiers. The railway, the motor car, the aeroplane care nothing for mountains, deserts, swamps or plains; and even the sea itself is only a tolerably good frontier." R. B. Mowat, *International Relations*, London, 1931, preface.

to destroy all life on the globe if we are unable to catch up with them in the social sciences. It is becoming increasingly clear that it matters comparatively little how splendidly a state manages its domestic affairs if it cannot escape the horrors of war. These facts have added greatly to the professional and humanistic appeal of the study of international affairs.

Although in a way a regionally delimited phenomenon, recent developments in the United States have had a remarkably far-reaching impact on the study of international affairs. It is widely agreed that the leadership of the United States in the Western World entails a great responsibility for which the Americans have not been too well trained. Their experience in diplomatic affairs is rather limited as compared with that of other great nations. Under these circumstances, it is only natural to believe that careful study and adequate education offer a means to prepare the citizens for the responsibility suddenly thrust upon them.[10] The efforts made in this direction have had considerable repercussions also in other parts of the world, as ideas fortunately have an extraordinary ability to penetrate the obstacles of political borders.

The motivations to a study may not merely determine to a greater or lesser extent the focus of interest, but also otherwise affect the professional handling of the subject. An analysis of the various categories of international studies seems to confirm this assumption. And it appears as if very strong or narrow motivations may also further tendencies which are undesirable from a purely scientific point of view.

A considerable part of the research in international affairs may be regarded as a by-product of national vindication and power politics. In this case, strategic considerations and economic affairs are often given great, or even undue, attention. Many studies in diplomatic history have been national in motivation, and often too much so in outlook as well. But, on the other hand, even though the immediate purpose may be narrow, the results may occasionally have far-reaching scientific impor-

---

[10] These ideas are very clearly expounded by Walter Lippmann in the article "The Shortage of Education" in the *Atlantic Monthly*, May, 1954.

tance. Many findings in international communications, for instance, have been obtained as a direct consequence of the battle for the mind of man, but the strange thing is that some of them are, nevertheless, highly interesting also from a general scientific point of view.

It appears that the overwhelming impact of the security problem has not had a favorable effect upon the academic handling of international affairs. The literature has naturally been extensively concerned with this basic problem of mankind. It seems strange that man has done wonders in his endeavors to master the forces of nature, and yet the human mind has failed in dealing with the ever-present nightmare of war, although wise men in all ages have been greatly concerned with the matter. And the desire to reform the existing state of affairs and to prevent catastrophes may, however respectable the underlying motives, at times have been too strong to allow sober reflections and scholarly thoroughness.[11] The horrors of war are usually duly emphasized, but the causes of armed interstate conflict are quite often rather speculatively dealt with; mere description of international events interspersed with scholarly exhortation is frequently practiced. It is more or less agreed that the influence of the great peace foundations and the peace movement may, to some extent, have stimulated a missionary zeal in the study of international affairs, which unfortunately has not always been an unmixed blessing.[12] It is also noteworthy that a great deal of the literature in this field has been written by practitioners of legal studies, which usually have a norm forming influence. But the value of

---

[11] Cf. E. H. Carr, *The Twenty Years Crisis 1919—1939*, second edition, p. 8.

[12] "The institutes of international affairs now existing throughout the world are at once an outgrowth of the nineteenth century peace movement and a revolt against it. Products of modern scientific temper and a more experienced understanding of world politics, the institutes are working towards international peace, not through the moral propaganda of earlier societies, but by inquiring into the complex nature of international relations and by the dissemination of accurate information." Carnegie Endowment for International Peace, *Institutes of International Affairs*, New York, 1953, p. 1. This statement referring to the operation of institutes indicates very well the development of international studies.

blueprints for a better world may occasionally have been overestimated.

It is, however, irrefutable that the dissemination of knowledge may have far-reaching consequences, since it may operate as a determinant of action and affect people's behavior. Scientific exposition of conditions generally regarded as untenable may evoke a desire to improve the position. Ignorance and confusion, on the other hand, may be serious obstacles to more confidence and tolerance, without which peaceful relations among nations are hard to obtain.[13] It is, therefore, a highly significant and encouraging fact that there actually is an increasing demand for better understanding of the complicated, if not perplexing, international aspects of the world, which ought to be met in the best possible way. To respond to this challenge is in itself a worthy aim.[14]

There is also, it seems, a more immediately practical objective. The expanding trans-boundary activity increases the demand for well-qualified personnel in a number of government agencies, such as foreign service, trade and finance, social and cultural affairs and defence. A similar development is taking place in private institutions engaged in overseas activity. Above all, it is essential to educate able leaders, as well as citizens interested and competent to guide and criticize them.[15] In view of the fatal consequences of serious mistakes in international politics, there is hardly any other field equal in importance.

Lastly should be mentioned one objective which is as yet rarely recognized. It is no longer sufficient to educate people to be citizens merely of national states. It is becoming increasingly

---

[13] "The history of mankind", writes Professor R. B. Mowat, "is the history of tolerance. First individuals had to learn, or were made, to tolerate each other. Churches took centuries to learn the lesson. Nations are still only in the process of learning it. Tolerance is not simply a mental condition or attitude. It requires knowledge and understanding. . . . The study of international affairs aims at achieving the knowledge and understanding of facts and problems, through which the tolerance and cooperation of nations are attained." *International Relations*, p. VI.

[14] This is declared to be a major aim of several recent writers. Cf. N. J. Padelford & G. A. Lincoln, *International Politics*, New York, 1954, p. VI.

[15] For a discussion of this matter see Quincy Wright, *The Study of International Relations*, pp. 65—82.

clear that we are also citizens of one and the same world. We need the intellectual and spiritual ability to adapt ourselves to the technological and social facts of an integrating world; otherwise we shall hardly be able to cope with the political problems with which we are confronted by this development.[16]

Although the importance of feelings and sentiments should by no means be ignored, it seems natural that the student of international affairs, in the capacity of scientist, should address his achievements primarily to reason. The significance of his work will necessarily be dependent on the role of reason in the dealings between nations. It is a foregone conclusion that the study of international affairs should endeavor to guide the development of interstate relations in a direction beneficial to mankind.[17] But there are greatly varying opinions as to what

---

[16] The working party set up by the Executive Board of UNESCO at its twenty-eighth session, November, 1951, agreed that education for world community was essential, and that a program of such education should, in its opinion:

1. "Make it clear that unless steps are taken to educate mankind for the world community, it will be impossible to create an international society conceived in the spirit of the Charter of the United Nations.
2. Make clear that states, whatever their difference of creeds and ways of life, have both a duty to cooperate in international organizations and an interest in so doing.
3. Make clear that civilization results from contributions of many nations and that all nations depend very much on each other.
4. Make clear the underlying reasons which account for the varying ways of life of different peoples both past and present, their traditions, their characteristics, their problems and the ways in which they have been solved.
5. Make clear that throughout the ages, moral, intellectual and technical progress has gradually grown to constitute a common heritage for all mankind. Although the world is still divided by conflicting political interests and tensions, the interdependence of the peoples becomes daily more evident on every side. A world international organization is necessary and it is now also possible.
6. Make clear that the engagements freely entered into by the member States of international organizations have force only in so far as they are actively and effectively supported by those peoples.
7. Arouse in the minds, particularly of young people, a sense of responsibility to this community and to peace.
8. Encourage the development of healthy social attitudes in children so as to lay the foundations of improved international understanding and co-operation."
International Social Science Bulletin, Vol. IV (1952), p. 149.

[17] Cf. F. S. Dunn, "The Scope of International Relations," *World Politics*, Vol. I (1948—49), p. 142.

lines of development are most beneficial to mankind; and it is a moot point whether the student of international affairs can, any more than his colleague in the physical sciences, be sure that his findings are used for purposes, and in accordance with scales of values, which he accepts.

The Inevitable Antagonism between Specialization and Generalization

The two major opposing trends which may be called specialization and generalization are apparently inherent in all science and, therefore, date back to times immemorial. They are, by their very nature, interdependent and interacting. Their functions are, in a way, opposite; yet they supplement each other, as the one favors detailed examination, while the other brings the detailed information into its proper context.

We know this phenomenon from all of the general sciences, notably history.[18] It is very evident also in sociology. This discipline was developed largely as a reaction to a desire for a broader outlook on the nature of human society; but it soon gave way to the forces of specialization, split up into an increasing number of sub-disciplines, and more or less failed to fulfil its function as an integrating science. The implications of these trends are, from the point of view of methodology, highly interesting, if not fundamental.

The study of international affairs is at present strongly marked by the trends towards specialization and generalization. But since there has until recently been no general science of international affairs, the tendency has been to divide the subject matter among an increasing number of established academic disciplines. In this way, important aspects of state interaction, which previously could be only haphazardly surveyed, or were altogether ignored, are being exposed to analysis and examination. There are, however, still many highly important areas which are very superficially dealt with; and some improvement

---

[18] G. J. Renier, History. Its Purpose and Method, London, 1950.

in these fields should not be considered beyond the range of possibility.

The division of the subject matter of international affairs among an increasing number of disciplines[19] is apparently not due merely to some peculiarity in administrative practices of higher centers of learning; there may be well-founded professional reasons for it. It should, on the other hand, be underlined that the main problems on which the study naturally focuses, like the security problem, do not coincide with the academic divisions of learning. They may have a variety of aspects which fall within the borders of several disciplines. To cope with this problem, it has, in recent years, become usual to study parts of several disciplines which have a bearing upon international affairs. But only in cases like law and economics is it fairly clear what are the contributions of the various disciplines to the common field; and there is seldom a clear-cut literature at hand. Recent moves to improve this situation[20] have so far proved only moderately successful.

There is, however, an important—more or less opposite—line of development. Out of the concerted efforts to explain international affairs by many methods and techniques, there has emerged a body of knowledge which tends to take the form of a distinct discipline. The need for an over-all view tends to work in the direction of coordinating and integrating studies, and thus a new general subject is being developed, which is commonly given the name of international relations. Naturally, this science in the making is not to be regarded as a self-sufficient academic creation. It is more or less dependent upon the findings of other branches of learning, even on some of the physical and biological sciences. This kind of interdependence is a natural characteristic of science. The question has been raised under what category of learning this new

---

[19] This matter is further dealt with below in chapter I. Reference may also be made to Grayson Kirk, *The Study of International Relations in American Colleges and Universities*, New York, 1947; and to Quincy Wright, *The Study of International Relations*, New York, 1955.

[20] Cf. Grayson Kirk, "Materials for the Study of International Relations," *World Politics*, Vol. I (1948—49), p. 426 ff.

discipline should be classified.[21] This question seems to be more than a mere matter .of terminology. However, international relations as conceived and outlined in part II of this study is clearly a social science.[22]

In the beginning, courses on the new subject dealt mainly with problems of security. These introductory courses have often been the forerunner of textbooks, which give the best indication of the lines along which the incipient discipline is developing. Many mistakes have been made; and, as usual when something new is to be created, much opposition has been, and is still being, met. But in spite of all, significant progress is being made. At a few American and British universities the new subject is acquiring a fairly clear-cut shape. It has not yet, however, become a traditional part of the university curriculum. Its fate is largely dependent upon the individual professor who shapes and teaches it. And there is as yet no agreement on its outline, although a good many solutions have been offered. On the whole, however, the subject matter dealt with in the various textbooks reveals an increasing degree of uniformity.

The Search for Better Techniques

The growing interest in methodology is, no doubt, a highly encouraging phenomenon. This kind of problem has, for various reasons, become more and more pressing. The contributions to the common field of international affairs are being made from so many disciplines that it is really very difficult to know how they should be coordinated or assimilated. The old academic arrangements seem unable to cope satisfactorily with the situation. The growth of a new discipline entails much groping for new frames of reference, and new conceptual tools are being developed, which naturally also create a good deal of confusion.

---

[21] The question has been raised whether international relations should be conceived as a science *stricto sensu*, as a "policy science", or as a branch of humanistic study. Cf. C. A. W. Manning, *International Relations*, p. 28.

[22] As to the meaning of the term *social science*, see p. I, note 1.

Encouraged by the progress made in some social sciences like sociology, students of international affairs have begun to pay increasing attention to new techniques of research. Fortunately, many problems have been rendered less difficult by the fact that improved facilities have been placed at the disposal of the research scholar. Essential source materials for documentary research have become more easily available. Improved news services[23] and inventions in communications like broadcasting, as well as better means of travel and observation, are all playing an important part in rendering the task of obtaining fairly reliable data much easier. No less important is the great improvement in statistical materials, which have become much more reliable, and available to a far greater extent than before, particularly as a result of the work done by the agencies of the United Nations. Questionnaires and interrogation techniques are being elaborated and used on an increasing scale. On the whole, it is technically feasible, to a much greater extent than previously, to treat current affairs in a somewhat scholarly manner.

The progress is generally smallest in older disciplines like history, which reveal comparatively little improvement in methodology.

New subjects like international communications,[24] on the other hand, are more consistently searching for better techniques and modes of approach, particularly because they are operating in new fields where the old techniques may not work very well. The infant science of international relations has obviously not yet been able to produce its own techniques to any appreciable degree; it is still relying on those of the older related disciplines. It is, of course, feasible to speak of some basic techniques which are applicable, to varying extent, to all of the social sciences.

The achievements of the physical and biological sciences have called forth much well-deserved admiration and anxiety. The

---

[23] It seems that the establishment of press libraries is highly useful, but this practice has so far been followed only in a few places.

[24] Cf. *Public Opinion Quarterly*, Special Issue on International Communications Research, Winter 1952—53.

question has, therefore, been raised as to why the techniques which have produced these marvelous results in the natural sciences cannot be used with success also in the social sciences.[25] It appears, however, that the great difference between the subject matter of the physical sciences and that of the social sciences is often insufficiently considered. There is, in fact, reason to believe that only moderate use can be made of the methodological findings of the physical sciences, and that the social sciences will have to rely on their own techniques adapted to the subject matter dealt with. The efforts made by sociologists to improve the research techniques should provide the student of international affairs with many useful suggestions. Progress seems, however, to be hampered by the heterogeneity and vastness of the field. It remains to be seen whether the development of international relations as a special subject will provide opportunities for improved research. There is reason to entertain hope in this respect.

---

[25] For a discussion of this question see Felix Kaufmann, *Methodology of the Social Sciences*, London, 1944, chapter X.

PART I

THE DEVELOPMENT OF THE STUDY
OF INTERNATIONAL AFFAIRS

INTRODUCTION

It is generally agreed that the study of a single subject, like international law or international economics, is too little for a broad understanding of international affairs. History offers by far the widest scope, but it is widely agreed that the traditional subject called diplomatic history is unduly narrów. The historical study of international affairs must be considerably extended and remodeled to give the necessary background knowledge of world politics. Such a remodeling meets with difficult methodological problems, but it can undoubtedly be done. In fact, many of the topics which are now being dealt with in the new subject called international relations can, and probably should, be included in the study of history. However, the situation in several countries today seems to be that the historical study of international affairs is being slowly superseded by rival disciplines.

Two methods have gained increasing ground in recent years. One is to choose a field of concentration comprising the international aspects of several disciplines, which in the following pages is called the multidisciplinary method.[1] The other is to study international affairs as a distinct discipline, adopting a general and unitary approach to the subject matter. We are still in a transitional period when it is rather difficult to form a well-founded opinion of what course we should steer. It is, however, clear that even though we should be able to develop a well-proportioned subject dealing with international affairs in general, we cannot

---

[1] For a discussion of this matter see F. S. Dunn, "The Scope of International Relations," *World Politics*, Vol I (1949), p. 142 ff.

do without the more penetrating analysis of the specialized subjects.

If we choose the former alternative, we should naturally like to know which disciplines have substantial contributions to make to the general field of international affairs, and what are the contributions of the individual disciplines. These questions can be properly answered only by specialists in the respective fields, but the generalizer must nevertheless grope along as best he can.

If we are interested in international relations as a distinct discipline, we are bound to inquire what kind of subject this is, and with what kind of subject matter it deals. We shall, however, soon discover that finding the answer to these questions is extremely difficult. It also follows from this fact that the next logical question, namely what are the shortcomings and advantages of the two methods, cannot easily be answered.

It would seem natural to approach the questions empirically and investigate the prevailing tendencies in countries leading in the field;[2] and although literature on the subject is still very inadequate, we will try to examine briefly the lessons which experience has to teach us with the object of clarifying certain basic methodological questions.

------

[2] The General Conference of UNESCO, at its fifth session in May-June, 1950 decided to undertake surveys in several countries of the types of courses and method of instruction in the social sciences, including international relations. With wha connotation the term *international relations* was used was not made clear. Mos of the contributors took it, however, to mean international affairs in general. In fact they had to conceive of it that way; otherwise their report might have been extremely brief, since international relations as a distinct discipline was hardly taught at all in their countries.

Inquiries were made in eight countries, and on the basis of the material thus obtained, a main report was made by a general rapporteur, who, before completing his work, obtained comments on the report from a wide range of persons having special experience in the matters of which it treats. The book thus produced reveals considerable variations from one country to another, and the general rapporteur has apparently had difficulty in arriving at clear-cut general conclusions. Cf. C. A.W. Manning, *International Relations*.

CHAPTER I

THE MULTIDISCIPLINARY METHOD

It is only natural that the problems of external affairs have, except for rare instances, loomed rather large in the intellectual life of practically every nation. The struggle against surrounding peoples for existence has, by the very nature of things, been a major concern of the ruling members of every independent political unit all through the ages. And this state of affairs is likely to remain at least as long as the international society retains its anarchical character.

Some disciplines, which include aspects of international affairs within their subject matter, have roots far back in ancient civilizations, while others were developed only a few decades ago, and still others are actually in the making. The points of view are usually more or less influenced by prevailing philosophies,[1] as well as by the preoccupations and conceptual tools and techniques of the individual sciences. And we more often find that the foci of interest are determined by recent historical experience or concern with contemporary international problems. In this sense the study of international affairs tends to retain considerable current political interest.

Educational Arrangements

The wide and complicated subject matter of internationa affairs presents difficult problems both in research and in education. During the last decades considerable experimentation

[1] This matter has not been sufficiently studied. For a brief discussion of this kind of question, see E. H. Carr, *The Twenty Years Crisis 1919—1939*, London, 1946, Part Two.

has taken place with a view to arriving at improved procedures, and disagreement among the specialists as to the merits of the various arrangements is still very common. It seems as if prejudices and the resistance to change offered by established practices in many cases hamper progress to an undue degree. On the other hand, there is good reason to proceed carefully and to examine the new devices properly, in order to avoid serious setbacks and unnecessary expenses.

The growing interest in international affairs in the 1920's had almost everywhere the initial effect that practitioners of the traditional disciplines felt inclined to pay more attention to those aspects of international affairs which they considered to be more or less akin or ancillary to the subject matter of their own disciplines. It was, in fact, possible for able educators to include a great deal under the old headings. It was more or less agreed that modern history offered the best opportunities, and there are still many authorities who maintain the point of view that the study of history can satisfy the needs of the student of international affairs when this discipline is properly arranged for that purpose. Recently political science has come to pay increasing attention to the field of international affairs, and in the United States international relations is usually regarded as a sub-discipline of political science.

Gradually, however, the idea was gaining ground that a specialist in international affairs must be a person who was able to master parts of several, if not many, disciplines. The subject was defined as the study not only of the dealings between governments, but also of the trans-boundary relations between non-official institutions and individuals, and of the principles underlying the development of these social phenomena as well.[2] This subject matter extended over a considerable number of academic boundaries. It was, in fact, an academic bundle, which included history, law, economics, political science, geography and sundry other subjects. A selection and coordination of the relevant subject matter were, however, to be obtained by

---

[2] Alfred Zimmern (ed.), *University Teaching of International Relations*, Paris, 1939, p. 7.

viewing the phenomena from a common angle—that from which the public affairs of the contemporary world can be observed.[3]

Only in a few countries does the faculty system allow the student to select freely from the established disciplines what he needs, since he will have to go through parts of at least three or four subjects to acquire what is considered to be a reasonably wide knowledge of international affairs, and these subjects are usually given in different faculties. Special arrangements are, therefore, usually needed. Even where the faculty system allows this kind of selection, some sort of coordination is desirable. During the last three decades it has become more and more common to combine, in various ways, subjects which have a bearing upon international affairs, to make it easier for students who want to specialize in this field, in spite of the fact that time-honored university systems in many countries present great obstacles to such arrangements.

In the United States, where the faculty system is very flexible, this development has gone furthest, and it has proved to be of considerable value. The arrangements chosen may differ substantially from one institution of learning to another. At several universities, schools of international affairs have been established. They may differ to a considerable degree both with respect to administrative arrangements and subjects given. It may, however, be said that courses in the history of international politics, international law and institutions, and international economics make up the more important parts of the curriculum in all of them, while a number of the other subjects may vary from one school to another. In some places, geography is given a very prominent place, while at others it is quite neglected.[4] There are usually also some language requirements. And since World War II, much attention has been given to

---

[3] *Ibid.*, pp. 6—13.

[4] Cf. School of International Affairs at Columbia University in New York and the Schools of International Studies at the John Hopkins University in Baltimore. There are, naturally, many variations from one institution to another also with respect to what is taught under the various headings.

area studies.[5] Some of these institutions are, however, only graduate schools, with no provisions for undergraduate training. The impression is that they are, on the whole, very practical in their teaching, aiming, to a large extent, at providing specialists for business and government services, where the need for well-qualified personnel has been rapidly increasing in recent years.

A considerable number of institutions operate programs in international affairs through interdepartmental faculty committees, which coordinate the studies and arrange interdisciplinary conferences and seminars.[6] The impression is, in fact, that at some universities the number and the variety of courses offered are almost bewilderingly great. In rare instances, a single course including parts of several disciplines may be given by specialists working together.[7] On the whole, American practices include an interesting variety of devices; but it may, perhaps, be said that the development of the study of international affairs is still more or less at an experimental stage where different methods are being tried.[8]

In Europe there is, as may be expected, considerable difference from one country to another. World War II hampered progress in the social sciences far more in Europe than it did in the United States, and during the postwar years most higher institutions of learning have struggled with great economic problems. On the whole, the study of international affairs may, therefore, have advanced further in the United States than it has in Europe. But if this is the rule, there are at least some important exceptions to it.

---

[5] In some cases, institutes for area studies have been set up. A great power needs a considerable number of specialists for the various regions of the world. In this volume, however, we are not considering area studies as part of the subject matter of interstate relations except when they include the international affairs of the respective regions. It is believed that the internal affairs of a country do not become part of interstate relations simply by the fact that they are studied by a foreigner.

[6] This method is practiced at, for instance, the University of Chicago, Harvard University, and the University of California.

[7] This technique is practiced at the Woodrow Wilson School of Public and International Affairs at Princeton University.

[8] For further information on the various practices in the United States, see *The Study of International Relations in American Colleges and Universities* by Grayson Kirk.

In Great Britain the development has not moved in the direction of making special arrangements for inter-disciplinary study. Several universities have, in fact, taken a still further step and established chairs of international relations. It seems, however, that opportunities for concentration on this field at the undergraduate level are still rather limited.[9]

Some countries in Continental Europe have made excellent arrangements for concentration on international affairs. Here, too, international history, international law and organization, international economics and political geography are the principal subjects. International relations as a distinct subject does not seem to have been introduced in any of the countries. The term *international relations* is used, but it actually denotes a more or less orthodox chronological presentation of international affairs.

In France, where the rigidity of the faculty system presents considerable obstacles to selecting the needed subjects, the special device called the university institute is being used as a medium for coordinating the relevant disciplines.[10] The candidates qualify for a diploma. In some respects this kind of institution resembles the American school of international affairs. A somewhat similar arrangement has been practiced at the graduate level in Switzerland for several decades.[11]

In Germany, great attention is given to the subject of international affairs.[12] But none of the institutions seems to have made arrangements for a concentration on the field comparable to the American school of international affairs. The impression is that here, too, several institutions are considering a reorgani-

---

[9] Geoffrey L. Goodwin, *The University Teaching of International Relations*, pp. 109—126; and C. A. W. Manning, *International Relations*, particularly pp. 15—16.

[10] Cf. the Institut des Hautes Etudes Internationales founded in 1923 and reorganized in 1946. Although an autonomous body from an educational or pedagogical point of view, it is administratively attached to the Faculty of Law of the Paris University. See C. A. W. Manning, *International Relations*, pp. 92—93 with regard to courses given.

[11] Cf. Institut Universitaire des Hautes Etudes Internationales at the University of Geneva.

[12] Among the institutions may be mentioned in particular Deutsche Hochschule für Politik in Berlin-Schöneberg.

zation and extension of the study. The same may be said of the situation in Italy.[13]

Some Scandinavian universities have established special degrees which offer a wide choice of subjects from which the student of international affairs can benefit.[14] But it may still bc very difficult to find a sufficient number of suitable courses within a reasonable period of time.

It thus appears that there are various multidisciplinary arrangements for meeting the increasing need of better knowledge in the field of international affairs. But it is, at present, very difficult to give a comparative appreciation of their merits on the basis of the available literature.[15]

At the Conference of Representatives of Universities, held under the auspicies of UNESCO at Utrecht in 1948, it was recommended that all universities not already possessing chairs or departments, and not otherwise providing for teaching and research on the subject of international affairs, be urged as soon as possible to establish such chairs or departments, or to make other provisions for such systematic teaching and research.[16] However, there are not only the difficult pedagogical questions to consider; in many cases, the greatest problem is one of cost, and universities, particularly in Europe, seem, as a rule, to be rather conservative institutions, which only slowly adopt new practices.

Methodological Implications of Specialization

The number of disciplines which have a bearing upon international affairs has increased with truly amazing speed during

---

[13] Geoffrey L. Goodwin, *The University Teaching of International Relations*, pp. 81–84.

[14] For example, the Magister Artium degree at the University of Oslo.

[15] It will be noted that the general rapporteur of the UNESCO project on the teaching of international relations, Professor C. A.W. Manning, has, for good reasons, been very cautious on this point.

[16] *Report of Preparatory Conference of Representatives of Universities*, UNESCO Publication 228, Paris, 1948, pp. 33—34.

the last decades.[17] To the nuclear subjects, diplomatic history, geography, international law, and economics have been added international organization, demography, sociology, social psychology, anthropology, area study, international communications, and many others. This dismemberment of the subject matter confronts the student and the teacher with embarrassing problems, and the traditional multidisciplinary method no longer looks so convincing as before.

It is undoubtedly possible to obtain a working knowledge of three or four of the most relevant disciplines, but there may still be some highly important uncovered ground. It might, then, seem natural to bring in the findings of still more subjects; but to proceed along this line is far from easy, particularly as long as there are only few attempts by specialists to describe, in concise form, the contributions of their subjects to the general field of international affairs. In any case, the rapid increase in the number of disciplines which are in one way or another concerned with international affairs makes it practically impossible for the generalizer to get a clear view of the whole field, since one can never approach omniscience.

Every discipline tends to develop its own way of looking at things, and this departmentalized mental technique may assuredly have great value. Each discipline can provide penetrating insight into that part of international affairs of which it treats. But there is also the possibility that the technique of a speciality may prove to be a barrier, reducing the student's capacity for grasping other aspects of the field or for forming an over-all picture. This characteristic of the academic disciplines is clearly indicated by their tendency to develop their own concepts and terminology, although some may go further than others in this respect. In fact, the semantic gap between the various academic fields may become so broad that it is almost unbridgeable except by the expenditure of much time and labor.[18]

---

[17] James T. Shotwell, "The Study of International Relations," *Institutes and Their Publics*, pp. 8—12.

[18] Quincy Wright (ed.), *The World Community*. See the comments made in the foreword by the Director of the Norman Wait Harris Memorial Foundation concerning the experience gained at the Institute on the World Community.

There is also the important psychological factor of professional chauvinism to consider. Time and again, one can observe
how, in contemplating an international situation, persons
trained in a traditional field may not only reveal a striking
ignorance of aspects outside their own branch of learning, but
may emerge so prejudiced as to disclaim outright the importance of factors lying outside their own professional area, this
area being often defined in the narrowest of terms. There can
be no doubt, however, that in this instance tolerant cooperation
will prove superior to narrow-minded isolationism.

Increasing specialization has certainly made it possible to
bring new aspects of international affairs into the light and to
penetrate deeper into the subject matter; but at the same time
the findings of science have become so scattered and the picture
so confused that it is almost impossible to know how far we
really have proceeded in our endeavor to explain the phenomena of our vast and complicated field. It is noteworthy that,
in spite of the multiplying of disciplines, there are still many
highly important aspects of international affairs which receive
little or no attention. And the present state of confusion complicates the task of locating the extent of these loopholes, which
is one of the major functions of theory. Thus for several reasons
the need of arriving at a fairly clear over-all view is making
itself felt with increasing strength, and the desire of acquiring
a better understanding of the interplay between the various
factors determining the nature of international problems is
becoming more and more widespread.

CHAPTER II

A SCIENCE IN THE MAKING

Although still largely overshadowed by the trend towards specialization, there is also a line of great promise towards integration. It is still poorly marked, and occasionally sprawls out into almost undistinguishable paths, but viewed over a period of some years, it leaves no doubt about the direction in which it is running. Pioneering work of different kinds on the road towards a reasonably well-integrated new branch of learning, covering some major aspects of interstate relations, has been done at several centers of learning. The Americans seem to have displayed the greatest initiative, but the variety of approaches is rather bewildering. In Great Britain, too, much serious thought has been devoted to the question. In other European countries, however, there has been greater caution in departing from the methods offered by the old and well-tried disciplines.

The development of a new branch of learning given the name of international relations has so far been primarily an Anglo-American phenomenon; that is true. But it would be a great mistake to assume that no contributions have been made by other nations as well. Indeed, it would be a curious paradox if the science of international relations, in contrast to other sciences, were not more or less international in origin and development. Political borders have never been complete barriers to ideas. Moreover, although international relations is a new branch of learning, many of its component parts are very old. And it is not easy to trace to the ends the roots of a discipline examining problems with which man has grappled since time immemorial.

In the interwar period, conditions for a cross-fertilization of ideas were relatively encouraging. The League of Nations' International Committee on Intellectual Co-operation, almost immediately after its establishment in 1922, paid special attention to the problem of finding suitable methods for education in international affairs. In 1926 it instructed its principal executive instrument, the International Institute of Intellectual Cooperation in Paris, to inquire into the possibility of bringing about the coordination of existing national and international organizations concerned with the teaching of international affairs.[1] Two years later the Institute convened in Berlin a meeting of experts to discuss this matter. On the recommendation of these experts, the so-called International Studies Conference was instituted. This method of bringing together educators and scholars proved to be of the greatest value. Mention must also be made of the Geneva School of International Studies and its initiative in bringing together teachers, and no less important was the activity of the European Center of the Carnegie Endowment for International Peace.

During the 1930's by far the most promising advances were, without doubt, made in Great Britain and the United States, and these countries have kept the lead since World War II. This progress seems, however, to have been partly due to the fact that a large number of distinguished scholars from the Continent took refuge in these countries and in many ways invigorated their intellectual life, perhaps more in this field than in any other.

The Unitary Approach in Education

In Great Britain, where university practices encourage the establishment of chairs by donation, a few enthusiasts have, by endowment, taken the initiative in introducing into the university curriculum a subject called international relations. They

---

[1] International Institute of Intellectual Co-operation, League of Nations, *The International Studies Conference. Origins, Functions, Organization*, Paris, 1937. The activity of this institution is further dealt with below in Part III.

did this partly because they adhered to the old belief that better understanding of world affairs might enhance the chances of peace. But it has been left largely to the individual professors to find out what should be included in this new subject.[2] The solutions as to the choice of subject matter, and the appropriate methods for obtaining an understanding of that subject matter, which the various educators have chosen, differ considerably.

On the whole, attention seems to have been concentrated primarily on the history of international politics and the development and functioning of international institutions.[3] This tendency may be partly due to the belief that education in these aspects of interstate relations may best serve the cause of peace. There are, however, some highly important exceptions to this rule, namely the programs in international relations at London University. Here a great step towards an independent discipline has been taken, and the points of view are indicated already by the title, "Structure of International Society," given to the elementary course. In the programs both at the University College and the London School of Economics, sociological concepts are adopted to a great extent. The curriculum at the University College appears to be marked by some influence from German sociology, particularly the ideas of MaxWeber.[4] The program at the London School of Economics is somewhat more philosophical in approach. But sociological and psychological concepts and viewpoints are also given due consideration.[5]

---

[2] C. A. W. Manning, *International Relations*, Chapter V.

[3] S. H. Baily, *International Studies in Modern Education*, London, 1938, and Geoffrey L. Goodwin, *The University Teaching of International Relations*, Oxford, 1951, pp. 120—122.

[4] The nature of the program is indicated by the work *Power Politics* by G. Schwartzenberger, which is largely used as textbook.

[5] In an introduction, the context of the study is discussed, and the relevance and necessity, in the study of international relations, of the companion disciplines —history, economic geography, political theory, and international law—are dealt with. Then follows a section on "Basic Ideas." It contains a discussion of the notion of an international society and single world order, as well as the notion of international right and wrong. The points of view appear to be somewhat colored by concepts from the philosophy of law.

In the United States, an increasing number of courses labeled "international relations" were given fairly early in the interwar period,[6] and this development has continued since the war. They are mostly introductory courses, varying considerably in content. The greater number of them are given in departments of political science.

In spite of notable variations in choice and treatment of subject matter, investigation shows that the bulk of the materials in these courses falls under a few main items: There is usually a discussion of the state system, which includes a brief survey of its evolution as well as of the various techniques and agencies by which states conduct their relations with each other. Next, a description and evaluation of the factors which affect the power of a state are given with the object of conveying to the beginning student a reasonably clear understanding of the fact that the sources of national power are many, complex, and, to a large extent, inter-related, and that they vary greatly from one state to another, and, over a period of time, within the same

---

The greater part of the course is given under the section called "International Politics," which has the following items:

The behavior of states—the needs, aspirations, and anxieties of states and the responsibilities of statesmen; motivations of state behavior; traditional and environmental factors conditioning the outlook of states. Internal elements—the interplay and interdependence of politics at the domestic and international levels. The mutual impact of states—means and methods of pressure in the relations between states. The grading of the powers—the ever-shifting balance of influence and authority in diplomatic exchanges and the factors on which it depends. Relationships between states—points of contact and of friction between peoples; the conditions of misunderstanding; the basic beliefs and the ruling enthusiasms of mankind and their influence upon the attitudes of states; man's urge to make a better world and the conflicting modes of its expression.

The last section of the course is entitled "Institutional Elements" and deals with the nature of international institutions. Cf. C. A.W. Manning, *International Relations*, p. 95.

Three more advanced optional courses deal with philosophical and psychological aspects of international relations, the interplay between politics at the domestic and international levels, and the sociology of international law. Cf. *International Relations*, pp. 95—96.

[6] Farrell Symons, *Courses on International Affairs in American Colleges, 1930—31*, Boston, 1931; Edith E.Ware, *The Study of International Relations in the United States, Survey for 1937*, New York, 1937.

state. Some attention is, as a rule, also paid to the international position and foreign policy of the great powers, and a rather hurried summary of recent international history is usually included. An almost compulsory part of the course is the development of international organizations and collective security. Together with this item, some basic facts concerning the application of law in the international society are usually also discussed.[7]

It goes without saying that this vast subject matter can be only summarily treated in an introductory course. But it may be possible to convey to the student at the beginning a sound notion of the complexity of international relations. It may be made clear that international affairs is not really strictly divided along the lines of academic division, but that the factors of international politics are many and often inter-related.

In some cases, the development from this general intro-ductory course has gone far in the direction of a new, distinct discipline[8] of international relations, even though it may be given in one of the older departments, particularly that of political science.[9] An increasing number of chairs of internation-

---

[7] Cf. Grayson Kirk, *The Study of International Relations*, pp. 27—31.

[8] The Yale Institute of International Studies, which was established in 1935 seems to have done most useful pioneering work. Here the philosophical concep of power politics, sociological concepts of interaction, as well as geopolitical notion and modes of analysis were cleverly applied in the development of new sets of thought Cf. E. S. Furniss Jr., "The Contribution of Nicholas John Spykman to the Study of International Relations," *World Politics*, Vol. IV (1952), p. 382 ff.

[9] As an example of a fairly well-integrated course, which in fact may be called the embryo of a new discipline, may be mentioned that on international politics given at the department of political science at Princeton University. Here, too, geographical and sociological concepts are rather strongly represented.

Considerable attention is given to the motivating forces and objectives under-lying the foreign policies of states, although it is still necessary to rely, to some extent, on hypotheses for the explanation of these matters. Particularly realistic is the section on the tools, techniques, and strategies which states employ in their efforts to achieve their foreign policy objectives. It includes a discussion of diplomacy, information, and propaganda or psychological warfare, miscellaneous cultural impacts, economic factors, subversion, and military war. The factors which determine the capability of states to attain their aims are also carefully treated. Somewhat more conventional are the sections on the behavior and relationship patterns resulting from the inter-al relations is also being established in the United States. But the subject matter given at these chairs still varies considerably from one to another.

Although there are an increasing number of highly interesting textbooks, the individual educator in international relations as a unitary subject is still largely responsible for the kind of subject matter he presents. And he has to attain, in one way or another, a reasonably clear-cut view as to what the new subject should be like. Since as yet very few educators have been originally trained in international relations as a distinct discipline, and since hardly a single one of the older disciplines will provide him with the necessary knowledge, it appears that some working knowledge of the peculiar techniques and subject matter of several social sciences is required in order to arrive at an applicable synthesis.[10] This qualification is required even when there is only the question of coordinating various relevant sciences.

It is, however, not easy to acquire the needed knowledge, even if the economic means are provided. There is no short cut to the extremely difficult field of international relations, no matter how well the course of study is planned. But a great many difficulties are undoubtedly due to the fact that the field is still in its initial, experimental stage, with blurred boundaries and hardly any academic recognition.

In recent years many countries, particularly the United States, have made considerable economic provisions for advanced study in international affairs, and several pedagogical devices are being tried. Participation in conferences or seminars of sufficient duration, devoted to systematic exploration of general problems to which each member can contribute from his own field, seems to be one of the best solutions. Of particular interest are seminars especially devoted to problems of

---

action of states and the norms and mechanisms that regulate or purport to regulate the relationships of states.

This course is given with increasing depth of analysis and scope from the introduction through the graduate levels.

[10] For a discussion of this matter, see C. A. W. Manning, *International Relations*, Chapters II and VII.

coordination and integration or other problems of methodology, when representatives of several relevant disciplines are participating to explain the matter from the point of view of their respective subjects.

It has also been long realized that periods of service in governmental institutions or international agencies may stimulate a sense of realism and further the ability to apply theoretical knowledge to the interpretation of political events and situations.[11] However, opportunities for such service are rather limited, particularly in minor states; and in unfavorable cases, they may merely result in dull routine work at a low level, which may be less rewarding than the scanning of newspaper pages.

---

[11] Cf. Grayson Kirk, *The Study of International Relations*, Chapter IV.

CHAPTER III

THE TREND AS INDICATED
BY THE LITERATURE

When in the second decade of this century, small beginnings towards a new branch of learning were made, there was a strongly felt lack of suitable textbooks. To satisfy this demand, there was written, in London in 1916, a book entitled *An Introduction to the Study of International Relations*,[1] which must be among the very first works of its kind. It contains chapters on the history of international politics since 1815, the causes of wars, international economic relations, international law, political relations between advanced and backward peoples and, finally, international affairs and the growth of freedom. To textbook writers in the 1950's it may not seem very impressive, but it was, after all, a prudent and suggestive attempt to arrive at a synthesis. There later appeared works which were more narrow in scope. A textbook entitled *The History and Nature of International Relations*, which was published in the United States in 1922, assumes that the fundamentals in a scientific study of international relations are the nature of diplomacy, history of diplomacy, the agents of diplomacy, legislative intervention in the conduct of international politics, and methods in diplomacy[2]. It should, however, be added that some of the above mentioned topics were remarkably well written.

---

[1] A. J. Grant, I. D. I. Hughes, Arthur Greenwood, P. H. Kerr, and F. F. Urquhart, *An Introduction to the Study of International Relations*, London, 1916. In the foreword it was stated that "The Council for the Study of International Relations found itself hampered in beginning its work by the lack of books on international relations suitable for use in study circles and classes."

[2] E. A. Walsh (ed.), *The History and Nature of International Relations*, New York, 1922. See particularly pp. 1—31.

All through the 1920's, by far the greater part of the subject matter presented in textbooks on international relations consisted of historical surveys and elements normally included in the study of international law.[3] But the scope was gradually expanded. Disciplines such as economics including some demography and particularly political geography increased their share in the subject matter. In 1925 a writer stated that he proceeded on the hypothesis that a field of international relations existed which was almost as distinct from international law as the study of American government was from that of constitutional law.[4] However, strong emphasis was still placed on problems of security, and international relations was defined as discussions of policies which resulted in the clash of interests, and of the methods by which these clashes could be avoided.[5]

During the past twenty years a considerable number of textbooks on international relations have been written. As one might expect, many of them have grown largely out of materials which were originally given in courses. By far the greater part of this literature has appeared in the United States. Great differences still exist, but, on the whole, the tendency is towards increasing uniformity with regard to the subject matter included.

The Framework of the Study

The framework chosen for the study is of fundamental importance. In this respect, considerable experimentation has taken place and is still taking place, but some fairly clear contours have emerged. The tendency is toward greater uniformity also on this point. Relatively few authors have, however, endeavored to describe properly the scene of action or the framework of their study. Their views on this matter are often merely implied.

---

[3] Cf. James Bryce, *International Relations*, London, 1922; Herbert Adams Gibbons, *Introduction to World Politics*, New York, 1923.

[4] R. L. Buell, *International Relations*, New York, 1925, foreword.

[5] *Ibid*, foreword.

The study of international law does, in a way, presuppose a notion of an international society, and one would almost automatically think of society in connection with law, since law functions in society. Looking at the subject from this point of view, it seems possible to speak of the functions of international law in an international society, or in the society of states, and of the sociology of international law. During the first quarter of this century, several writers on international law adopted this approach in their works.[6]

For the specialist in international law who was desirous of expanding his subject to a study of international relations, the notion of an international society naturally came to form his frame of reference. This framework was conceived of as a society of states.[7] "The term *Nation* has been used throughout this volume as an equivalent of State; it has no reference to race. It denotes those political entities which compose international society and which are the immediate concern of the Law of Nations."[8] This was the view of an author who undoubtedly deserves to be called one of the very first authorities on the incipient system of learning. Attention was focused on the nature and interests of the state as studied in this context.[9] Only slowly was the scholar who had had his training in international law able to expand substantially beyond the traditional boundaries of this discipline.

Particularly in the United States the so-called state system concept has come to be much applied, and its development is given much space in nearly every textbook on international

---

[6] Cf. Max Huber, *Die soziologischen Grundlagen des Völkerrechts*, Berlin, 1928
Franz Wilhelm Jerusalem, *Völkerrecht und Soziologie*, Jena, 1921.

William E. Rappard, *International Relations as Viewed from Geneva*, New Haven, 1925.

It may, however, also be argued that international law has been national in the sense that it has emphasized sovereign rights rather than world responsibility, and has given more attention to neutral rights and obligations than to notions of collective responsibility. Cf. Quincy Wright, *The Study of International Relations*, p. 69.

[7] For a critical analysis of this concept by an authority on international law see P. E. Corbett, *Law and Society in the Relations of States*, New York, 1951.

[8] P. M. Brown, *International Society*, Princeton, 1923, p. IX.

[9] *Ibid.*, p. 14.

relations. Sociological and legal concepts have been mixed and formed into a new dish usually classified under political science. A leading authority assumes that "the phenomena of international politics can be dealt with most fruitfully if they are envisaged as aspects of the whole pattern of political behavior and power relations which has developed inWestern civilization. This pattern may be designated as the Western State System, i. e. the total complex of attitudes, values, habits, and behavior patterns which have a bearing on the contacts between the states in the Western world."[10] The term *Western State System* seems to imply an embarrassing limitation. However, the viewpoint as to geographical delimitation is clarified by the statement that "the particular and specific problems of contemporary international politics can be dealt with meaningfully only if they are considered in the light of the whole state system of the modern world."[11]

During the last decades sociological concepts, viewpoints, and interpretations have come to play an increasingly important role in the study of international relations. Basically, the sociologist thinks of the world as constituted of cooperating and competing groups which must find their adjustment through the balancing of behavior and satisfactions.[12] This view seems to merge almost automatically with the functional approach of the student of international law, and it appears also possible to match it with the attempt of some historians to treat the history of mankind as the study of the rise and fall of civilizations over the globe. In the 1930's it was increasingly common to think of international relations in terms of international sociology, where the structure of the society of states, its processes of

---

[10] Frederick L. Schuman, *International Politics. An Introduction to the Western State System*, first edition, New York, 1933, p. XIII. The influence of American sociology is very strong on this statement of program but perhaps less evident in the subsequent treatment of the subject matter, where traditional legal and historical materials are given considerable attention.

[11] *Ibid.*, p. XIII. As to more recent viewpoints, attention may be drawn to the chapter written by F. L. Schuman in *Contemporary Political Science, Publication No. 426 of UNESCO*, Paris, 1950, pp. 578—580.

[12] L. L. Bernard and Jessie Bernard, *Sociology and the Study of International Relations*, p. 71.

association and disintegration, and the norms, moral and legal, which guide behavior in this social nexus, are the principal foci of interest.[13] But, naturally, there is often considerable disparity between the ambition and the achievements of scholars.

However, the trend has moved in the direction of including entities other than states in the framework termed international society. In the early 1940's an authority defined international relations as "the relations between groups, between groups and individuals, and between individuals, which essentially affect international society as such, i. e. its development, structure, and working." And he states that "the study of international relations is a special branch of sociology, which is concerned with those phenomena that essentially affect international society as such."[14] In a later work he has further elaborated the conception of international relations as the study of the international society "with the full stress on the synoptic character of this study."[15] Recently two other textbook writers have "attempted to synthesize the study of political behavior and social action with an analysis of international relations as one manifestation of group aspiration."[16]

Awareness of the shrinking of the globe in terms of transport and communications and the increasing interdependence of its people has also made its influence felt on the framework of the study of international relations. It has been realized that the major problems of international politics are global in nature, can be solved only on the basis of global cooperation, and must,

---

[13] Cf. statement by Alfred von Verdross and other authorities at the eleventh session of the International Studies Conference. Sir Alfred Zimmern (ed.), *University Teaching of International Relations*, Paris, 1939.

[14] George Schwartzenberger, *Power Politics*, London, 1941, p. 25. There seems to be some relationship between Dr. Schwartzenberger's views and the ideas of Max Weber propounded particularly in the work, *Wirtschaft und Gesellschaft*, Tübingen, 1925.

[15] Schwarzenberger, *Power Politics*, second edition, London, 1951, p. XVI. Dr. Schwartzenberger is one of the very few who have given a systematic description of the structure of the international society as conceived by the author.

[16] Ernst B. Haas and Allen S. Whiting, *Dynamics of International Relations*, New York, 1956, p. VII

perforce, be studied in a global perspective. A somewhat more dynamic concept than the usual notion of a state system seems to be emerging, which emphasizes the urgent need for developing an attitude of political discovery so as to establish political units more in accordance with the facts of life than are those which we have at present.[17] The contours of this "human world concept" are, however, still rather dim.

The global nature of international relations has been revealed also by the findings of political geography. The study of geography has had to face the fact that the world has, militarily and economically, become a unit area.[18] It has been realized that technological developments have made it increasingly possible for the great powers to conduct their political and military strategy on a world-wide scale, and that the foreign policy of any one of them can best be analyzed in a global perspective.[19]

Basic Assumptions about Political Behavior

From the earliest times there has been a tendency to form assumptions about political behavior, in the light of which political phenomena are interpreted.[20] They may be, or may pretend to be, derived from interpretations of historical phenomena, but quite often they appear to have grown primarily out of strong political or economic interests.[21] During the last half century, which has witnessed the development of international relations as a branch of learning, there has been a far-reaching

---

[17] Linden A. Manden, *Foundations of Modern World Society*, Stanford, 1947.

[18] George T. Renner, *Global Geography*, New York, 1945. See particularly pp. 14—15.

[19] Cf. Nicholas J. Spykman, *America's Strategy in World Politics*, New York, 1942.

[20] Frank M. Russel, *Theories of International Relations*, New York, 1936. This work is an attempt to present the most significant ideas concerning international affairs that men have had since the earliest times, analyzed in the light of environmental influences.

[21] Cf. E. H. Carr, *The Twenty Years' Crisis 1919—1939*, London, 1946, particularly pp. 41—62.

change in point of view, characterized by a shift in emphasis from the harmony of interest assumption to the power politics assumption—or from utopia to realism, as some authors prefer to describe it.

Emphasis on power as basic to politics in general may be traced back at least to Greek philosophy and history.[22] But it was the pernicious rivalry among the Italian small states as pawns in the game of the great powers during the fifteenth and early sixteenth centuries which evoked the first really penetrating analysis of the struggle for power in politics.[23] The subject has occasionally been dealt with in one form or another by students of political philosophy through the centuries. Early in the 1920's, a distinguished analyst and advocate of democracy declared that since states are, so to speak, in a state of nature towards each other, with no law or superior power able to enforce law, the thing called justice is merely the interests of the stronger.[24]

It was, however, not until the 1930's that this kind of tenet gained really great attention in academic quarters, although it may have been fairly consistently practiced by statesmen all through the ages. The need for what was called a realistic outlook on international affairs, as opposed to the conception of the world in terms of abstract assumptions or in terms of what one would like it to be, now came to be strongly emphasized. An American authority writing in the early 1930's declared that he proceeded on the assumption that political science, as one of the social sciences, was concerned with the description and analysis of relations of power in society— i. e., with those patterns of social contacts which are suggested by such words as *ruler* and *rules, command* and *obedience, domination* and *subordination, authority* and *allegiance*.[25] How he adopted this point of view in his study of international affairs may be illustrated by the statement that "the contemporary efforts to

---

[22] Cf. Thrasymachus in the first book of Plato's *Republic;* see also the fifth book, chapters 85—113, of Thucydides' *History of the Peloponnesian War.*

[23] The influence on political philosophy of Niccolo Machiavelli's *Il Principe*, finished in 1514, appears to have been great indeed.

[24] James Bryce, *International Relations*, pp. 197—198.

[25] F. L. Schuman, *International Politics*, first edition, p. XII.

insure peace through idealistic verbage and international organization were evaluated in the light of the fundamental patterns of power in the Western state system."[26]

The disappointment at the achievements, or rather the failures, of democracy and its apparent inability to meet emergency conditions, the startling success of dictators, and ruthless treatment of political opponents in authoritarian states seem to have invigorated the conception of politics as a struggle for power. Political leaders were postulated as political animals seeking power as the businessman seeks wealth.[27] And within a philosophical framework, the dynamics of society was explained by regarding the desire for power as a primary force.[28]

Above all, the breakdown of collective security and the frustration of the hopes and aspirations which it encouraged seem to have had profound consequences and widespread repercussions. The optimistic assumptions expounded by the supporters of and believers in international cooperation and organization were regarded as utopian and exposed to considerable criticism.[29] "The characteristic features," wrote one authority, "of the present crisis, seen in the light of the twenty years between 1919 and 1939, has been the abrupt descent from the visionary hopes of the first post-war decade to the grim despair of the second, from a utopia which took little account of reality to a reality from which every element of utopia seems rigorously excluded."[30] In its extreme form, this school of thought states that, acting squarely on behalf of himself, the individual meets with opposition from the society, but in the service of the state the satisfaction of the desire for power is placed at the top of the hierarchy of values, and in this setting the individual's *animus dominandi* seems to have no less than the world as its object.[31]

---

[26] *Ibid.*, p. VIII.

[27] George E. G. Catlin, *A Study of the Principles of Politics*, London, 1930.

[28] Bertrand Russell, *Power, a New Social Analysis*, London, 1938.

[29] Cf. Reinhold Niebuhr, *Moral Man and Immoral Society*, New York, 1932, and Karl Mannheim, *Ideology and Utopia*, New York, 1936.

[30] E. H. Carr, *The Twenty Years Crisis 1919—1939*, second edition, p. 224.

[31] Hans J. Morgenthau, *Scientific Man vs. Power Politics*, Chicago, 1946; see particularly pp. 192—200.

While some authorities on international relations adhere to the conviction that all politics is a struggle for and wielding of power,[32] there are others who explain the dominating role of power in international politics as due largely to the anarchical nature of the world society. As long as there is no effective means of restraint in the world society, groups tend to do what they can rather than what they ought. Under these circumstances, certain patterns of behavior become dominant: armament, power diplomacy, power economics, regional and universal imperialism, alliances, balance of power, and war. That is power politics.[33] The most noteworthy aspect of this kind of politics as compared with that taking place in a well-organized society seems, however, to be the predominant role of physical force or violence.

The impact of the war tended to increase the view that international politics was merely the brute wielding of power.[34] And the struggle between the communist and non-communist blocs has had a similar influence by focusing attention on the tactics of the cold war.[35] There has, however, always been a strong opposition to this way of conceiving the nature of international politics.[36] The so-called idealistic school has cleverly argued the view that there may also be a considerable element of idealism and sense of fairness prevailing in the dealings between nations.[37] During recent years the extremists have been inclined to moderate their views to some extent.

---

[32] No one has put this more clearly than H. J. Morgenthau: "International politics, like all politics, is a struggle for power. Whatever the ultimate aims of international politics, power is always the immediate aim."-*Politics Among Nations, The Struggle for Power and Peace*, New York, 1949, p. 13. See also Thorsten V. Kalijärvi, *Modern World Politics*, New York, 1942, Introduction.

[33] G. Schwartzenberger, *Power Politics*, second edition, p. 13.

[34] The change in attitude is clearly revealed by the work, *Modern World Politics*, edited by Thorsten V. Kalijärvi, New York, 1942.

[35] Cf. Robert Strausz-Hupé and Stefan T. Posony, *International Relations in the Age of Conflict between Democracy and Dictatorship*, New York, 1950.

[36] Among the strongest attacks on the so-called realistic view may be mentioned Lizzie Susan Stebbing's, *Ideals and Illusions*, London, 1941.

[37] Arnold Wolfers, "The Pole of Power and the Pole of Indifference," *World Politics*, Vol. IV (1952), pp. 39—63.

On the whole, the tendency seems to be away from extreme dogmatic-philosophical interpretations and towards an empirical investigation—to the extent possible—of the character of international politics.

The fact that international relations, as a separate branch of learning, has developed primarily in countries where extreme Marxian doctrines have had relatively few proponents may partly explain why these views have never been strongly represented, although their influence may occasionally be noticed. That may be true, for instance, in the case of the conflicting assumptions about man's scope of independent action, where opinions range from the assertion of the absolute free will of man to choose his own course of action to the denial of any independence at all on the part of the political leaders, who are thought to be so tied up with the environment in which they act that they are merely the instruments of social forces over which they have little or no control. Almost equally conflicting views have been held about the role which reason and irrational forces play respectively as regulators of human action. Such assumptions may, because of their very nature, be explicitly or implicitly maintained, to a greater or lesser extent, by every writer, but they have never formed the philosophical foundation upon which the entire work has been based to the same extent as has the concept of power politics.

The Major Topics

With regard to the subject matter studied, development has, on the whole, been in the direction of greater originality and uniformity. It is no longer merely a mixture of materials from sundry older disciplines. Some aspects of international affairs are being studied from new points of view, while others which were previously almost completely neglected have been taken up for examination.

The works on international relations which appeared during the years from 1916 to 1925,[38] most of them intended as text-

---

[38] Cf. above pp. 34—35, notes 1—3.

books for some educational institution, were, unlike later publications on the subject, all small books, although they represented valuable contributions to the difficult task of establishing a
new branch of learning. During this initial period it was, however,
not possible to advance substantially beyond knitting together
parts of traditional subject matter from history and international
law and, to some extent, also from international economics.

During the later 1920's and early 1930's some more carefully
written—and, in many ways, excellent works—appeared.[39]
Very much space was, however, still devoted to the various
aspects of diplomacy. American authors, in particular, paid much
attention to imperialism; and to all, nationalism was a major
concern. From then on, textbooks on international relations
began to reveal greater originality than before, but they were
still rather unsystematic with regard to content.

In the 1930's, with the development of the state system and
the international society as frames of reference for the study,
considerable progress was made. But from then on, the conviction that international politics was merely a struggle for
power began to make itself increasingly felt in the choice and
treatment of the subject matter. While previously emphasis was
on policies which might result in clashes of interests, and on
the methods by which these clashes could be avoided, attention
was now focused on the nature of power politics.

Since international politics was explained merely as a struggle
for power, a penetrating analysis of the motivating forces of
state action might seem more or less needless.[40] There were,
however, some strong opposing tendencies. For a long time
much attention had been paid to causes of war and the nature of
national interests.[41] And primarily from this point of departure,

---

[39] R. L. Buell, *International Relations*, New York, 1925; P. T. Monn, *Syllabus on International Relations*, New York, 1925; R. B. Mowat, *International Relations*, London, 1931.

[40] Cf. the limited space given to this matter by Hans J. Morgenthau in *Politics Among Nations*. He does, however, distinguish within the struggle for power among three kinds of motivation towards imperialism. See pp. 34—42.

[41] The matter of national interests was taken up and ably discussed by Charles A. Beard in the work, *The Idea of National Interest*, New York, 1934.

the student of international relations had turned his eyes to several highly important determinants of action in the field of interstate politics. Foremost among these motivating forces was probably nationalism. "Nationalism is the primary force in the Western state system, shaping the attitude and the action of its members toward one another,"[42] states one authority in the early 1930's. And nationalism was made responsible for many kinds of disputes, such as quarrels about frontiers, struggles about economic resources, and, in particular, problems of self-determination. The motivations towards imperialism were, likewise, carefully explained by several authors, especially the importance of raw materials, as well as commodity and investment markets.[43] Other factors dealt with were racial intolerance and ignorance, ethnic problems, and migration policies. But during recent years less space has, on the whole, been devoted to these matters, although they have not been dropped entirely except in rare instances.

Ideological forces, on the other hand, were somewhat neglected during the first decades of this century. Since then they have been given increasing attention.[44] The same may be said about traditions, educational ideals, and principles.[45] Impulses from German geopolitics, as well as sociological concepts of the struggle for power, were among the factors which in the United States led to stronger emphasis also on geographical and demographical phenomena.[46] They were interpreted partly in terms of motivating forces, partly in terms of capability to wield power and attain foreign policy objectives. Another stimulus in the same direction came during World War II, when the need for sound evaluations of the enemy's power

---

[42] F. L. Schuman, *International Politics*, first edition, p. 277.

[43] See R. L. Buell, *International Relations*.

[44] H. J. Morgenthau, *Politics Among Nations*, Chapter V.

[45] Norman J. Padelford and George A. Lincoln, *International Politics*, New York, 1954, pp. 305—328.

[46] The Yale Institute of International Studies seems to have made its influence felt to a considerable extent in this field. For an example from one of the latest books of how geographical and demographical phenomena are dealt with, see N. J. Padelford and G. A. Lincoln, *op. cit.*

potential tended to increase the study of the elements of power.[47]

For a considerable period of time, the processes by which the foreign policies of states are formed were rather neglected. In fact, many of the best books left this matter out entirely. The increasing interest in what is called policy-making, which has prevailed for some years in the United States, has in general led to increasing emphasis on this important part of the study of international relations. Some of the recent books in the field have fairly extensive chapters on this subject. For practical purposes, they are usually confined to a discussion of the procedures followed in the United States, the Soviet Union, and the major European states.[48]

Instruments of foreign policy and their application have of course been dealt with from the very beginning; but in the 1920's this item was, as a rule, limited merely to describing the instruments and procedures of diplomacy. The introduction of the concept of power as basic to international relations apparently had, in this respect, a broadening influence. While it tended to reduce interest in the problems of motive forces, it encouraged the study of the means by which the states wield their power. At the end of the 1930's, a reasonably systematic study of the ways and means of foreign policy appeared.[49] The use of military and economic power, as well as power over opinion, was analyzed in a new and highly interesting manner. Since then the study of this matter has been considerably elaborated, particularly in the United States, and there is a high degree of similarity between the approaches chosen by the various authors.[50]

Some books have fairly systematic chapters on the strategies upon which the powers base their foreign policies.[51] The prin-

---

[47] Reference may be made to R. Strausz-Hupe and S. T. Possony, *International Relations*, New York, 1950; and H. J. Morgenthau, *Politics Among Nations*.

[48] Cf. N. J. Padelford and G. A. Lincoln, *International Politics*, Part III.

[49] E. H. Carr, *The Twenty Years Crisis 1919—1939*, London, 1939.

[50] As examples from British and American literature may be mentioned G. Schwartzenberger, *Power Politics*, second edition, chapters 10 and 12, and Strausz-Hupé and Possony, *International Relations*, Part III.

[51] Under the influence of sociological thinking, these matters are also dealt with as patterns of behavior in the international society.

ciples of balance of power and policies of alliance are more or less carefully treated by all writers on international relations.[52] This is what we might expect in view of the predominant role these matters have played, and are still playing, in international politics. And they have, for a long time, been major topics in diplomatic history. Some other strategies involve, to a greater extent, questions of international law. They have, therefore, been primarily dealt with by specialists in this field, from which they have been introduced into the study of international relations. Students of international relations are, however, inclined to discuss them from points of view different from those of the lawyer. Such strategies are neutrality, the establishment of buffer zones, and guarantees,[53] which may collectively be called policies of isolation.

Since international relations as a special field to a large extent grew out of subject matter in which the student of international law is interested, it is not surprising that from its early stage this discipline should be much concerned with such matters as the law of nations and the settlement of international disputes, as well as the history, structure, and functions of international institutions, collective security, and other means of reducing the danger of war, such as limitations of armaments.[54]

The disillusionment felt at the breakdown of collective security in the 1930's, in particular, appears to have encouraged a more critical analysis of the effectiveness of international law and institutions. And under the impact of sociological thoughts, the student of international relations came to look upon the various control media in the international society more from the point of view of social function,[55] and to examine their ability to fulfill the functions attributed to them. Nor is he

[52] Cf. books from different periods like P. M. Brown, *International Society*, chapter XII; F. L. Schuman, *International Politics*, first edition, chapter II; and H. J. Morgenthau, *Politics Among Nations*, first edition, parts 4 and 7.

[53] G. Schwartzenberger, *Power Politics*, second edition, chapter 11.

[54] For examples from the 1920's, see P. M. Brown, *International Society*, chapters III, VII, VIII, and XI; and R. L. Buell, *International Relations*, Part III. These authors devote a major part of their works to these subjects. For an example from the 1930's, see F. L. Schuman, *International Politics*, Book Two.

[55] Cf. G. Schwartzenberger, *Power Politics*, second edition, pp. 210—250.

any longer interested merely in international institutions as means of collective control of or restraint on indiscriminate use of power by the individual members of the world society. He is also aware of the fact that some of them have other functions, which can actually be carried out only by world-wide cooperation. While the chapters devoted to subject matter traditionally classified with international law have, on the whole, been reduced to a considerable extent, the problem of organizing the world society is still dealt with at length in most textbooks.

It might be expected that the influence of sociology would stimulate the study of non-legal norms of behavior, but that apparently has not been the case to any appreciable degree. Some aspects of this subject have been studied by various disciplines. Particularly in the field of philosophy of law there has developed an interest in international morality, and anthropology has, in recent years, attempted a comparative study of norms of international conduct. But such matters are only rarely given careful consideration in books on international relations.[56] In a considerable number of American works they are almost entirely omitted, although it may be argued that they are dealt with implicitly in all studies of international affairs.

Very often books on international relations contain large sections on recent history. It seems to be a widespread opinion that "given such a war-torn and otherwise fluid world as that of today, no study of international politics can wholly escape being dated."[57] But it may be argued that an undue amount of space is frequently devoted to this matter, in view of the fact that it is equally well, if not better, treated in courses on general history. Sometimes attempts are made to analyze, in an historical perspective, the main trends in the world society. This might seem to be a legitimate task for the specialist on international relations *eo nomine*, but it is, naturally, a difficult one which requires extensive historical knowledge. There are,

---

[56] For an interesting discussion of this subject, see Schwartzenberger, pp. 202—250.

[57] W. R. Sharp and Grayson Kirk, *Contemporary International Politics*, Washington, 1940, Vol. I, p. IV.

obviously, many other subjects, too, which may preferably be analyzed in an historical context.[58]

Regional descriptions were included in some of the first books, and this tendency has been stimulated by the great interest in area studies developed in the United States during World War II.[59] The arrangement of the subject matter may vary considerably. Usually the United States, the Soviet Union, and the British Commonwealth are selected for separate analysis. Other parts commonly included are the Far East and the Middle East. The regional studies of textbooks may frequently be written as symposiums, and the aspects of an area which are chosen for analysis may vary greatly from one author to another. Usually writers endeavor to describe the region from the point of view of its importance in world affairs.

The educational value of area study may be incontestable, but it does not seem to form an organic part of international relations conceived as a separate branch of learning. It is, however, true that there are regional peculiarities and interests which must be taken into account if world affairs are to be properly understood. And the importance of finding the best ways of depicting these regional variations can certainly not be denied.

★ ★ ★

It is hoped that this brief survey indicates sufficiently clearly that there is a quite large and rapidly increasing body of literature on a subject which neither resembles traditional studies in history, nor is organically related to other topics dealt with in departments of political science. It has, particularly in its initial period, sucked lifeblood from several disciplines, notably diplomatic history and international law; but today we are bound to regard it as a science in the making. Its position in the family of academic disciplines is still rather uncertain, but it has proved to be so tenacious of life that we are entitled to look upon it as a sound response to a clearly felt need for new modes of analyzing those aspects of human social life which we call international affairs.

---

[58] This matter will be further analyzed in Part III.

[59] For an example from a recent textbook, see Charles P. Schleicher, *Introduction to International Relations*, New York, 1954.

PART II

ELEMENTS OF INTERNATIONAL RELATIONS: A PROPOSAL FOR A MODEL OF ANALYSIS

INTRODUCTION

Although considerable advance in the direction of a new branch of learning has already been made, there is still much uncertainty as to what the subject of international relations should be. Of fundamental importance is the framework to be chosen and the approach to be adopted. One fact seems to be clear. It is becoming increasingly obvious to people in all countries that international affairs, in our time of jet propulsion and nuclear energy, broadcasting and television, are world-wide in scope. The foreign policy strategies of the great powers must be more or less global because the field of action is no less than the world. Measures taken in one area must be planned not only on the basis of the conditions prevailing on that spot, but also, to a varying degree, with a view to the situations in other parts of the world. And most, if not all major international problems, like matters of economics or security, can be lastingly solved only on a world-wide basis either by voluntary cooperation or by dictation.

Although the statesman as well as the scholar is only slowly accommodating himself to the new states of affairs, the fact remains that the technological integration of the world is probably the greatest social phenomenon of our age, and its consequences are inescapable. The question then arises whether it is possible to analyze such a vast subject as world affairs in a scholarly manner. How can we abstract relevant aspects from this tremendous field in a way which reduces it to manageable proportions and yet retain something so essential that it indicates the true nature of the subject? Is it possible to find some common denominator for such a heterogeneous matter?

It is natural to look to old and well-tried disciplines for guidance in this question. There are, for instance, political geography, cultural sociology, and anthropology, whose problems of limitation and abstraction resemble, in many ways, those of the science of international relations. It is, moreover, interesting to note that the frameworks so far used in the study of international relations, namely the international society conceived as the society of states and the concept of a state system, which, in fact, appears to be little more than another name for the former, are world-wide in scope. It may, however, be argued that there are other actors than states in world affairs, a fact which suggests a broader frame of reference than the society of states; moreover, the dynamics or rapid change of the state system itself may conceivably be analyzed more easily within the context of the world society.

Which aspects of the world society are most important to the student of international relations may, within certain limits, be a matter for discussion. Only scientific experience can produce a reasonable degree of agreement on this matter. In this respect the new subject resembles nineteeth century sociology. It may, in fact, be useful for the student of international relations to acquaint himself with the works of the founders of sociology, who were largely concerned with the task of defining, on a theoretical basis, the subject matter of the developing science. However, this search for and discovery of new objects of study does not cease when a science has been firmly established. There seems in every science to be a tendency to turn to new fields as it is gaining ground.

There is even the possibility that international relations, like sociology, may tend to split into a number of separate studies, and, in doing so, may more or less fail to fulfill its primary function as a coordinating and integrating discipline. Any undue tendency in this direction can probably best be forestalled by delineating the new discipline as clearly as possible and giving it a logical coherence which will reveal beyond doubt its importance as a general science.

CHAPTER IV

THE ROLE OF THE NATURAL
ENVIRONMENT

It is regarded as a foregone conclusion that the actors in world politics must, in planning their behavior, pay due attention to the character of the natural environment, since the latter offers opportunities or forms obstacles, and under certain conditions even sets limits. In stating this we do not, of course, in any way mean to ascribe anthropomorphic qualities to inanimate nature, or to maintain any kind of teleological environmentalism. And it is duly realized that the importance of the natural environment is profoundly modified by a large number of highly complicated social phenomena, particularly technology.

When the above stated attitude is adopted it seems logical and advantageous to begin the study of international relations by a survey of the more important ways in which the natural environment enters into the study.[1] Firstly it should be mentioned that the term *natural environment* has various meanings.[2] Here it is used only in its conventional sense, and may be defined as the primordial earth as modified by man and nature. More specifically it has been stated as consisting of the following twelve elements: climate, flora, fauna, land forms, soils, mineral resources, ground water resources, water features, the ocean and its littoral, size, form, and location.[3] This may, however, be a too wide definition. It seems to be a moot point

---

[1] Some aspects of the subject will be dealt with in chapter XI.

[2] For a discussion of the various meanings see the penetrating study, *Man-Milieu Relationship Hypotheses in the Context of International Politics*, by Harold and Margaret Sprout, Princeton, 1956, p. 14.

[3] C. Langdon White and George T. Renner, *Human Geography: Ecological Study of Society*, New York, 1948.

whether the size and the configuration of a state's territory should be looked upon as part of the natural environment. They are actually created by political borders, and may, therefore, be regarded rather as part of the socio-cultural environment in which the actors in world affairs operate, and their role may, perhaps, be more conveniently discussed under such topics as the main structure of the world society and the capability of states. The same appears to be true of some aspects of location. It seems possible to speak not only of geographical location but also of social location. The former may be defined in terms of physical geography, while the latter may be defined by relationship to such social phenomena as the principal avenues of transport, great centers of administration or production, and other politically or strategically important subjects, notably states. For instance, the highly favorable location of London during the last centuries is clearly the result of an interplay between socio-cultural and geographical factors. The former are usually subject to relatively rapid change. This means that the geographical position of a city or a country, which is favorable from an economic or strategic point of view under a given social or political pattern, may become unfavorable if changes occur in this pattern. In this way many busy and prosperous cities have been reduced to oblivion or disappeared entirely from the map, but we are strangely enough often inclined to forget this obvious fact.

If we further assume that the repercussions of major events in international politics in our day can be world-wide, and that the foreign policies of the great powers have to be more or less based on global strategies, then the natural environment in which the actors in international politics operate comprises ultimately the entire earth. Time-honored geographical concepts are, undoubtedly, very useful for the explanation of the subject, and much help can surely be obtained from specialists in the various branches of geography, particularly from students of political geography.[4] Geographers and historians have, in

---

[4] "The field of study which the political geographer rightly claims in this connection is the relationship between the external activities of the states and the planetary physical stage in which they are set . . .

one way or another, paid much attention to this matter since ancient times. It is, however, fairly certain that we also need new concepts which correspond better to the character of international politics in the second half of the twentieth century, and the student of international relations may be able to make significant contributions to this field.

It might seem that man has now achieved such a complete mastery of the forces of nature that the significance of the natural environment can be disregarded; but this would undoubtedly be a dangerous fallacy. It is, however, necessary to observe the greatest care in forming conclusions about the relationship between man and nature, since many social factors have to be taken into consideration. Moreover, the natural environment itself is not an entirely stable phenomenon.

Changes in the Natural Environment

The processes of change which nature itself initiates, notably variations in climate, may,[5] according to some authorities, have had profound cultural effects, undermining the position of some civilizations and improving that of others. But even if such hypotheses may be correct, which is sometimes rather doubtful, the processes have usually been so slow that their effect upon international affairs was hardly perceptible for decades or even for centuries. There are, however, some exceptions to this rule. An example from our own time which may be mentioned is that the decrease of the permanent ice cover of the Arctic Ocean has,

---

"The aspect of inter-state relationships with which political geography is primarily concerned, then, is that which arises out of the relations between physical conditions and human activities on a global scale, and which finds expression in the foreign policies of the constituent states. These relationships fall into a global pattern which is susceptible to change, but which reveals underlying conditions which are worthy of analysis."— A. E. Moodie, *Geography behind Politics*, London, 1947, pp. 59—60.

An almost classical study of political geography is *Geography and World Power* by James Fairgrieve, 8th ed., London, 1941.

[5] Ellsworth Huntington and Stephen Sargent, *Climatic Changes. Their Nature and Causes*, New Haven, 1922.

in relatively few years, considerably improved the possibility of navigation north of the Siberian coast; and this fact is, of course, of great economic and strategic importance. It may also be mentioned that hurricanes, floods and earthquakes may make great, although only local, changes in the environment.

More important from the point of view of contemporary international relations are, however, the processes of change in the natural environment which are effected by man. Most conspicuous is probably the political importance of the great canals which have been dug through narrow strips of land. It may suffice to mention merely the great ones which divide Africa from Asia and South America from North America.

The modification of coastlines may attract less attention, but when we realize the importance of the many more or less artificial harbors, we will agree that this man-made change in the natural environment also deserves admiration.[6] And considerable areas of land have been reclaimed from the ocean by the building of dykes, and turned into fertile land.

Rivers have been diverted and regulated, lakes have been filled up or drained, and marshes and swamps have been turned into arable land. Changes have been made in the quantity as well as the quality of ground and surface water. Passages have been cut through mountains and under sea and river bottoms. Hills have been leveled. The quality and quantity of soils have been greatly changed through the ages, in some cases to such an extent that the appearance of particular localities has been considerably altered. Soil erosion, in particular, may in many places be a serious problem. Mention must especially be made of the great political consequences of depletion of mineral deposits due to economic exploitation.

Minor alterations are effected even in climatic elements. The character of the air can be considerably changed, particularly over densely populated industrial areas. Attempts are being made to induce precipitation artificially, and promising results have already been achieved. A recent but very

---

[6] To a particular category, but certainly very important from a political point of view, belong temporary artificial harbors of the kind used by the invasion forces during World War II.

important problem is the increase in the radioactivity of air and soil as well as the effect of fission materials on living organisms.

Highly important also are changes in that aspect of the natural environment which is often called the biological environment, and which refers to plant and animal life. By his activity through the ages man has profoundly affected the flora of most, if not all, of the regions of the globe. Vast stretches of forested land have been changed into grassland or arable land, and a large number of plants and trees have been spread to new regions. Some species have been eradicated, while others have had their areas greatly reduced.

This situation is equally noteworthy in the case of animal life, at least from the economic point of view. Some economically important species, like certain kinds of whales, have been exterminated or seriously reduced in number, while others have been decimated merely because hunting them is a popular psort. On the positive side is man's increasing ability to destroy harmful insects and animals. Especially important is the progress made in techniques of destroying disease-carrying insects and animals, such as mosquitoes and rats. This ability has enabled man to make effective use of previously almost uninhabitable regions and to improve sanitation in densely populated areas to a considerable extent.

Many of these processes of change have been set in motion unintentionally. In his eagerness to exploit the riches of nature and to manufacture, man has produced harmful results which he has not been able to foresee. Rivers, air, and ocean fringes have been polluted, sometimes with very unpleasant effects. Ruthless deforestation has, in some cases, brought about not only changes in local climate but also very harmful soil erosion. But all these problems seem insignificant as compared to those with which we are confronted by the development of atomic industry.[7] To deal efficiently with them will require worldwide cooperation.

[7] William L. Thomas Jr. (ed.), *Man's Role in Changing the Face of the Earth*, Chicago, 1956. This great symposium deals with the subject from points of view which the student of international relations may find interesting.

Physiographic Factors in World Affairs

In the following pages we will endeavor to indicate by a few examples the relevance of physiographic factors in world affairs. There are many other aspects of the subject which deserve attention, and it may well be that the examples which have been selected here are not the most important.

Some interesting political contingencies follow already from the distribution or layout of land and sea on the globe. Only less than one third of the earth's surface is land. Two large continents,[8] Eurasia-Africa, covering 83 million square kilometers, and the Americas, about half that size or 42 million square kilometers, surround in the north the mostly ice-covered Arctic Sea and radiate southwards in a tripartite fashion to 35° south latitude in the case of Africa and as far as 60° south latitude in the case of South America. By far the greater part of the former continent is located to the north of the Tropic of Cancer, while the latter is roughly divided by that line. Then there are, in the southern hemisphere, the somewhat smaller continent of Australia, covering 8.9 million square kilometers, and the ice-covered and uninhabited Antarctica, which is 14 million square kilometers.

This means that by far the greater part of the earth's land surface is located in the northern hemisphere, and that the Arctic Ocean forms a kind of mediterranean sea between the culturally most advanced regions of the world, which are likewise the seats of the most powerful political units. The land of the southern hemisphere is largely located in climatically unfavorable regions, where there are no strong powers. World affairs are, therefore, primarily controlled from the northern regions, and it can be safely concluded that no major change in this situation is likely to occur in the near future.

A noteworthy strategic aspect of this situation in the air age is the fact that planes based in the Arctic can reach most of the important targets in the world, and this opportunity is

---

[8] The term *world islands* has often been used since it was coined by Sir Halford MacKinder some forty years ago. But the term *continents* will be preferred in this study because it seems to convey a more accurate notion.

being increasingly exploited in modern strategy. It is interesting to note how an increasing number of strategic maps are based on the polar projection, where the North Pole forms the center.

The political and military implications of this distribution of land and sea on the globe are particularly significant in the case of the Americas. For some decades American states were able to pursue a policy of neutrality in European conflicts. However, even in the first quarter of the twentieth century this policy became—largely as a result of technological progress —untenable. But the continent could still avoid being a battleground in a major war or the target of large scale bombing, thanks to its distance from the Eurasian-African continent. During the two World Wars its industry could be operated and developed unhampered by war damage. Today, advance in transport has reduced, if not eliminated, this possibility, and it is increasingly feared that in case of a major armed conflict the New World may have to rely on its own resources.[9]

The configuration of the land masses is also an important matter, since it affects the delimitation of political units. Coastlines are often political borders, but the sea may also unite. This has been true particularly in times when the means of sea transport have been relatively favorable as compared with those of land transport. The configuration of the land masses, moreover, affects the course of trade routes. Particularly important are bottlenecks between oceans or seas where ocean trade is constricted. Gibraltar, the Malaccan Straits, and the Straits of Bab el Mandeb are important cases in point. Sea transport has usually offered not only greater opportunity for a concentration of power than land transport, but also a greater freedom in choice of route. At these bottlenecks such choice is lacking. There are abundant examples from modern history of how the possession of such points entails great strategic and economic advantage, although in our day of strategic bombing they have become more vulnerable to attack. Man-made canals fill the same role, and so, in a way, do isthmuses, even

---

[9] *Accessibility of Strategic and Critical Materials to the United States in Time of War and for Our Expanding Economy, Senate Report No. 1627,* Washington, 1954, p. 28.

if they are not cut through by canals. This has been particularly well illustrated by the narrow strip of land between Asia and Africa.

Mountain ranges occasionally play a highly significant role as political and cultural barriers. The great, apparently tertiary, folding which extends from the Mediterranean Sea eastwards to the Chinese plain, almost dividing Eurasia in the north-south direction, and branching south into the Indo-Chinese peninsula, dividing India from the Far East, has had, and still has, in spite of great advance in the means of transport, a political importance which is rarely overestimated. Its effect as a barrier is, moreover, enhanced by the partly adjacent Dry Belt of Asia, which extends westward into the Saharo-Arabian Belt. Among other mountain ranges which have played important roles in history may be mentioned the Alps and the Pyrenees.

Land transport is apparently affected even more than sea transport by physiographic factors. Certain passes, valleys, or plains, serving as bridges between important regions, have for centuries been traditional roads of migration, or routes for military campaigns and for trade, in spite of considerable changes in transportation techniques. Although they may offer great economic advantage, notably for traders, their military importance has often made it a mixed pleasure to inhabit such localities.[10]

The direction in which states have expanded, or are inclined to expand, can occasionally be defined in terms of geography; either the route or the objectives may be geographically determined. Russia, for instance, has for generations, irrespective of regime, carefully considered any opportunity to thrust foreward in the direction of the Yellow Sea and has tried to extend her sphere of influence towards the Mediterranean largely because of the commercial and strategic value of coastal zones. Another example which may be mentioned is that the Far Eastern nations have fairly consistently expanded southwest in the direction of Indo-China. A large number of other interesting cases can be found in the history of colonial expansion.

---

[10] Lucien Febvre, *A Geographical Introduction to History*, London, 1932, p. 316 ff. See also Hugo Hassinger, *Geographische Grundlagen der Geschichte*, Freiburg, 1931.

Finally, some general remarks may be made on the role of accessibility, which is usually of considerable social and political importance. High accessibility may favor economic life and, on the whole, have a stimulating cultural effect. But it cannot be concluded that low accessibility has only unfavorable effects. It may enable a nation to avoid being drawn into international conflicts against its will, and the percentage of its energy which is spent on military affairs can thus be kept at a relatively low level. However, accessibility is the result of a number of factors, only some of which, like topographic features, island position or climatic elements, are geographical. The others are social and, therefore, subject to relatively rapid change.

Climatic Factors

The social and political significance of climate has been the subject of long controversies.[11] All authorities seem to agree that climate is a most important factor in social life, but there is little agreement about how or to what extent it affects human affairs. It is obvious that there is a relationship between climate and vegetation as well as animal life, and together such factors are, of course, of the greatest importance for the cultural conditions and way of life of every nation. It is interesting to note that the areas of highly advanced civilizations coincide to a large extent with areas of favorable climate.[12] Such phenomena have induced several students to form rather deterministic social theories, but it is obviously necessary to tread warily, since there are many complicating factors.

We are here concerned with the importance of climate merely from the point of view of world affairs; and two important facts immediately attract attention; namely, that there is not, and never has been, any really strong power in the tropics,

---

[11] Lucien Febvre, op. cit., p. 91 ff. In referring to this in many ways excellent book, it should be added that it may not be entirely unbiased.

[12] Ellsworth Huntington, Mainsprings of Civilization, New York, 1945, Part III. Highly interesting, though possibly controversial, is the author's view on the psychological consequences of geographical factors, cf., Chapters 18—19.

and that most of the polar areas have, until recently, been almost inaccessible. In these regions, which together cover a large part of the earth's surface, man must use so great a percentage of his energy to overcome the difficult geographical problems that only a moderate quantity is left for creative work.[13]

The tropics are underdeveloped, and, in the case of Africa, still largely colonial areas. All the peoples of this part of the world may, and should, achieve political independence some day, but they seem not likely to play a really prominent role in world affairs. The arctic and subarctic regions have, partly because of their geographical proximity, been incorporated in the states of the northern temperate zone. But these lands, too, are, to a great extent, still unexploited, primarily as a consequence of their severe climate. The greater part of Antarctica is also occupied by the northern states, and here only the resources of the sea have been exploited so far. But it is becoming increasingly possible and necessary to make use of the economic resources of all these parts of the world. Very significant also is the fact that military considerations have made it necessary to establish bases in localities where man has previously hardly trodden.

It is, moreover, noteworthy that there are only relatively small areas of fertile land in the temperate zone of the southern hemisphere. The parts of Australia, Africa, and South America which are situated in these latitudes are, to a considerable extent, desert. It thus appears that climate combines with physiographic factors in increasing the political preponderance of the northern temperate zone.

Geographical difficulties of the kind mentioned on the previous pages have been increasingly reduced by modern technique and science.[14] This development is clearly revealed particularly in the polar regions. But climatic problems may still be very great, for instance in the case of transport and the art of war, not only in the polar regions, the tropics, or in desert areas, but also in somewhat more hospitable areas. The

---

[13] S. F. Markham, *Climate and the Energy of Nations*, Oxford, 1944.
[14] E. P. Hanson, *New World Emerging*, New York, 1949.

classical example of this fact is, above all, Russia. Such phenomena have, naturally, a considerable indirect political importance.
While for some time there may have been a tendency to form
rather naively deterministic hypotheses about the relationship
between man and nature, there seems today to be some inclination to underestimate the importance of geographical factors.
Even in our atomic age man is still largely an earth-bound
creature, who, in planning his actions, must pay due attention
to the character of his natural environment. And this fact offers
the analyst many clues to an understanding of the policies of
nations.

The Political Importance of Resources

The importance of resources is so fundamental and all-
embracing that it neither can nor need be dealt with anything
like exhaustively within the framework which the study of
international relations can adopt. It may suffice to draw attention merely to some major aspects of the subject.[15]

Natural resources reveal particularly well both the profound
importance of geographical factors and the fact that the significance of the latter may be fundamentally affected by matters
of technical culture. The tremendous oil resources of the countries adjoining the Iranian Gulf were of little use until they
could be exploited by Western techniques. The uranium deposits
of Northwestern Canada would probably have meant nothing
to the Indian tribes even if they had known about them. But
the possession of essential resources by peoples capable of using
them means strength and welfare; and their outstanding political importance is unmistakably indicated by the role they have
played as issues of war. In one way or another, nations have
all through the ages been fighting for the wealth of the world.[16]

---

[15] The subject is dealt with also in Chapter XI.

[16] In the vast literature on resources, the student of international relations may
find interesting a book like *World Resources and Industries. A Functional Appraisal of
the Availability of Agricultural and Industrial Materials* by Erich W. Zimmerman, New
York, 1951, particularly part I.

Also, resources reflect the dynamics of human social life. One particular type may be essential for some time; then another takes its place. Tin, copper, and iron have, in turn, been the pivots of technology. The same is true of the resources of power. Coal has been largely outmoded by petroleum, which, in turn, may be rivaled by atomic power. Food resources which are mostly based on plant and animal life reveal a somewhat greater stability.

The dependence of technical civilization upon metals and sources of power seems to explain why they coincide to a considerable degree. The countries bordering on the North Atlantic are—or at least have been—on the whole fairly well supplied. This fact partly explains their strong industrial and political position. In addition, they have for several generations controlled, to a large extent, the distribution of the resources which are produced in other parts of the world. This is particularly true of strategic materials like oil and the more important kinds of ore.

The production of highly industrialized countries is so great and varied that some of its ingredients must be brought from abroad, and the dependency on foreign supply tends to increase as some resources of highly industrialized regions are being depleted. Mineral resources in particular are distributed rather incongruously with consumption, and hardly any country is self-sufficient in all fields.[17] More than a third of the world's output of minerals seeks foreign markets. Of this production petroleum, iron ore, and coal constitute the bulk. It is particularly here that politics comes into the picture.[18] Nothing indicates this better than petroleum, which, in fact, is rather a newcomer as a major strategic raw material. Not until the early interwar period did it become clear that petroleum would increasingly supersede coal both in industry and as fuel for ships. Great Britain was then quick to intensify its diplomatic activity to gain control of the fields, and the British had remark-

---

[17] Not even an area like the Western Hemisphere is self-sufficent in all fields. Cf. *Accessibility of Strategic and Critical Materials to the United States in Time of War and for our Expanding Economy. Senate Report No. 1627,* Washington, 1954, p. 34 ff.

[18] L. Herman Beukema et. al., *Raw Materials in War and Peace,* New York, 1947.

able success for some time. The United States was somewhat slower to enter the gamble, because it had vast resources at home. But it eventually became clear that the United States could not rely merely on domestic supply, and during recent years this country has become the strongest rival for the available resources of the world. A similar situation has occurred in the production of iron ore. The great domestic deposits are largely depleted. It is calculated that by 1960 the United States will need to import about 50 million tons.

Increasing nationalism and the spread of socialist ideas have, in recent years, complicated the situation. The technically poorly developed producers of raw materials reveal an increasing desire to control the output themselves; and since these countries are short of capital, nationalization of the industries seems to have a particular appeal, even in states where socialist ideas are not too popular. The nationalization of the petroleum production in Mexico and the energetic attempt to do the same in Iran are examples of this trend. Even when the production is in the hands of the citizens of the producing country, they often prefer to live abroad and register their companies there to obtain reduction in taxation. The extent to which the natural resources are in the hands of foreigners is almost unbelievable, even in some countries which have enjoyed political independence for generations. This is true notably of some South American states.[19] A strong reaction to this state of affairs could not be avoided. Growing nationalism is bringing about changes, as is indicated by the nationalization of the tin industry in Bolivia and of the Suez Canal. On the other hand, there may be some doubt as to whether all of these countries have already acquired the economic strength and the technical ability to develop their resources satisfactorily.

The distribution of resources for food, shelter, and clothing compares, on the whole, better with consumption than does that of the resources for heavy industry, and the possibility of adjustment to obtain greater self-sufficiency in case of emergency

---

[19] United Nations, Department of Economic and Social Affairs, *Foreign Capital in Latin America*, New York, 1955.

is, on the whole, better. But there are many instances of discrepancy between production and consumption which entail great political consequences. The Far East and India, for example, have for a long time been largely dependent upon the rice production of Indo-China. But the greatest case of dependency on foreign production of foodstuffs is apparently Great Britain. The political and military implications of this situation are very far-reaching indeed, and the possibility of exploiting them has for more than a hundred years been the preoccupation of military experts in rival countries.[20]

The relationship between the means of subsistence and the size of population varies to a very great extent from one region to another; and the difference in ability to utilize the available resources enlarges still more the difference in wealth among the nations. This important aspect of the world society is attracting increasing attention, and it is generally agreed that to find a suitable solution to this problem is a prerequisite to friendly and reasonably stable relations among the peoples of the world.[21]

However, the problem goes further. Many experts in the field believe that within the not too distant future the resources of the earth will simply not suffice for all of us, and they have warned that the rapidly growing population of the world is increasing the demand for means of subsistence at a dangerous speed, while on the other hand mineral resources are being quickly depleted in technically advanced regions, and agricultural production is being seriously affected by erosion and other causes of reduction in the fertility of the soil. Others are maintaining that man's inventiveness certainly will be able to solve the problem.[22] And, in fact, the history of inventions

---

[20] Important in this respect is the fact that the import of the United Kingdom is so widespread that no single country supplies more than 13—14 per cent of her total import.

[21] Gunnar Myrdal, *International Economy; Problems and Prospects*, New York, 1956.

[22] Roderick Peattie, "Are You a Malthusian? A Review and a Bibliography of Recent Readings," *Journal of Geography*, Vol. 49 (1950).

seems to encourage the optimist.[23] Advance in technical culture enables man to exploit the resources of the vast tropical and polar regions, which so far have been largely out of reach. Consolation may also be drawn from the fact that, if need be, the growth in population can be checked by other means than the traditional ones—war, pest, flood, earthquake, and the like.

---

[23] Athelstan Spilhaus, "Control of theWorld Environment," *Geographical Review*, Vol. 46 (1956), p. 451 ff.

CHAPTER V

THE HETEROGENEITY AND DYNAMICS
OF THE WORLD SOCIETY

When we turn our attention to what may be called the socio-cultural environment in which the actors in international affairs operate, we are confronted with a very complicated subject matter. Human social life varies not only from one region to another, but even within relatively small areas. Moreover, the phenomena are subject to rapid change, which makes observations from earlier generations of reduced value for the interpretation of contemporary affairs. On the whole, these two characteristics of the subject matter, diversity and instability, complicate scientific operations to a large extent.

Spatial Variations in the Pattern of Culture

It is generally agreed that the some two and a half billion peoples of the earth, in spite of variations in such matters as body build, skin color, and limb proportions, all belong to the same species. But their way of life may vary greatly from one region to another. A large number of cultures[1] have been recognized, scattered over most of the earth's land surface. There are certain human and social needs which every culture must satisfy, but otherwise the patterns of behavior tend to

---

[1] According to some authorities, at least a thousand. The term culture may be defined as a set of behavior patterns more or less common to the members of a group of peoples, and which is passed down from one generation to another and taught to children, while it is constantly liable to change. Cf. John Lewis Gillin and John Philip Gillin, *Cultural Sociology*, New York, 1948, p. 139 ff.

reveal more or less spatial variation. Perhaps nothing indicates this heterogeneity of human culture better than the partition of the world society by an incredible number of apparently wholly useless linguistic barriers, which look like remnants of social practices developed thousands of years back in ages when the globe was sparsely populated and inter-society contacts were negligible as compared with present day conditions.

Sustenance and shelter are provided in a great many ways. There is little resemblance between the crude windbreaks of aboriginal Australians and the glass skyscrapers of the great cities in the Western world, except that they are both shelters for human beings. The difference in the foodstuffs eaten by the inhabitants of the extreme Arctic and the meals served at an exclusive Paris restaurant is certainly also great; or compare the dress of a Pygmy with that of a Greenland Eskimo. And in between such extremes there are almost infinite shades and variations.

Social structure and economic activity reveal an almost equally great diversity. There are societies which depend for their subsistence upon primitive techniques for extracting what they need from materials offered by the environment in their natural state, like the gathering of fruits, seeds, and leaves. And there are the highly industrialized societies with their advanced technology and great centers of production, where everyday life has become mechanized and monotonous almost to a dangerous degree.

This diversity of culture reflects, to a considerable degree, the environmental differences between the various parts of the earth, to which man must adapt himself. As pointed out in the preceding chapter, the climatic elements and the topography of a region, its natural resources and its location with respect to trade routes, etc., affect, more or less, the character of economic activity as well as many other social phenomena including political activity.[2] And the geographical picture changes greatly

---

[2] C. Langdon White and G. T. Renner, *Human Geography: Ecological Study of Society*, New York, 1948.

from the icy Arctic to the dense rain forest of the Torrid Zone, from the luxuriant monsoon coast to the dry and almost lifeless desert, from the plains at sea level to mountain plateaus at some 20,000 feet.

But there are also other forces at work. Societies are made by an interplay between man and nature. Apparently more important than the impact of the natural environment is the inventiveness of the human mind. Numerous examples from the history of civilizations seem to support this assumption. Regions of Europe which today are highly developed and over-populated industrial areas were once the hunting ground of cliff dwellers; and only a few generations ago the great production centers of the Middle West in the United States— technologically the most advanced districts of the world— were the fields of roaming Indians. The natural resources were there, but technical knowledge had not yet reached such a state of perfection that they could be put to good use in the same way as today. However, in spite of all this, geographical factors may help to explain why some peoples are still living in the culture of a stone age, while others have learned to fly through the air and to split the atom.

When we turn to religious and intellectual life we likewise find many variations, and sometimes profound and apparently irreconcilable differences. As a rule, it is extremely difficult for a stranger to understand and appreciate fairly the views and feelings of a people; and it is a commonplace assertion that mankind is almost hopelessly divided into conflicting groups, which demand the loyalty of the individual; it is assumed that common values are almost lacking. This may, however, be an exaggeration of the real state of affairs. Obviously, there is no denying that it is extraordinarily difficult to reconcile views; but in spite of all these disagreements, a serious examination may prove that basically peoples all over the world have quite a few values in common. Although acquired drives may vary greatly, some fundamental biological similarities remain. And it is significant that the commandments of the advanced religions to which nearly all of mankind belongs are basically very similar. They all prohibit killing, stealing and lying; and they share the common ideals of justice and peace.[3] It is, moreover, important that this great variety of human social life is being diminished. The trend is clearly towards greater unity.[4]

Actually the important thing, from the point of view of the student of international affairs, is not merely to remember that great regional variations in culture exist, but also to realize that they are sociologically quite natural. The fact that a people behaves differently from the way we are used to does not necessarily mean that it is funny or backward. It is usually hard to say whether one way of life is higher than another, because that depends on what scale of values we use. But the level of technical culture is, as a rule, easy to ascertain; and we may say that a people behaves barbarously according to more or less universally accepted standards of conduct and human values. In a rapidly integrating world, which irresistibly makes distant peoples more or less dependent on each other, it seems essential to adopt this point of view; otherwise, it will be difficult to obtain the degree of tolerance needed for a reasonably successful cooperation.[5]

Implications of Accelerating Dynamics

Viewed over a reasonably long period of time, human society reveals not only striking regional variety but also remarkable fluidity. It seems, in fact, that the whole mosaic of social life over the earth is subject to continuous change, some societies being more stable than others. In some civilizations the change may be almost imperceptible for centuries, as has been the case with some great societies in Asia; and the societies of primitive peoples living in the tropical rain forest might seem even more static if protected against influence from outside. But they all change over a long span of time.

---

[3] Norman Bentwich, *The Religious Foundations of Internationalism*, London, 1933. It is, however, possible to point to some minor exceptions to this rule; and there may, of course, often be great discrepancy between theory and practice.

[4] Cf. below Chaphter VII.

[5] Problems of evaluation are dealt with in Chapter XVIII.

It is difficult to find out what initiates the change in a society. Among the more important factors may be mentioned technological inventions, discovery of new resources, new ideologies and religions. Other factors are changes in population and wealth, or dynamic personages, and political changes.[6] Particularly important seem social models which have a great appeal to the masses, like the one advocated by communism.

Evolution may not always mean progress. There are periods of retrogression and decay,[7] at least in some sections of society. But on the whole evolution has, with accelerating speed, moved in the direction of greater mastery by man over the forces of nature. For the peoples who have a written history the main trends can be fairly easily discerned.

The increasing acceleration of social dynamics is in fact an amazing phenomenon, which we can fully realize only when we use the long perspective of the anthropologist. Nearly a million years seem to have elapsed before man reached the stone age culture, while the steps from there to the "atom age" have been taken in a few thousand years. According to the conclusions reached by anthropologists, it took man several hundred thousand years to learn domestication of animals and plants; and viewed against the existing stage of culture these inventions involved a profound social revolution, since they apparently led to the transition from migratory bands to more or less permanent settlements. In the same way, the introduction of domesticated animals and sailing boats as means of transport must no doubt have meant a great step forward in the long process of learning to cope with the forces of nature. Yet it all seems insignificant as compared with recent developments.

In our own time and society the processes of increasingly rapid change have in several ways become a serious worry. It is not always easy for man to adapt himself to the miracles

---

[6] William Fielding Ogburn, *Social Change with Respect to Culture and Original Nature*, New York, 1928.

[7] Arnold J. Toynbee deals in his monumental work, *A Study of History*, with more than twenty civilizations covering a time span of about 6,000 years.

which he creates; they usually involve complicated unforeseen problems.

The fluidity of human society tends to counteract regional variations and cultural isolationism. Even in ancient times, when the means of transport were incredibly poor as compared with present-day conditons, the movement and the mingling of the races were truly amazing. It may suffice to recall the waves of invaders who entered America from the north and spread over the continent, the sailors who traversed the great oceans, and the horsemen who swept over the vast Eurasian plains. The ensuing intersociety diffusion of cultural elements appears to have been considerably greater than generally realized. Thus, underneath the variations there are also deep-rooted and far-flung relationships;[8] and the effect of accelerating dynamics upon the processes of cultural diffusion is becoming increasingly marked.

Of particular interest are the implications of social dynamics on the methodology and ability of the social sciences. The variety and dynamics of the subject matter naturally entail that it is hard to obtain scientific propositions of general validity.[9] In this respect the social scientist is confronted with problems somewhat different from those of the student of physical sciences, who can deal largely with inanimate and, as a rule, far more static subject matter. We must really question to what extent it is possible to arrive at universal rules in the social sciences.

---

[8] Kaj Birket-Smith, *Geschichte der Kultur*, Zürich, 1946.

[9] The implications to the research process of this situation are discussed in Chapter XVI.

CHAPTER VI

THE MAIN STRUCTURE OF THE
WORLD SOCIETY

Some sort of social and political organization is apparently necessary even for the most primitive people. As civilization has developed, man has organized himself in various kinds of self-governing groups growing in size and complexity from small migratory bands to the clan, the tribe, and lastly the various types of states,[1] which again are subdivided into many kinds of groups varying greatly in size and character. By organization man improves his ability to satisfy his biological demands and other needs and aspirations. And as the technological processes become increasingly complicated, the need for cooperation tends to increase at a rate which raises great problems of organization and adaptation.

It is supposed that a realistic study of international relations should include endeavors to understand the organization, or lack of organization, of the world society. If we lack an elementary knowledge of the context in which international politics takes place we shall hardly be able to understand its character properly.[2] We will, therefore, in the following pages make some suggestions as to what points of view may be chosen for this kind of analysis.

---

[1] "What is a nation or a state but a group of people associated for certain purposes?" Linden A. Manden, *Foundations of Modern World Society*, Stanford, 1947, p. VIII.

[2] Geography provides much essential data and numerous useful concepts for analysis of this subject.

The State System

The principle unit of the world society, and the one with which the student of international relations is primarily concerned, is the politically sovereign group which we call the state. The number of states has slowly decreased, while the size and interdependence of such sovereign groups have tended to increase.[3] There has, however, not been a straight development in this direction. The crumbling of empires has entailed a temporary increase in the number; and the adoption of the principle of self-determination and national unity has had a two-way effect, leading in some cases to the union of small states, in others, to the breaking up of great powers into smaller units. But when we view the development over a long span of time, it seems clear that the trend has been towards fewer and larger states. During the last years the number of independent powers has varied around one hundred. They cover, with their territories, practically all the land of the globe. Even the most remote corners of the polar regions have been claimed; only the oceans and the air above them are the common property of mankind.

The tremendous difference in size is indicated by the fact that the greatest state, the Soviet Union, covers 22.27 million square kilometers, or about one sixth of all the land surface, while the smallest one,[4] Monaco, has an area of 1.5 square kilometers. The size and form of the territory may have great political and military importance. Most of the states have a continous territory, while some, notably the British Empire, are scattered over several continents. The cohesion of such political units is naturally exposed to disintegrating forces and largely dependent on transport. The intercontinental type of state has, on the whole, been losing ground in recent years. The location of a state with respect to lines of transport, economically or strategically important regions, densely populated

---

[3] See below, Chapter VIII.

[4] The Vatican State is only 109 acres, but it is a question whether it can be regarded as an ordinary state.

areas, major centers of administration, or other important objectives is a very important factor in its life.

All sovereign states are subjects of international law, which postulates equality among them—that is to say, equality before the law. The law is the same for great and small states. Theoretically, it does not provide the one with any privileges as compared with the other. With respect to power and influence, however, there is the greatest of difference between, for example, the kingdom of Nepal and the republic of the United States of America.[5] But so it is among the subjects of municipal law, too. Equality before the law does not mean equality between the rich and the poor with regard to opportunities and influence.

There has been a tendency to think of states merely as nation states. But there are, of course, a considerable number of states which are multinational, sometimes with all ethnic groups enjoying at least theoretical equality. It is interesting to note that the influence of empires where one nation is ruling over others, commonly more backward peoples, has been declining. Only fifty years ago a large part of the world, with a population of between six and seven hundred millions, was so-called colonial areas ruled by the European great powers. The national liberation of these peoples has proceeded with such speed that little more than 100 million peoples still have a colonial status. This development has entailed a temporary increase in the number of states. In some cases the independence of a state may be merely nominal. One important reason for this may often be economic dependence upon a great power, although the relationship between great and small powers has changed.[6] It follows from the variety of human social life that states may differ in a great many other ways. It may suffice to mention merely the many types of government.[7] Boundaries of states are often geographical in nature, sometimes merely

---

[5] H.Weinschel, "The Doctrine of Equality of States and its Recent Modifications," *American Journal of International Law*, Vol. 45 (1945).

[6] Cf. below, Chapter VIII.

[7] For a brief discussion reference may be made to G. Schwartzenberger, *Power Politics*, Chapters 3—7.

ethnic. They may have been drawn up arbitrarily, or they may even have come about by mere chance.[8]

The ranking of the states is an aspect of fundamental importance. Since the element of power is so strongly dominating in the world society, the order of the hierarchy of states is more or less clearly arranged according to the striking power in conflict. This is true at least insofar as the greater powers are concerned. Decisive influence in world affairs is vested only in a few great powers, which tend to be surrounded by spheres of influence consisting of minor or small powers. Perhaps it may be said that the number of states wielding decisive influence in international politics has been decreasing in recent years.

That a large number of small states can exist at all in a society where the political problems in the final instance are so often—or we may perhaps say, as a rule—decided by the actual use, or by the threat of use, of sheer force might seem curious.[9] However, small states within the sphere of influence of a great power may enjoy relatively favorable conditions provided they do not reveal an interest in political or social systems antagonistic to that of the guardian state; and, of course, steps will be taken to prevent them from entering into too close relations with rival great powers. However, the character of the guardian power's political regime as well as the degree of tension in international politics may considerably affect the extent of actual independence which can be obtained.

Small states often constitute buffers in border zones between the spheres of influence claimed by the great powers. They may then enjoy considerable freedom of choice in their foreign policy. In some cases they may even be able to play one great power against another. But they are, on the other hand, severely exposed to intriguing, internal disintegration, and weakening of morale by the subversive activity of the rivaling great powers. In such cases the small powers are actually the battle-ground

---

[8] Thomas H. Holdich, *Political Frontiers and Boundary Making*, London, 1916; Stephen B. Jones, *Boundary Making*, Washington, 1945.

[9] Cf. Schwartzenberger, *Power Politics*, pp. 104—112.

of the cold war between the major antagonists in world politics, and to resist the destructive forces may require considerable internal social and political strength. As an example from recent history may be mentioned Iran. It is as a matter of consequence almost unavoidable that such states become pawns in the game of power politics. And changes in the pattern of power or balance of power may mean that they almost disappear from the political map. This has happened, for instance, to Poland, which is a middle power. When a small state is able to maintain actual independence for a long period of time in the midst of rivaling great powers, it seems to serve a political function in the international society. It may, for example, serve as a buffer state, which one or several of the great powers consider useful, and therefore support. Switzerland may be given as an example of this situation; particularly instructive is Great Britain's historic interests in preserving the integrity and independence of the Low Countries.[10]

It follows from the dynamics of the world society that the ranking of the powers is very unstable. Civilizations and empires have risen and fallen, and the centers of the greatest cultural advances have moved from one area of the world to another. The political pattern is, in fact, subject to a more or less continous change, although there are also strong forces making for stability. Long-established political units seem to have considerable ability to resist change even if they are badly outmoded by the trend of events.

It is interesting to note that advancing technology may at one time favor one area; then another region may benefit. Science and technology may change the possibilities of exploiting the natural resources. The crop-raising opportunities of the river valleys in the Near East could be exploited at a comparatively early stage of cultural development. It took a much longer time before man could exploit the resources of Western Europe so that this part of the world was brought to leadership in world affairs.

---

[10] Royal Institute of International Affairs, *Political and Strategic Interests of the United Kingdom*, London, 1939, p. 12 ff.

In a somewhat similar manner the technique of warfare may change the strategic position of a country. The island position of Great Britain made it possible for several hundred years for her to devote a relatively small part of her manpower and economic resources to defence. And in the existing political and social pattern her peoples seemed almost predestined to become naval and trade minded. The geographic factors which gave her a priviliged position in the era of naval empires may be less advantageous in the era of air power.[11] Or, put in other words, progress in the art of war, which, of course, is merely part of a more inclusive technological development, may at a certain stage favor one country, then at the next stage favor a country having a different geographical setting.

Shift in power may, to some extent, also be due to changes in the natural environment. The building of canals may increase the strategic and economic importance of an area. Drainage of swamps, extirpation of harmful animals or insects, and reduction of endemic diseases improve a region, while reduction of resources by, for instance, deforestation, soil erosion, or depletion of mineral deposits has the opposite effect. But more often the causes of major shifts in power must be sought in political, economic, and social changes. There are numerous examples which prove that the establishment of a new political regime may have far-reaching effects upon the power-potential and international ranking of a country.

Finally, it may be mentioned that change in the ranking of the powers by actual expansion of territory and subjugation of other peoples is not yet an entirely outmoded practice. Historical experience indicates, however, that such states tend to be unstable unless the ethnic groups are being properly merged socially in each other. Powers which have been able to undertake major expansions have usually enjoyed a technical superiority, notably in military affairs.

The real or alleged objectives of expansion have been numerous. Frequently they have been to obtain a better strategic

---

[11] Cf. this year's British "White Paper" on the reorganization of the armed forces. See also E. J. Kingston-McCloughry, *Global Strategy*, London, 1957, Chapter IV

position by the improvement of frontiers. The notion of strategic frontiers has played an important role in international affairs.[12] But when such objectives have been achieved, the scene has frequently been set for still further demands and more expansion. Of other objectives may be mentioned access to raw materials, markets, and lanes of transport. In many cases colonial expansion can be classified under this category. Occasionally the expansion is undertaken in order to prevent the occupation of a certain territory by an enemy. Poland has had some very unpleasant experiences in this respect. Under the impact of nationalism, it has been a frequent objective to bring about union of people of the same nationality.[13] This kind of expansion is well known from modern European history. Another strong motivating force is pressure due to overpopulation. Japanese expansion in recent decades may, to some extent, be classified with this type. It is also conceivable that a regime may try to improve its position by focusing people's attention on an adventure in foreign policy. Such motives are naturally difficult for the research scholar to ascertain. Cession of territory and the granting of independence to parts of a state are usually done merely as a matter of necessity. A state may be faced with such strong disintegrating forces, like growing nationalism supported by rival powers, that it may seem advantageous or necessary to end the struggle by a contraction of the frontiers, with ensuing reduction in military commitments. This is what has happened in recent years to the British Empire.

Interstate Groups

The common practice of pooling resources for defence against a common enemy has occasionally led to a lasting union, but as a rule such relationships have a rather fleeting character. And this leads us to another important aspect of the structure of the world society.

---

[12] Lucien Febvre, *A Geographical Introduction to History*, p. 297 ff.
[13] Norman Hill, *Title to Territory*, London, 1945.

All through the ages international societies have tended to be loosely organized into systems of alliances or power-political groupings transcending state borders. As international politics has expanded and come to have a global character, such systems of alliance have become correspondingly wider. Until recently, some great powers have tried to conduct a policy of neutrality and remain outside such super-groups in international politics. But it is becoming increasingly clear that the world society has now reached a degree of integration which makes this political technique almost impracticable. Today only minor states, favorably located, manage to maintain a policy of neutrality.[14]

Such super-groups have tended to become increasingly versatile both with regard to structure and to functions. A state can be a member of several defence organizations. This is a form of political integration to which we have so far paid little attention. The United States, for example, is today simultaneously a party to NATO and SEATO, as well as a member of the Inter-American Treaty of Reciprocal Assistance. The members of the European Council form a kind of union which may be given as an example of an intergovernmental organization with a variety of non-military functions; and its members, with a few exceptions, are also parties to NATO. Some organizations like the Pan-American Union have a geographical delimitation and may be fairly stable. Others, like the Arab League, have a linguistic and cultural basis.[15] Still others, like the great communist and non-communist coalitions, have what may be called a socio-political basis.

Another highly important aspect of the world society is the large social and spiritual groups[16] created by the division of mankind into different religious and philosophical systems. Their borders may remain fairly stable for long periods of time.

Attempts have been made to divide mankind on the basis of general cultural, notably religious, traits into civilizations,

---

[14] Egypt may be mentioned as an exception to this rule; but it may be argued that its neutrality in World War II was rather precarious.

[15] Some of them are further dealt with in Chapter XII.

[16] Toynbee has called the higher religions societies of another species. *Civilization on Trial*, New York, 1948, Foreword.

and to use this kind of social entity as the "unit" of historical study. There is much to say in favor of this method as compared with the practice of choosing the nation or the state as the "unit of history".[17] But such social groups are apparently not sufficiently clearly delimited for the study of international relations, and their borders tend in some ways to become increasingly blurred. Moreover, in our day of revolutionary change, their social structure is subject to rather great variations. How much will, for example, the Sinic Society of China[18] be transformed in the course of a few years of communist rule? There are, however, indications that civilizations may become increasingly important as units of the world society. Interesting in this respect is the tendency to speak of an Atlantic civilization as a super-group with which the European and American peoples may identify themselves.

It may also be justifiable to mention briefly the increasing number of non-governmental organizations,[19] some of which are very old, but most of which have been established in recent decades. Their members are individuals, institutions, or organizations in a variety of states. They are operating independently of the governments of the states to which their members belong; therefore, they have been called non-governmental. Their functions may vary greatly. Perhaps most of them may be looked upon as humanitarian in character. Some of them, at least, have a structure and function which make it reasonable to regard them as kinds of loosely organized social groups in the world society. Others are more universal, and their administrative setup may develop in the direction of world institutions.[20]

---

[17] Arnold J. Toynbee, *A Study of History*, Vol. I, p. 17 ff.

[18] Of living civilizations Professor Toynbee mentions Western Christendom, the Orthodox Christian Society, the Islamic Society, the Indic or Hindu Society, and the Sinic Society. Cf. *A Study of History*, Vol. I, p. 51 ff. It thus appears as if religion is the basic criterion for his division of mankind into civilizations.

[19] L. C. White, *International Non-Governmental Organizations. Their Purpose, Methods and Accomplishment*, New Brunswick, 1951. For a brief, somewhat lexical description, reference may be made also to the *International Yearbook* and *Statesmen's Who's Who*.

[20] Cf. below p. 118

Regional Variations in Social Structure

Regional variations in social structure affect, of course, international affairs to a very great extent, since they form part of the background to policy orientation. But at the present state of social science research it is rather difficult to undertake a reliable classification and arrangement of the social phenomena involved.

The fundamental difference between communist and capitalist states is surely very conspicuous; but to describe in detail this difference may be less easy than it seems. And between these two extremes there are all sorts of shades and variations.

In some moderately developed regions society reveals a fairly clear stratification. And even some rules of thumb may be useful as a kind of memento. It may, for example, be said with some qualifications that in great parts of South America there is a small class of landowners and military officers who rule the country, and a large proletariat of Indians and Mestizos, while the "middle class" is small or almost lacking. And an authoritarian type of government is common. A somewhat similar social structure exists in certain parts of Asia, for example in the Middle East. Elementary information on this kind of phenomena is readily available in geographical studies, and an increasing number of area studies are improving our knowledge in this field substantially.

Comparative analysis of advanced societies is on the whole more difficult, since they have a more complicated structure. The trend toward greater uniformity[21] may reduce the problems involved in this kind of study, but that will in any case be a slow process.

Social structure appears to be more or less correlative to the degree of industrialization, which may also form a basis of classification. But there is still much pioneering to do in this field. The advance made by sociological research will be

---

[21] Cf. next chapter.

of the greatest importance.[22] However, the student of international relations needs, more than anyone else, information about this subject, and he will have to carry on this study to the best of his ability. The task is formidable—that is true—but the "globalization" of international politics unavoidably confronts the student with this kind of problem.

[22] A project on comparative social analysis is being undertaken at Princeton University, and there is reason to expect that it will produce results of interest to the study of international relations. Cf. Marion J. Levy Jr., *The Structure of Society*, Princeton, 1952; see particularly the preface.

CHAPTER VII

ASSOCIATIVE AND DISSOCIATIVE TRENDS

Since the world society is subject to continuous change, and this change is taking place with increasing speed, it is naturally of the greatest interest for the student of international relations to have an idea of the various trends and the forces behind them. Already in the 1930's some writers, who were influenced by sociological thinking, maintained the view that the integration and disintegration of the world society should be regarded as an essential part of the subject matter of international relations.[1] This is, however, very difficult subject matter, although the source materials, notably the statistical data available to the research scholar today, open up opportunities which no one could dream of some decades ago. Moreover, when social science turns to new aspects of human society, the agencies engaged in providing data are also likely to pay attention to these subjects.

Integration

The advance of technology and science during the past hundred years has resulted in a multiplying of the physical contacts between the nations. Most conspicuous in this process is the development of transport and communication facilities on the one hand and the means of mass production of low-price commodities on the other. International exchange of goods has been extended to embrace practically the whole world,[2] and the volume and variety of the world trade have increased

---

[1] Cf. above, p. 37. The literature on the subject is still rather limited. The author has found the views of Professor Quincy Wright suggestive. Cf. below, p. 93, note 20.

[2] Cf. Eugene Stanley, *World Economy in Transition*, New York, 1939.

tremendously. The value of exports and imports for all the countries of the world has been more than tripled during the past twenty years.[3] Ocean shipping has increased from 470 million metric tons loaded and unloaded in 1929 to 710 million tons in 1954; and the number of net ton-kilometers carried by railway has been doubled during the same period.[4] Particularly amazing is the progress in civil aviation,[5] and the introduction of jet propulsion is calculated to triple the capacity within a few years.

In spite of numerous inventions of synthetic materials and a tireless inventiveness in the production of new articles by the individual countries, economic interdependence seems, on the whole, to increase. The need of highly industrialized states for raw materials and the consumption of advanced nations have become so varied that hardly any of them is entirely self-sufficient in resources.[6] Even superstates like the Soviet Union and the United States are deficient in some essential raw materials. They also find it advantageous to import certain kinds of manufactured goods, since the conditions of production for the different articles may vary greatly from one country to another, and thus create the prerequisites of profitable trade. A world-wide and complicated system of finance has been developed to facilitate trade and the flow of capital between the countries. But there have been, and still are, also some serious retrogressive tendencies at work.

Migration has been technically facilitated, although politically it is still being very much hampered.[7] It is naturally difficult to form a well-founded opinion of its role as integrator and diffuser of cultural elements, though great it certainly is. A very dreary aspect of modern migration is the great number

---

[3] *The Statistical Yearbook of the United Nations for 1955*, p. 386.

[4] *Ibid.*, p. 315 ff.

[5] As an example may be mentioned that passenger-km. increased from about $3/4$ million in 1937 to 33 millions in 1955 in the United States.

[6] Cf. *Reports on Operations of the International Materials Conference*, Washington, 1951—1953. See also *Raw Materials in War and Peace*, issued by United States Military Academy, New York, 1947, Chart I.

[7] Max Sorre, *Les migrations des peuples*, Paris, 1955.

of refugees and displaced persons who have lost their homes as a result of war and revolution.[8]

Travel has been immensely increased and facilitated by improvements in transport, international banking, and the development of travel agencies. Large-scale tourist travel, which has come up only during the last 70—80 years, has become an economic and cultural factor of great importance.[9] Its influence on the views and minds of people is naturally very difficult to ascertain; but that, too, is undoubtedly a matter which deserves some attention.

Even the fields of entertainment and sports are contributing increasingly to the development of international intercourse. Better public and private arrangements have been made for international exchange of art and literature; and opportunities to study abroad have been much improved, not merely for scholars, artists, and teachers, but also for other occupations as well. In recent years it has become increasingly common to arrange these matters by international agreements.[10]

The very fact that there are now four times as many people living on the earth as there were some two hundred years ago is another important aspect of integration, since it necessarily means that they are brought into closer contact with each other.[11] And continued increase is to be expected.[12] This fact obtains additional importance when compared with the amount of resources available. It seems as if only by wise use of the earth's wealth will there be enough for all of us.[13] This means better world-wide cooperation and planning.

[8] H. M. M. Murphy, *Flight and Resettlement*, Paris, 1955.

[9] *The Statistical Yearbook of the United Nations, 1955*, p. 344 ff.

[10] See UNESCO publication *Study Abroad, International Handbook, Fellowships, Scholarships, Educational Exchange*.

[11] The population of the world in 1750 has been estimated at 694 millions and in 1940 it was 2406 millions. *The Statistical Yearbook of the United Nations.*

[12] In the years from 1920 till 1954 the population of the world had increased from 1810 millions to 2652 millions. *Statistical Yearbook of the United Nations 1955*, p. 36. It should, however, be remembered that the statistical data for some parts of the world are still unreliable.

[13] *Political and Economic Planning, World Population and Resources: A Report by PEP*, London, 1955.

Most astounding is, perhaps, the development of communication media.[14] Not only is it a prerequisite to continued technological and social integration, but it now also offers remarkable opportunities for becoming familiar with other peoples' ways of life and for learning how they look at important common problems.[15] The greatest obstacles are no longer echnical, but rather political and in the form of censorship.

Some of the problems involved in this kind of study are, however, rather difficult. It is relatively easy to ascertain the development of the technical media for dissemination of information, but it must be admitted that we know relatively little about the ways in which ideas migrate and opinions are formed.[16] And we need far better knowledge about the degree of agreement among peoples concerning major issues in politics, although the techniques for this kind of study have been considerably improved in recent years.

Disintegration

The trends of social evolution are far more complicated than they may appear at first glance. It is really very difficult to follow their circuitous paths, and in doing so the theories of dialectical philosophy are almost automatically brought to mind, because opposite tendencies seem inherent in human social life. There are not only trends of integration, but also deep-rooted and strong disintegrative forces at work.

---

[14] For the increase in the numbers of letters and telegrams during the period 1929—1954, and in telephones in use during the period 1932—1954, see *Statistical Yearbook 1955*, p. 351 ff.

[15] Robert C. Angell, "International Communication and the World Society," *The World Community*, edited by Quincy Wright, Chicago, 1948; see also *Ibid.*, p. 161 ff.

For figures about the tremendous increase in radio receivers, newspapers, television sets, and the use of film see *United Nations Statistical Yearbook*, 1955, p. 593 ff. Particular mention must be made of the UNESCO publication, *Basic Facts and Figures. International Statistics relating to Education, Culture and Mass Communication*, Paris, 1956.

[16] From the rather scanty literature may be mentioned Charles Y. Glock, "The Comparative Study of Communications and Opinion Formation," *The Public Opinion Quarterly*, Vol. XVI, p. 512 ff.

As long as little or no international protection can be given to individuals, group attachment and loyalty, which easily engender a sense of group superiority, necessarily tend to remain unabated. They should be looked upon as natural social phenomena, which are likely to survive even if a high degree of political unification of the world be attained. But they may take highly different forms, some being more harmful to international conciliation than others.[17] It is, moreover, an interesting phenomenon that groups other than the nation seem to woo increasingly the loyalty of peoples, notably political parties or movements having a more or less clearly delimited class basis. On the whole it may also be assumed that increasing direct and indirect contacts between peoples may further the ability to understand and appreciate each. other's peculiarities and conceivably reduce national chauvinism and racial prejudice; but, on the other hand, there is always the possibility that such contacts may work both ways and create friction and disputes as well. Wars have more often been fought between neighbors having closely related cultures than between nations situated far apart.[18]

It is a significant fact that class affinity not only produces solidarity with colleagues abroad, but also entails that the animosity to social and political opponents is equally international. The intolerance toward adherents to unappreciated religions, political ideologies, and social systems does not end at international political borders. This is all the more important since the global struggle between political ideologies based mainly on social and political interests, or the use of such ideologies in the power politics of the great powers, is an outstanding characteristic of our time. The world is being divided into seemingly incompatible social and political systems. And the strengthening

---

[17] "The central question is not, as so many assert, nationalism versus inter-internationalism. The fundamental issue is what kind of nationalism can best serve the interests of the peoples of the world, and what kind of international organization can most efficiently minister to man's need."—L. A. Manden, *Foundations of Modern World Society*, Stanford, 1947, p. VII.

[18] G. M. Stratton, *Social Psychology of International Conduct,* New York, 1929, p. 127 ff.

of the authority of the state, so common in most parts of the world today, accompanied by rigorous regulation of economic activity and severer security measures against the increasing danger of subversive activity, favors substantially the forces of disintegration. It seems, in fact, almost ironical that the chances for better contact and cooperation among the nations, which technology is creating, are largely nullified by iron curtains, security measures, and trade barriers.

It may also be noteworthy that inventions are used for many, and often contradictory, purposes. It cannot be denied that, for instance, the media of mass communication are frequently utilized to achieve ends which are generally given a low moral esteem. The impression is, in fact, that in international affairs they are more often used in the service of power politics than for the impartial dissemination of knowledge. As for the role played by the media of mass destruction, no comments need to be made.

There has, however, been ideological and religious intolerance in the world before, which has led to widespread and prolonged struggle. The religious wars are among the bloodiest and most ruthless in the history of mankind. But peoples of different religious creeds have gradually learned to tolerate each other. It is theoretically conceivable that the major social and economic systems of our age may be gradually modified towards each other, and, like the religions, eventually learn to practice a reasonably peaceful coexistence. It is not insignificant that there is today an awakening understanding of the global community of interests which the technological integration of the world and the invention of horrible means of mass destruction have made painfully real. What is more, a sense of global fellow-feeling is increasingly encroaching upon the spirit of economic exploitation and political subjugation, which has been manifested, in particular, by programs of assistance to the poorer nations. This activity may be stimulated by the dissemination of reliable information about the conditions under which peoples in the various parts of the world are really living. The combined effects of such tendencies may be more powerful than generally realized.

The immediate obstacles to cooperation are largely political; that is true. They may vary in character from iron curtains maintaining rigid seclusion to almost unnoticeable border markers and mere formalities in customs and passport control. However, the roots of the problems are, as a rule, not merely political; they may be of a social, economic, or even a psychological character.[19]

Increasing Homogeneity

The international social integration has, in many ways, a considerable standardizing effect. Architecture, clothing and many other kinds of cultural equipment tend, within certain limits, to become standardized for large parts of the world. And this tendency is, perhaps, even more marked in the field of entertainment. It may suffice to mention movies and various kinds of play. Also in the social services there is a trend towards similarity and standardization. The achievements of science and technology are spread over the world, and may strongly affect, for example, the health services and medical treatment. Mass production and trade have considerable ability to make for homogeneity. Important, although usually more difficult to discover, is also the work of imitation, whose chances are being improved by the increase in social contacts.[20] The effects of these social processes can be most easily observed among primitive peoples like the Eskimoes, but they can be noticed to a greater or lesser extent practically everywhere.

This is by no means a new phenomenon. Geographers have for a long time been aware of the great standardizing effects which, for instance, the cultivation of plants and the domesti-

---

[19] "The fact that deeper and more fundamental causes underlying the political are not recognized, when they exist, is usually due to the circumstance that the average newspaper reader or radio listener is not trained in sociological analysis and makes up his mind from headlines and the dramatic and personal element in the news." L. L. Bernard, *War and Its Causes*, p. 377.

[20] Cf. Quincy Wright, "Modern Technology and World Order," in the volume *Technology and International Relations*, edited by W. F. Ogburn, Chicago, 1949.

cation of animals have.[21] Also, the processes of production reveal a similar trend. "It is certain that in some ways the primary tendency of civilization is to uniformity."[22] The processes of standardization seem, on the whole, to be faster in the field of material equipment than in those of intellectual and religious life. But there are great obstacles to standardization also in the case of material equipment. The ways in which peoples provide for habitation and dress and earn their living are naturally more or less dependent on the natural environment in which they live.[23] The great difference in wealth is likewise a check on the trend towards more social homogeneity. The spread of the communist model of society over large parts of the world is likely to entail considerable social leveling and standardization, although it will surely be more or less modified by the society upon which it is imposed. But this is naturally a matter which is still inadequately studied.

Religions, which dominate the life of primitive peoples to such a large degree, are, undoubtedly, very resistant to change. But it is a very significant fact that they have for a long time revealed a distinct tendency towards greater tolerance. And some optimistic observers assume that our generation witnesses a concord among intellectuals which is unprecedented since the age of Humanism and eighteenth century Enlightenment.[24] But it may perhaps be argued that this view is slightly at variance with the ideological clashes of our time. However that may be, it seems certain that the processes of standardization are, to a varying degree, at work in most fields.[25] Even customs and manners are subject to this trend.

While there may be much to say in favor of these processes of standardization, they probably also entail some consequences

---

[21] P. Vidal de la Blanche, "Les genres de vie dans la géographie humaine,' *Annales de Géographie*, Vol. XX (1911).

[22] Lucien Febvre, *A Geographical Introduction to History*, p. 158.

[23] Cf. above p. 71.

[24] G. A. Borgese, *Foundations of the World Republic*, Chicago, 1953, p. 32.

[25] For a study of these problems from a sociological point of view, reference may be made to Hornell Hart, *Towards Concensus for World Law and Order*, New York, 1950.

whose value seems definitely controversial. Superior cultures override and break up ways of life less capable of resistance. People living in a civilization little above that of the stone age may within the time-span of some decades be forced to accommodate themselves to ways of living which it has taken their masters thousands of years to attain.[26] It goes without saying that such social processes are hard to get through. But historical evidence indicates that the transformation of a society can take place with amazing speed.[27]

Even in advanced societies integration and standardization can proceed too fast.[28] We are different, and should, perhaps, remain so in order to make our greatest contribution to the improvement of the world in which we are living. And a world society in which the needs and aspirations of the various peoples can be satisfied to a large extent should also be able to elicit a considerable degree of loyalty, even though it reveals many shades and variations of social life. Yet we are inevitably united by technology, which we cannot master without co-operation.[29]

---

[26] "Social Implications of Technological Advance in Underdeveloped Countries. A Trend Report and Bibliography," *Current Sociology*, Vol. III, No. 1.

[27] Mention may be made of the social revolution that has taken place in countries like Japan, Turkey, Russia, etc. Some of the regions which have remained rather backward until now may be able to modernize at a greater speed than generally assumed.

[28] Margaret Mead, "World Culture," *The World Community*, ed. Quincy Wright; see also *Ibid.* p. 57 ff.

[29] Other aspects of the subject are dealt with in chapters X and XI.

Interesting, although regional in scope, are also the increasing integration and standardization, notably in military affairs, which are taking place in interstate groups; cf. chapter VI.

CHAPTER VIII

THE CHANGING POLITICAL PATTERN

International relations as a discipline has sometimes been defined as the study of international power politics. Whether that be a fruitful definition or not, the groupings of the powers, their character and changes, are certainly a basic part of the subject matter. The powers are incessantly trying to arrange the political pattern of the world society for their own benefit. The game is mainly in the hands of the very largest ones. The small states have a limited scope of action, which sometimes decreases to nothing. Then there is the slower and less perceptible social and economic change, which also affects the political balance fundamentally.

The political pattern of the world is dealt with by several disciplines like political science, political history, and notably political geography. The last mentioned discipline professes to devote major attention to the subject.[1] Previously, it used to adopt a rather static approach, which seemed to be of reduced value. But recent students of political geography have tried to deal with the phenomena in a more dynamic manner. Whether the science of international relations is able to adopt new points of view which may justify its transgression of academic borders remains to be seen.

The Development of World Politics

The assumption that a global outlook is necessary for a proper understanding of international politics in our day of world-wide interdependence is one of such far-reaching impli-

---

[1] Samuel van Valkenberg, *Elements of Political Geography;* see particularly the preface.

cations that its meaning needs still further explanation and historical demonstration.

It has been suggested that the delimitation of political units may, to a large extent, be a matter of geographical factors, or, in other words, political units may often tend to develop within a geographical framework. Mountain ranges, deserts, rivers and seas, swamps and marshes, as well as thick forests, have been barriers which reduced the intercourse and mingling of the peoples. But technological progress has brought about great changes during the course of time. Rivers and seas which once were barriers have become lanes of transport and media of unification. The Danube, for instance, was once a frontier of the Roman Empire, and then it became an important line of transport and a unifying element of the Dual Monarchy. Seas like the Mediterranean and the Baltic were barriers between peoples at a primitive stage of technology but became means of transport and unification when seafaring improved. Then their importance in this respect declined as land transport was improved and in some ways outmatched sea transport. Dense forests which were once serious obstacles to intercourse have been cleared, and swamps have been drained to make easy passage. As progress is being made in flying techniques, even the highest mountains are losing much of their capacity as barriers. As man's mastery of the forces of nature has been increased, the areas of social and political intercourse have expanded. But the development is not illustrated by an entirely straight line. There have also been periods of retrogression and disintegration.

The independent groups of a region, whether they be tribes, clans, or states, have tended to form together a kind of social nexus, which may be called spheres of group interaction. The most noteworthy ones of ancient times are those of China,[2] the Indian peninsula,[3] and the Mediterranean region.[4] The

---

[2] Of literature in English, reference may be made to Chi Li, *The Formation of the Chinese People*, Cambridge, Mass., 1928.

[3] N. N. Law, *Inter-State Relations in Ancient India*, London, 1920.

[4] For a brief survey see the brilliant chapters written by M. Rostovtzeff in *History and Nature of International Relations*, edited by E. A. Walsh, New York, 1922.

groups of such a sphere might live in a prolonged state of rivalry, developing systems of alliances and balances of power. In some cases the whole region might be more or less firmly united under a single sovereign for a long period, during which peace might be preserved. When a high degree of unification was attained, as in China and the Roman Empire, a cosmopolitan spirit was developed, and the sovereign tended to be regarded as the ruler of the world, although strong efforts, in fact, had to be made to ward off intruders at the frontiers.[5] Remnants of such spheres of group interaction may still be recognized, even though their number and character have changed. Since they tend to be dominated by the strongest power, it is usual to speak of spheres of influence.[6]

Such spheres of group interaction, which, because of their integration, also constituted a fairly uniform civilization or "Kulturkreis", have tended to expand their area. The Roman Empire established commercial relations as far as China. The Moslem civilization made its influence felt over the greater part of Asia and North Africa. The Mongol Empire extended in the thirteenth century from Russia to China and India and made it possible for traders to traverse most of the continent. But even though the area of social and political contact was greatly expanded in such cases, there still remained other fairly important

---

[5] It has been assumed that the evolution of the international societies of the past reveals considerable similarity from one region to another. It is supposed that there has been a trend towards a fairly stable balance of power, which has remained for a long time. Then there have been periods of increasing rivalry, marked by military inventions favoring the offensive; and the smaller states have been gradually eliminated. The development has moved in the direction of a bi-polarization of power, and ultimately towards universal conquest by one of the competing parties. A period of comparatively stable rule has generally been the outcome of this centralization of power. But then the empire has been exposed to strong disintegrating forces, like corruption and insurrection, and eventually decayed. (Cf. Quincy Wright, "Modern Technology and the World Order," *Technology and International Relations*, ed. by W. F. Ogburn, p. 189 ff.). The number of cases studied are too few, and the comparative study of history probably still too inadequate to allow trustworthy conclusions, but such observations are, nevertheless, interesting.

[6] Cf. the approach used by Nicholas J. Spykman in *American Strategy in World Politics, The United States and the Balance of Power*, New York, 1942.

spheres of group interaction with which no political contact was maintained, apparently because the means of transport were too poor. Even the most far-reaching upheaval in one sphere might remain for a long time almost unnoticed in the others.

It was destined to be the task of the Europeans to develop the means required for the conquering of the continents and to fulfill the amazing achievement of making international politics world politics. After increasing trade and sea travel, particularly in the Mediterranean, had brought about suffcient improvements in ships and navigation techniques, and the Renaissance had stirred the spirit of adventure and curiosity, the scope of action could no longer be confined to minor seas like the Mediterranean, the North Sea, and the Baltic. The time had come to challenge the great oceans. Out of the economically and politically dismembered Europe,[7] there emerged political units of greater strength and social cohesion, the national states, which from the fifteenth century and onwards, under fierce competition and ruthless struggle, extended their influence to all the continents of the world.[8] By their superior technology and military techniques they were fairly easily able to subjugate and rule over the non-European peoples.

During the second half of the 19th century, by a powerful forward surge, motivated and made possible by the industrial revolution and its achievements, notably in the field of transport, the limits of international politics were extended to include the most desolate regions of the world.[9] In terms of politics our globe became a strange and complicated system of balances, where a major shift in power or a political disruption in one part could have more or less strong repercussions on other parts

---

[7] For a careful study of how this dismemberment hampered economic activity, reference may be made to Eli F. Heckscher, *Mercantilism*, London, 1935, 2 vols.

[8] A study of this process as seen from the point of view of the geographer is made by Johan Gunnar Andersson, *Hur vi erövrade jorden. De geografiska uppteckterna gjenom tidsåldrana*, 2 vols., Stockholm, 1953.

[9] For a highly interesting discussion of this phenomenon see "The Unification of the World and the Change in Historical Perspective," in the volume *Civilization on Trial* by Arnold J. Toynbee.

of the system. The European sphere of state interaction had been expanded to encompass the entire world. There were no longer isolated major scenes of action.

Along with the political expansion, Western transport and trade were rapidly extended and increased. European traditions were taken all over the world by traders, emigrants, and missionaries. But the civilizations of Asia and Africa were, in the main, able to survive and retain their peculiarity. It appears that the Asiatic ones had the strength to resist the impact, while the African ones were, on the whole, too different to be able to adopt European ways of life to any great extent. In spite of increasing economic and technological interdependence among the nations, humanity remained spiritually and politically disintegrated to a very large degree. And this was true even of Europe, the nucleus of the expansion. But this partition no longer means isolation from the repercussions of political and economic upheavals in world affairs.

The technological integration of the world continues. During recent years even the polar regions, which have resisted most strongly the intrusion of man, have been firmly included in the sphere of international politics.

The New Political Pattern

In our own time two trends are particularly outstanding. One is the concentration of power in two so-called superstates, the United States and the Soviet Union. This phenomenon is often called the bi-polarization of world power. The other trend is the elimination of colonial rule with the ensuing decline of the colonial empires, and the establishment of a considerable number of, at least for the time being, relatively weak states in the former colonial areas.

Scholars have for some time paid attention to the trend towards fewer and larger political units,[10] since it might justify

---

[10] Hornell Hart, "Technology and the Growth of Political Areas," *Technology and International Relations* by W. F. Ogburn.

the belief that eventually the development will move in the direction of a world state. There have, however, also in former times been mighty empires like those of Charlemagne and Ghengis Khan. But none of them were really well integrated as compared with the superstates of our own time; that was technologically and socially impossible. They were all more or less created by conquest; and many, but not all, of them were relatively short-lived.

The expansion of political units and the creation of empires have undoubtedly been related to, or dependent on, the invention of new means of transport and warfare,[11] which have made conquest and subjugation possible or at least easier. But the establishment of durable political units is obviously dependent upon a considerable number of so-called contact-inventions, by which the states can be transformed into well integrated and coherent societies. And the invention of new means of transport and communication seems always to be merely part of a much more inclusive cultural development. The whole process is very difficult to understand. It may, however, be assumed that technological progress is making it possible to govern efficiently political units of increasing size. Of special significance is the progress in aviation, which is far less dependent on physiographic factors than are land and sea transport. In fact, the tremendous industrial capacity required for mass production of standardized commodities as well as for the production of modern weapons and airplanes, not to speak of atomic weapons and rockets, can be attained only by very great states.[12] On the other hand, it seems as if the threat of atomic warfare necessitates decentralization not only of industrial plants, but also of the administrative functions of the state.

The trend toward a bi-polarization of power in world politics has been strengthened by the forming of the great military alliances, The North Atlantic Treaty Organization and the Warsaw Pact. Actually, it may be said that the nineteenth century

---

[11] Hornell Hart, *The Technique of Social Progress*, New York, 1931.
[12] David Eli Lilienthal, *Big Business: A New Era*, New York, 1953.

pattern of power, in a way, remains; but the dimensions have become greater. During the nineteenth century, Great Britain could hold, as an island power, a strong, at times even a dominating, position in international politics as long as she was able to maintain the strongest navy in the world and at the same time could prevent the nations on the European Continent from being united. At the middle of the twentieth century the United States has, from some points of view, taken over the position of Great Britain, and Eurasia has taken the position of Europe. In fact, Europe may be regarded as merely a rimland of the greater Eurasian Continent, which it is essential for the United States to unite and strengthen and make an ally of in order to prevent a Eurasian union under the leadership of the Soviet Union. On the other side of the Eurasian continent, an American-Japanese Alliance may come to play the same role as the Anglo-Japanese Alliance did some decades ago, in spite of rivalry between the Americans and the Japanese in the Pacific area.

But the image is, nevertheless, different in several respects, and the pattern of strategy is another in the age of air power than was the case in the era of naval supremacy. Air bases, particularly those for strategic bombing, tend to become more significant than naval bases, although the latter are still highly important, and will, by necessity, remain so as long as the sea is a basic means of transport.

During the century between 1814 and 1914 the British Empire was able to establish a kind of Pax Britannica, having as its foundations naval and economic supremacy and, in fact, a rather fragile system of alliances and economic ties which was kept in operation by a highly skilled diplomacy. And it is true that, on the whole, the British policing was done with remarkable ability to abstain from interference in the social affairs of the peoples under its sway, although British political and economic doctrines spread to many parts of the world, in spite of the fact that they were made to meet the needs of Great Britain, and not those of other countries.

North America has hardly a sufficient margin of power to establish a comparable Pax America. This kind of historical parallel may be deluding. Britain's strongest continental rival during the greater part of the nineteenth century, France, had suffered a crushing defeat; nor was Russia a match for Great Britain, and Germany was not united until late in the century. America's continental rival at the middle of the twentieth century is a power which has come victorious out of war and has in recent years greatly increased its influence in world affairs; and more important still, it has a rapidly expanding industrial capacity and war potential.

Particularly noteworthy is the role which the Arctic has come to play in the new political pattern. On the map it looks like a no-man's land between the states of North America and the Soviet Union. But it is, in fact, now possible to establish air bases relatively near the North Pole, from which many of the more important targets in the world can be reached, since the most developed regions of the globe are located in the Temperate Zone of the Northern Hemisphere. But on the other hand, such bases can naturally be reached and attacked from many places on the rimland around the Arctic Seas. Their value seems, therefore, to be largely dependent on the relative perfection of the weapons of defence and attack, and also on whether their location can be kept secret.

On the whole, the progress in the art of war seems to give the one who attacks first the best chance of success. This fact endangers the situation and requires tremendous efforts for the construction of warning systems. Important in this respect is the geographical difference between the arctic regions of the Western and the Eastern Hemispheres. The vast areas of uninhabited land in the North American continent offer a greater chance of detecting an attacker before it reaches its target than can be obtained in the Eastern Hemisphere. In the Soviet Union important cities and industrial areas are located considerably further north than is the case in North America. But there, too, vital industry and mining tend to move northwards.

Recently also the Antarctic, the last continent of the globe to be brought into the whirlpool of international politics, has come more into the limelight. It is conceivable that important mineral deposits can be discovered in this vast region. But geographical conditions seem to prevent it from attaining a strategic significance similar to that of the Arctic.

The political liberation of colonial areas, which has been taking place during the last two decades, involves countries having about one-fourth of the world's population. This just and natural development has been facilitated by the fact that the European colonial powers have been seriously weakened by World War II; and it is itself both a cause and an effect of the changes in the political pattern that are taking place in our time. The rivalry among the great powers and the desire to obtain free access to the colonial areas for business enterprises have naturally also been important factors in this process. Stirred by awakening nationalism, the colonial peoples themselves have, under these conditions, been in position to put up such strong resistance to the rule of their former masters that it eventually became necessary to grant them political independence. The fact that the colonial peoples have made considerable advance in technical culture under the impact of Western civilization has been a great asset during their struggle for liberation. Whether their independence is real or merely nominal may, in some cases, be questioned. But only the greater part of Africa and some minor areas elsewhere remain politically really colonial. Such areas tend to be far more important in world politics as objects of action than as actors themselves.

It is still too early to form an opinion as to the great consequences which naturally must follow from the political liberation of one-fourth of the world's population. As compared with the population figures, all the new states have a very low power potential. But social revolutions may change this situation sooner than generally expected. Although their climate may not be favorable, their resources are, in some cases, considerable. Moreover, their resources include oil and various essential minerals, on which the European states and even North America are dependent. It seems, therefore, safe to say that further development in these parts of the world will highly affect the balance between the Western coalition and the communist bloc.

Very interesting is the phenomenon that while the older colonial empires are breaking up, and a number of weaker states are being created in the former colonial areas, the trend seems to move somewhat in the other direction in the more advanced regions. Here the tendency appears rather to be a further inclusion of the smaller states into the orbit of the greater ones. The new type of empire has the appearance of a super-power, with smaller states forming a surrounding zone of influence. The progress of technology, which makes for increasingly large plants and markets, and particularly the development in military technique and in instruments of war, tend to make the small states relatively smaller and more dependent on the neighboring great powers. But it is very difficult for a great power to include culturally highly advanced nations, which have enjoyed political independence for generations or even for centuries, into its sphere of influence. Such partnerships will reflect the difference in strength and influence, and any professed equality and mutually declared observation of sovereignty and independence tend to become nominal. When such small nations feel that they have been humiliated, and that their elementary rights have been encroached upon, they may become reluctant allies.

The prevailing situation is largely a result of World War II, and it is naturally rather unstable. The defeated great powers are rapidly recovering strength. It may be assumed that the role of Europe and the Far East in world affairs will increase substantially in the coming years, but Europe is not likely to regain her pre-war status[13] unless a drastic concentration and coordination of her potentialities are achieved.

Irrespective of temporary changes in the political pattern, the integration of the world will, no doubt, continue irrevocably. And it is a question to what extent the political and technological developments can run in more or less different directions. Many students of international affairs assume that the political development is bound to move in the direction of a kind of world government. In that case the great problem of our age seems to be whether this process is going to take

---

[13] Cf. P. M. S. Blackett, *Military and Political Consequences of Atomic Energy*, London, 1948, p. 67 ff.

place along orthodox lines — that is to say, by war and conquest — or whether it can take place by peaceful changes in the political pattern of the world society. For a long time it has been argued that the instruments of war have become so horrible that they actually exclude the danger of armed conflict. Perhaps we have now reached a stage when this argument holds good, but the idea is not entirely convincing. It may be worthy of notice that World War II was fought without the use of poison gas, although the belligerent parties had prepared for that kind of warfare.

In the 1930's the International Studies Conference devoted much attention to the question of whether major changes in the political pattern can take place peacefully,[14] and several books on this matter were prepared.[15] But systematic and clear-cut studies of the political pattern, its nature and changes, are lacking.

A proper understanding of the phenomena involved seems to require that we be able to distinguish the forces and interests behind the existing state of affairs. Notably the role of the small states may be more complicated than it appears. Frequently they become objects of great power politics and are cast for roles in wide schemes over which they have little or no control. The fate of the small states of Eastern Europe is particularly instructive in this respect. Historical knowledge of how such things have come into existence may be useful if not essential.[16]

Changes in the political pattern are usually very complicated processes. A war may be merely the explosion caused by a long and manifold development. The crumbling of an empire may be the result of slow and deep-rooted processes in many parts of the world, which are far from easy to discover. Sometimes changes in the wealth of a power may be very significant. Production figures are readily available, but information about fluctuation in foreign investments is not so easy to get. It

---

[14] International Studies Conference, *Peaceful Change*, Paris, 1938.

[15] Frederick S. Dunn, *Peaceful Change. A Study of International Procedure*, New York, 1937; C. A. W. Manning, *Peaceful Change*, London, 1937.

[16] As an interesting example of a historical survey may be mentioned the symposium, *The World in March 1939*, in the series, *Survey of International Affairs*.

may, however, tell a lot.[17] On the whole, the prospect of getting better insight into the mechanism of such changes should improve with the progress of the social sciences. It is, in any case, an interesting subject from which we may learn more about the causes of armed conflict and the chances of avoiding it.

---

[17] The decline of France in the interwar period was indicated by her inability to maintain her strong economic position in Eastern Europe.

The drastic reduction of Great Britain's overseas investments during World War II was a most serious blow to her strength. Such economic ties mean not only wealth, but also strength. They are instruments by which power can be wielded and foreign policy objectives achieved. Cf. below, p. 136 ff.

CHAPTER IX

STANDARDS OF CONDUCT

Function and Efficiency of Law

International law has, for a long time, been a highly esteemed university subject, in which courses are given both in the study of law and in the study of politics. It might, therefore, seem unnecessary to deal with it also under international relations as a separate discipline; and that is, in a way, true. However, it is a fundamental characteristic of society that the rights and duties of citizens in relation both to one another and in relation to the state are defined by law. This arrangement produces greater social stability and provides increased security for the citizens. The character of the law is to some extent a reflection of the nature of the society in which the law operates. And, although law is a stabilizing and conservative element, it must be adapted to major changes in society.

Such considerations seem to indicate that the study of international relations, having the world society as its framework, cannot ignore international law as a social phenomenon. Although he may not be in a position to indulge in long-winded discussions on the relative merits of naturalist and positivist views on the ultimate authority of international law, or in detailed legal explanations, every serious student of international relations will have to inquire about the functions, efficiency, and limitations of law within the social environment which he calls the world society.[1]

---

[1] For a brief discussion of international law from these points of view, reference may be made to Quincy Wright, "Law and Politics in the World Community," in the volume, *Law and Politics in the World Community*, edited by George A. Lipsky, Berkeley and Los Angeles, 1953.

Because of its heterogeneity and anarchical nature, the world society presents some peculiar problems with regard to the common standards of behavior prescribed by law and morality. Lessons derived from advanced and well-integrated societies like most modern states can naturally be applied only with the greatest caution. There is no proper legislature to make laws, nor is there any authority to enforce the observation of what legal rules may exist. But in spite of all the qualifications that must be made, the influence of international law and morality as normative factors is undoubtedly great. It seems, moreover, to follow from the interdependence of law and society that the influence of law will increase with the growing integration of the world society.

The political pattern of the world society is confirmed in documents. Even the most ruthless subjugation of a defenceless people may be given the outward appearance of an agreement. A treaty is supposed to legalize and make more durable a political arrangement even if it be brought about by brute force. A victorious power or coalition will try to maintain its supremacy and privileged position by forcing upon the defeated a treaty which confirms the status quo. However, these kinds of agreements are, except for the formal procedures, not made on the basis of legal norms. They are not laws, but rather sorts of contracts.[2] Since there is in the world society no authority to enforce the observation of these kinds of agreements, except the parties that have made them to their own benefit, they are likely to be abolished when sufficient changes in the pattern of power have taken place.[3] Exceptions to this rule are cases where great powers regard a conflict as inconvenient and, therefore, put pressure to bear on small states to prevent them from violating an agreement, or when the United Nations guarantees the status quo. Only in few instances are territorial agreements truly voluntarily entered into.

---

[2] P. Jessup, *A Modern Law of Nations*, New York, 1949, p. 123 ff.

[3] For a brief discussion of the sanctity of treaties see E. H. Carr, *The Twenty Years Crisis 1919—1939*, second edition, pp. 181—192.

There are, however, situations when the states agree on what may be called actual lawmaking and prepare rules of lasting and general validity.[4]

The technique of treaty-making is also applied for the implementation of foreign policy strategies like the forming of alliances, guaranties of neutrality, and so on. And there is much to support the view that international law in the above given cases is actually used to sustain the supremacy of force and serve the strategies and tactics of the individual states.[5] But there still seems to be some resemblance to the use which the stronger parties make of law even in well-organized societies.

International law may, however, be looked upon from another point of view. In certain areas of international affairs, states have found it advantageous to acquiesce in the practising of rules which smooth their intercourse. This practice is based largely upon the working of the principle of reciprocity, which implies that an action may produce a counteraction of similar nature. There has, in the dealings among states, developed something in the way of customary law, covering matters like diplomatic immunity, and, in particular, problems arising out of the increasing technological integration especially evident in trade and finance, transport and communication. And international judicial institutions are, during their operation, producing an increasing body of case law,[6] although progress is hampered by the fact that the states still reserve the right to determine themselves what kind of cases they will bring before such judicial bodies. The principle of reciprocity may operate even in wartime. It is evident in rules about the treatment of prisoners, sick, and wounded, as well as in neutrality regulations.

---

[4] For example, the rules of maritime law agreed on at the conference in Paris after the Crimean War.

[5] G. Schwartzenberger, *Power Politics*, second edition, p. 206.

[6] Edvard Hambro, "A Case of Development of International Law through the International Court of Justice," in the publication *Law and Politics in the World Community*, edited by G. A. Lipsky. Cf. also E. Hambro, *Folkerettspleie*, Oslo, 1956.

If a state is willing to bring a case before an international tribunal, it is also likely to observe the verdict given. That is essential, since there is no authority capable of enforcing the decision of the tribunal against the will of the parties concerned. And experience proves that states, even in relatively important matters, may consider it politically convenient to refer a dispute to the International Court of Justice.

However, as long as the political structure of the world society remains basically as it is, as long as the world is split up into sovereign states with no supreme authority to enforce law, an international judicial system seems unable to cope with major conflicts. But in our day of rapid evolution the student of international relations will have to watch the trend of events so as to be able to appraise the capability and limitations of law in this highly dynamic social environment.[7]

Morality

In the whole field of international relations there is hardly a more evasive topic than international morality. Here the student cannot rely on the findings of an old and highly developed discipline as he can in the case of international law. Moreover, there is comparatively little factual research done. What studies exist are mainly philosophical. There is, indeed, much need for concise and reliable information about the sources, functions, and effectiveness of morality in the world society, particularly in view of the increasing importance of public opinion.[8]

Opinions on international morality range from a denial of its very existence, on the negative side, to the assumption that the same codes of morality which are valid for intercourse between individuals also apply to dealings between states, on

---

[7] In the vast literature on international law the student of international relations may find particularly suggestive works like Max Huber, *Die soziologischen Grundlagen des Völkerrechts*, Berlin 1928. H. Lauterpacht, *The Functions of Law in the International Community*, Oxford, 1933. G. Niemayer, *Law without Force, The Function of Politics in International Law*, Princeton, 1941.

[8] Cf. below, p. 215.

the positive side. It is, however, necessary to keep in mind that much of what is said about the matter is merely guesswork, wishes, or declarations of unfulfilled programs.

In our time of global politics, practically every nation professes its adherence to generally accepted moral concepts like justice, freedom, and equality of states, or reliability as to commitments undertaken. The greatest problem is to reach agreement on what is actually justice, freedom, legitimate interests of states, and so on. Moral excuses and grounds are pledged for almost any action, even the rudest type of power politics. And in international as well as in national politics, appeals are made to emotion and prejudices by means of moral slogans. This technique appears to work surprisingly well, because it seems comparatively easy to disguise political objectives in terms of morality for quite a long time. This is particularly evident in the case of war propaganda and declarations of war aims. The fact that this kind of lip-service is useful, is in itself important and interesting. But the weakness of this technique is soon revealed when it comes to matter-of-fact decisions.

A minimum of morality in the dealings between states as well as between individuals appears to be essential in order to avoid a perpetual and exterminating war against everybody. Looking at morality from this point of view, one may feel inclined to speak about its biological function of preserving life and society. On the other hand, ethical systems seem to spring in part from religious sources, or they are at least sanctioned by religion, from which they draw strength, since religion warrants that violation or disregard of its codes entails punishment either in life or in the afterlife. As there are several major religions which make their influence felt in this respect, it might be assumed that the sources of international morality are so heterogeneous that the prospect of widely different peoples coming to terms would seem rather small. But there may be no reason to draw such pessimistic conclusions.[9] It may, however, be noteworthy that during recent centuries nearly all the major actors in world politics

---

[9] Cf. above, pp. 72—73.

have represented a civilization based on Christian principles of morality.[10] This situation is apparently now being changed.

Much has been said about the difference between individual and state morality.[11] But this is apparently a misleading way of raising the question. What we really are interested in is the difference between the moral codes applicable to persons acting merely on behalf of themselves as individuals in a community, and those applicable to persons acting on behalf of autonomous political groups. In spite of fair declarations to the contrary, it is clear that there is a profound difference, which emanates so a large extent from the difference between the two kinds of society in which the moral codes are used. To make this statement is to suggest that morality is shaped in conformity to the society in which it operates. From this follows that to understand the character of moral codes or patterns of international conduct, we must understand the nature of the world society. It is, in this connection, necessary to stress the fact that the world society is still a poorly integrated and politically unorganized body, where each nation must, in the final resort, rely on its own strength, or that of its guardians, for protection. In this social environment, acts of inhumanity which would be severely condemned within a well-organized community, may, in fact, be looked upon as meritorious or even honorable. It is, moreover, essential to remember that just as there may be differences in the individual observation of recognized moral codes within a community, so there may be great differences when individuals act on behalf of states. It would also be unreal to disregard the possibility of variations emanating from cultural differences.[12]

---

[10] That may, with some qualifications, hold good even for the Soviet Union. Before World War II Japan was the only great power where Christianity was not the major religion. Its behavior in international affairs is very much like that of Christian great powers.

[11] Cf. E. H. Carr, *The Twenty Years Crisis 1919—1939*, second edition, pp. 157—161.

[12] Of useful literature on international morals may be mentioned Reinhold Niebuhr, *Moral Man and Immoral Society*, New York, 1933. L. S.Woolf, "International Morality," *International Journal of Ethics*, Vol. 26 (1916). G. Catlin and others, *Above All Nations*, London, 1944. N. Politis, *La morale internationale*, Neufchatel, 1943, Ruth Nanda Anston (ed.), *Moral Principles of Action, the Ethical Imperatives*, New York. 1953. See also Quincy Wright, *The Study of International Relations*, Chapter 27.

It is commonly assumed that public opinion is the guardian of morality, and the lip service of statesmen seems to confirm this view. But public opinion is a judge who often lacks the most essential documents of the case; and to obtain its acquiescence is frequently a question of marshalling the necessary instruments of propaganda.

But although we still lack clearly defined moral codes apart from the rules of international law, and although the facts can fairly easily be distorted by propaganda, there are certain actions which are universally regarded as outright violation of international morals. To this category belong armed aggression and subjugation of weaker nations, as well as ruthless treatment of opponents by such methods as murder, deportation, and large-scale confinement in concentration camps.

Violation of morals in a well-organized society is not necessarily punished on the basis of written law. Society has its own way of reacting. A highly relevant question is, therefore, how the members of the world society react to a violation of international morals. This question is very hard to answer, but speaking generally it may be said that violation of international morals may entail a loss of good-will and prestige, and the nation concerned may discover that less confidence is placed in the statements and declarations of its leaders, whether given at home or at international conferences.

However, the actual political consequences of this kind of reaction are not easy to define. Somewhat more palpable are the political reactions abroad in the form of changes in the relative strength of political parties. This is particularly evident in the case of communist parties, whose position may be substantially affected by the actions of the Soviet Union.[13] It is, moreover, possible that a serious violation of moral codes may cause small states, which are more or less free to choose their allies and guardians, to orient themselves away from the violator and toward his rivals. In this way the violator may be exposed to some sort of diplomatic isolation.

---

[13] As a recent example may be mentioned the reaction to the Russian intervention in Hungary in November, 1956.

CHAPTER X

THE DEVELOPMENT OF INSTITUTIONS

Most writers of textbooks on international relations[1] devote extensive space to the organization of the world society. But like international law, international institutions are now usually dealt with in separate courses and in special textbooks. It may, therefore, be argued that detailed discussion of the history, structure, and practices of the United Nations with all its agencies, as well as other international institutions, should not fall within the study of international relations in general.[2] However, the progress of civilization confronts man with ever new problems of cooperation and administration. Organized cooperation is not merely a device by which greater political power or more social welfare can be achieved; it is often simply a matter of necessity. This rule holds good also for a world society marked by increasing integration and interdependence of previously more or less sharply separated political entities. It appears that it would be from this point of view that the

---

[1] Among the latest textbooks may be mentioned Padelford and Lincoln, *International Politics*, in which about one-fourth of the book is devoted to a discussion of what is called "organizing the international community," and C. P. Schleicher, *Introduction to International Relations*, where practically one-third of the volume is concerned with the problem of "organizing the world society."

[2] It is supposed that regional alliances like The Arab League or even the North Atlantic Treaty Organization should not be included in a discussion on institutions. They have been dealt with in Chapter VI on the main structure of the world society, and they will be touched on in Chapter XI in the discussion on strategies of international politics. The administrative and political organs of these groups are naturally regional institutions, but we are here concerned with the institutionalization of the world society as such.

student of international relations should examine international institutions and the emergence of supranational institutions.

Not even internal security can, in our day of easy travel, be properly organized merely on a national basis. And how can world-wide systems of transport and communication be smoothly managed without international cooperation? It is also being increasingly realized that the interlocking system of trade and finance, which is so sensitive to shocks and changes, and where major disturbances may have global repercussions, demands an increasing degree of international planning and cooperation at both the private and the governmental level. Nor can the spread of contagious diseases be quickly checked, nor epidemics easily be brought under control, without the most efficient cooperation among the medical authorities in the various countries.[3] The value of cooperation has, on an increasing scale, been realized also in the case of many other social problems, like labor standards and nutrition. Nor should the international character of science be forgotten.[4]

Administrative Institutions

During the past hundred years a considerable number of international institutions have been set up to cope with the problems of an integrating world. Some are already universal, while others are hampered in their work by the fact that many important states, including even the Soviet Union, are still reluctant to participate.

In the field of communication such institutions deal with problems concerning postal service, telegraph, telephone, and broadcasting. The global nature of politics requires better and wider organization of the news service, and encouraging progress has been made in this field as well. In the field of transport,

---

[3] These phenomena are ably discussed by Linden A. Manden in his suggestive book, *Foundations of Modern World Society*.

[4] Amos J. Peaslee, *International Governmental Organizations. Constitutional Documents*, The Hague, 1956, 2 vols.

endeavors are being made to obtain better coordination, sanitary inspection, and equivalence and stability of rates.

In international economics, measures are being taken with regard to such matters as the stabilization of exchange and protection of copyrights, patents, and trademarks. Various arrangements have been made to facilitate the granting of loans and other forms of support to economically weak countries. The rapidly increasing populatio of the world and the depletion of vital resources for which substitutes cannot easily be made are confronting man with the choice between cooperation and planning for common welfare or a drop in the standard of living. As an example may be given common measures to prevent the extermination of animals which are vital as food resources or in some other respect. From the point of view of global politics, this growing need for cooperation to secure a better preservation of the resources of the world seems particularly significant.

In the field of social welfare, cooperation comprises such matters as the combating of diseases, improvement and standardization of labor conditions, and betterment of nutrition and child care. Considerable advance has been made towards an international police service for the detection of crimes and the maintenance of law and order.

In science new inventions like those in nuclear physics and meteorology have notably increased the need for trans-boundary cooperation. Also in education and cultural affairs in general, international cooperation and administration have been substantially promoted. Mapping of the globe and the provision of statistical data are being successfully undertaken by international agencies now working under the auspices of the United Nations.

The trend towards global cooperation is noticeable also in religious matters, a field where the world society has so far revealed great and rather dangerous disintegration. The tendency is indicated by such events as the founding of the World Council of Churches in 1948 and the establishment of the World Fellowship of Buddhists four years later.[5]

---

[5] Cf. Chapter XII.

Some agencies seem to owe their existence to a growing sense of duty and humanism rather than directly to the problems of integration, although there may be considerable interdependence between these motive forces. They cover such areas as education, technical assistance, emergency relief, settlement of refugees,[6] and the definition and protection of minimum human rights.

In a particular category belong the administration and development of unappropriated areas. This practice demands special attention, because it is a kind of political management by a world institution.[7]

It is interesting to note that some of the institutions created to serve the needs of an integrating world have initially been non-governmental, and none is more than inter-governmental. But their social function as world institutions has been underlined by the fact that they have been transferred to the United Nations, or such arrangements have been made that they can operate under its auspices. This coordination of the agencies under the United Nations reduces the danger of wasteful overlapping of functions and increases their ability to serve as an integrated part of the institutional superstructure of the world society. But here, too, the cleavage between the communist world and the western coalition is a seriously retarding factor.

In the whirlpool of international affairs these administrative institutions may not loom very large, yet they indicate a trend towards the institutionalization of the world society which certainly deserves great attention. And their indirect contribution to peace may be more substantial than is generally realized.[8] The pace of their development in number and in scope suggests that this is an important road to the unification of mankind.

---

[6] Graham Beckel, *Workshops for the World*, New York, 1954.

[7] Charmian E. Toussaint, *The Trusteeship System of the United Nations*, London, 1956.

[8] For an evaluation of these agencies from the point of view of world government and the maintenance of peace, reference may be made to P. E. Corbett, *The Individual and the World Society*, Publication No. 2 of the Center for Research on World Political Institutions, Princeton, 1953.

In recent years the increase in transboundary non-governmental organizations has been truly amazing.[9] Most of them apparently owe their existence to keenly felt human needs and a growing sense of duty. They, too, may reduce the barriers between the states and further good-will and a better understanding of differences as well as of common interests. Although non-governmental, they are by no means insignificant from the political point of view.

Political Institutions

The other major line of development, that of collective security and international jurisdiction, is by the very nature of things much older and far more conspicuous. The main aim is to provide security, and that is a much more difficult task than the ones with which the agencies mentioned above are concerned. Since their basic functions are the promotion of international security and the maintenance of law and order in the world society, political and judicial institutions[10] are, in a way, interrelated.

The idea of collective security, put very simply, is that if one member of the international society embarks upon armed aggression, all the others shall collectively resist him. Confronted with this situation, states will, it is assumed, prefer to have their disputes settled by international judicial institutions.

This seems to be a logical line of reasoning, and in its crude form this idea has been the basis of systems of alliances since time immemorial. It is really surprising that not until after World War I was the entire machinery needed for the smooth operation of collective security set up. The study of why it failed to work may still produce some useful lessons. Highly significant also is the fact that the disappointment felt at its inefficiency had far-reaching and deplorable consequences. But

---

[9] L. C. White, *International Non-Governmental Organizations. Their Purpose, Method and Accomplishments*, New Brunswick, 1951.

[10] It is assumed that the development of international judicial institutions can most conveniently be included in the discussion of international law.

the failures should not be allowed to obscure the achievements. After all, the League of Nations was able to cope with some disputes, and it served as a very useful forum of discussion and a medium of focusing attention on crucial issues. Perhaps the work of the Permanent Court of International Jurisdiction, too, was more important than is generally realized.

The experience gained with the League of Nations could be successfully used, and the machinery set up after World War II could be considerably improved upon as compared with its predecessor.[11] What is more, it looks as if the United Nations will be the first really universal institution of its kind. That it will develop in the direction of a supranational organ seems also possible. As things are, each state endeavors to exploit the United Nations for its own benefit. It may be argued that the individual parts of a confederacy also advocate their own interests in the national assembly. But there is, in this case, the difference that there is a top authority responsible for the whole. The substitution of lasting law and order for armed power politics requires a profound change in the structure of the world society—the transformation from an anarchical social body composed of sovereign political entities to something like a federal world state. What is needed then is not merely international institutions but supranational organs; and that is naturally a very long and difficult step to cover. What kind of problems an international institution like the United Nations is able to cope with seems impossible to determine merely by academic studies. The experience on which conclusions could be based is still very limited. Moreover, the dynamics of the world society seems to prevent the problems from recurring in precisely their old form.

When independent political units have voluntarily united, there has often been a common enemy threatening their very existence. That seems to be the only danger great enough to justify the abandonment of untrammeled sovereignty. There is, naturally, no such external enemy to the world society. The

---

[11] B. P. Potter, *An Introduction to the Study of International Organizations*, New York, 1948.

danger comes from within—from man's threat to destroy himself. This danger grows in proportion to man's ability to master the forces of nature. When such tools have been invented that virtually all social life on earth can be destroyed, then it becomes vitally important to prevent the handling of them by witless people. The question is how this can be done.[12]

All these governmental and non-governmental attempts to create international institutions are important phenomena, which certainly deserve attention from many more than the politicians and technical experts directly concerned. There is a great need for careful scientific examination of the world-wide processes which promote them. And in the case of international institutions, too, the rule applies that social phenomena can hardly be properly understood when studied detached from their social context.[13] When analyzed against the background of a world society in transition, the development of international institutions gets a wider meaning which may inspire realistic and patient hopes.[14]

---

[12] For a variety of views on the role of world institutions see Quincy Wright (ed.), *The World Community*, p. 259 ff.

[13] For some interesting points of view concerning the study of international institutions see Richard W. van Wagenen, *Research in the International Organization Field. Some Notes on a Possible Focus*, Princeton, 1952. Cf. also G. P. Speeckaert, *International Institutions and International Organizations*, Brussels, 1956.

[14] G. Clark and L. B. Sohn, *World Peace through World Law*, Cambridge, Massachusetts, 1958.

CHAPTER XI

THE BEHAVIOR OF STATES

When we speak of the behavior of states, we do not conceive of states as living organisms having, so to speak, a life and will of their own, as do some specialists on geopolitics.[1] From some points of view we would like to think of states as institutions, from others as groups. But these notions of the state do not preclude the application of the concept of state behavior. It should, however, be added that what we really are concerned with is collective action of individuals organized in groups called states, some individuals playing a far more important part than others. And we have already pointed out that the moral standards for such collective action, or for action on behalf of the group, differ from those appropriate to intercourse between individuals in a well-organized community. This may be regretted, but it appears to be a fact. We are concerned with different types of social organization and different types of behavior.

The analysis made in this chapter is based on the assumption that the actions and reactions of states can be explained partly from characteristics inherent in the states themselves, partly from the natural and social environment in which they exist, and finally from the characteristics of the individuals controlling government. It is necessary to allow for considerable variations from one state to another, and over time, within one and the same state. But it is a condition for the validity of the approach chosen in the following passages that some major characteristics are common for states in general.

---

[1] Cf. R. Hennig, *Geopolitik. Die Lehre vom Staat als Lebewesen*, Düsseldorf, 1928.

Although there are other bodies in the world society capable of wielding some influence,[2] major issues in international politics, like peace and war, require the involvement of states. The interaction of states is the major concern of the student of international relations, but not the only one.

Most of the topics outlined in this chapter have, in one form or another, already become traditional parts of textbooks on international relations, although there are few books, if any, which include all of them. The purpose of this brief presentation is to suggest how these topics may be logically arranged and to indicate from what points of view they may be most rewardingly studied.

Motive Forces

The study of the motive forces of state action naturally leads us to inquire what the functions of the state as a social creation are really like. Speaking generally, it may be assumed that the state has been developed as an instrument for the protection and promotion of the interests of its subjects. But opinions may differ as to what these interests actually are, and how they can best be furthered. It is also interesting to note that political power may quite often rest in the hands of a relatively small clique whose interests may be different from, or even conflicting with, those of the majority of the nation.

In an international society where physical force or violence is a dominating factor, mere self-preservation is necessarily much harder than is the case in a well-organized community. Since, however, the state and the nation are not entirely identical, the destruction of the state does not necessarily entail destruction of the nation. In fact, it very rarely does. A great nation hardly runs the risk of annihilation, although it may lose political independence for a short period of time, or may be split up into smaller units even though it has a strong social cohesion. Germany may be given as an example from modern

---

[2] They will be discussed in Chapter XII.

history. A small nation, on the other hand, may be entirely subdued, and the nationally most conscious sections of the population may be deprived of any opportunity to carry on nationalistic activity, and in severe cases even be expelled or deported. Something like this has happened, for example, to the Baltic peoples.

The struggle for self-preservation may take many forms, and even develop into expansion and domination. But domination may, according to some authorities, be itself a primary motive. There is, in fact, much to support the assumption that states tend to expand their influence as far as they can,[3] either by direct territorial acquisition[4] or by achieving actual control of other states, leaving them only nominal independence. Groups, as well as individuals, are inclined to pursue their own self-interests; and this is often done at the expense of others, particularly in a social environment where there are few restraining forces. Self-preservation on the one hand and expansion[5] and domination on the other are, then, two basic motive forces in international politics.

Another basic function of states is to protect and further the cultural interests—intellectual and spiritual as well as material—of its subjects. Nations are naturally eager to preserve and protect appreciated ways of life which they have obtained through ages of political and social struggle, through trial and error and hard-won experience.

Except for basic interests like security and prosperity, national interests may vary; and their identification depends to some extent on opinion and evaluation.[6] From this follows that they cannot easily be defined in a brief sentence.

---

[3] For a criticism of this hypothesis see Arnold Wolfers, "The Pole of Power and the Pole of Indifference", *World Politics*, Vol. IV (1952), pp. 39—63.

[4] Norman Hill, *Claims to Territory in International Law and Relations*, London, 1945; see particularly Chapter I.

[5] The theory of expansion has been most clearly stated by the geo-politicians. Cf. Friedrich Ratzel, "Die Gesetze des räumlichen Wachstums der Staaten", *Petermanns Geographische Mitteilungen*, Vol. 42 (1896), p. 97 ff.

But it seems also to be implicit in the notion of power politics.

[6] Lester Morkel and others, *Public Opinion and Foreign Policy*, New York, 1950.

For the purpose of illustration we may say that the motives and aims of interstate action can largely be explained by politico-cultural, economic, demographic, psychological and strategic factors. They vary, as a rule, considerably in character and relative importance from one state to another and, over time, within one and the same state, some being more permanent than others; but it holds good in every case that the behavior of states cannot be properly understood without analyzing it against such backgrounds.

Ideals, moral standards, and values affect the attitude and behavior of a nation and its leaders; that holds good also for action in the field of international affairs. However, even if the government of a great power, in a given situation, professes to act on the basis of general moral principles, there may be reason to look more closely into the matter, because such declarations may be convenient covers for more selfish ends. This is, of course, not to say that there have never been political leaders who have been idealists and whose actions have been prompted by moral considerations. A frequently mentioned example is President Woodrow Wilson.

Historical experience also may influence the attitude of a nation, notably towards its rivals, and affect its reaction to problems of international politics to a very great extent. The public opinion in France after the war with Germany in 1870 —71 may be a good example of this case.

How type of regime and political ideology may affect foreign policy is particularly evident in the case of the Soviet Union. As a rule, social affinities seem to make themselves felt to a large extent; and congenial regimes tend to secure their position by cooperation. We thus find a tendency to mutual support and cooperation among communist states on the one hand and among conservative democratic states on the other. But there are many complicating factors. In spite of ideological verbiage to the contrary, the desire for national independence makes itself felt also in communist states; and economic rivalry, for example, may seriously undermine the solidarity among the adherents of what has been called conservative democracy.

With regard to the economic factors, it may suffice to mention the classic examples of raw materials and commodity and investments markets, which have played a fundamental role in the history of international affairs. On the whole, economic motives seem to be playing a greater part in the foreign policy of capitalist states than in that of communist states; but naturally, it also depends on the extent to which a state is economically self-sufficient.[7]

Economic motives cannot be properly analyzed without taking into account the demographic factors.[8] The political problems are likely to be determined by the relationship between demand and supply: that is to say, between size of population and standard of living on the one hand and the available resources on the other. The foreign policies of the United Kingdom, Japan and Italy illustrate in different ways this matter. The impact upon foreign policy of demographic factors is felt also in various other ways. We know only too well from recent European history how fatal minority problems can be.

Strategic and economic factors are often so merged with each other that they can hardly be separated. This is the case, for example, with the provision of strategic raw materials. Among other strategic interests may be mentioned safeguard of lines of transport. This factor is particularly important to intercontinental states like the British Empire.[9] Another basic strategic interest, notably for the great powers, is to work for a favorable balance of power, and to prevent rival states from getting a foothold in vital areas. But the greatest of all strategic interests is, as a rule, the interest in preserving peace.

However, states exist in a social environment; they act and react. Their behavior is prompted not only by stimuli coming from within, but also by stimuli coming from outside; the

---

[7] For examples of how economic interests affect foreign policy, reference may be made to C. A. Beard, *The Idea of National Interest*, pp. 169—195.

[8] Pierre Renouvin, "L'histoire contemporaine des relations internationales. Orientation de recherches," *Revue historique*, Vol. 211 (1954), p. 234 ff.

[9] Royal Institute of International Affairs, *Political and Strategic Interests of the United Kingdom*, London, 1939.

action of a state is largely determined by that of others. This fact implies that the foreign policy of a given state, particularly that of a great power, can hardly be understood when studied isolated from the policy of rivals, and it stresses the necessity of the society concept as a basis of analysis.

The struggles between states engender much jealousy, suspicion, fear and hatred, which in turn make themselves felt as determinants of action.[10] The detrimental effects of these rather dismal aspects of international affairs tend to be increased by the fact that states are inclined to veil their aspirations and actions in secrecy. Important also are pride and prestige, which have often called upon national feelings for support and played a rather mischievous part in the life of nations.[11]

Perhaps the most illusive of all the factors influencing state behavior are the personal characteristics of the individual leaders controlling government. We may learn a great deal about the guiding principles and values of a society; yet the reaction of a political leader in a given situation may be determined by personal peculiarities such as ambition, pride, fear, or odd ideas, which defy any scholarly analysis and classification.[12] The extent to which such peculiarities can make themselves felt may naturally vary from one regime to another.

Statesmen normally act on the basis of the conception they have of the situation under consideration;[13] and it goes without saying that even leaders of great powers may occasionally form erroneous impressions of their opponents and act on the basis of untenable assumptions. This problem is complicated by the fact that it is extremely difficult to obtain reliable information about the opponent's intentions and capabilities. Not even the

---

[10] A sober scholar like James Bryce emphasizes strongly the importance of fear and jealousy. Cf. *International Relations*, p. 146.

[11] Interesting points of view on the matter of motive forces of state action are given by L. L. Bernard in the study, *War and Its Causes*.

[12] We can learn quite a lot about this matter from memoirs and diaries. A unique source of this kind is *Hitler's Tischgespräche im Führer Hauptquartier, 1941—42*, by Henry Picher, Bonn, 1951.

[13] Cf. Harold and Margaret Sprout, *Man–Milieu Relationship Hypotheses in the Context of International Politics*, chapter VI.

best intelligence service can provide all the needed information. There will always be some room for guesswork, and the uncertainty thus created increases the scope for psychological forces such as fear and suspicion.

Capability

Small states naturally do not feel inclined to enter upon such ambitious enterprises as do great powers. To mention this obvious fact is to suggest that capability affects motivation and the forming of foreign policy objectives. On the whole, the matter of capability is a dominating factor in international politics. It affects fundamentally the formulation of foreign policy, and requires a constant vigilance as to the ratio of strength among rivals. It is not the absolute but the relative capability that matters. Many, if not most, decisions to go to war have been made in order to prevent major changes in the interstate pattern of power. This is just another instance to prove how meaningless it would be to study the behavior of a great power detached from the social context in which it operates—that is, detached from the world society.

The capability of states is determined by many partly interrelated and varying factors. To begin with, mention may be made of geographical factors.[14] The location of a country may affect the conditions both for defensive and offensive operations. This is clearly seen by comparing states like Spain and Poland. The classic example of how location can be an important factor in military and economic affairs and perhaps even with regard to psychological phenomena is probably Great Britain.

Size is important with regard to, for instance, the chances of defense. This is well proved by the history of Russia. Shape, topography, and climate are likewise significant factors which must be considered when we examine the military position of a country. This may be illustrated by countries like Switzerland

---

[14] For a theoretical discussion of this matter reference may be made to Harold and Margaret Sprout, *op. cit.*, p. 39 ff.

and the Netherlands.[15] We have, however, already pointed out that the significance of these factors is being steadily reduced by man's increasing ability to master the forces of nature. It may suffice to mention merely the progress made in transportation techniques and the improvement of the means of mass destruction.

The above-mentioned phenomena have for ages been carefully examined by students of military affairs.[16] Somewhat less attention seems to be given to what may be called their non-military aspects. Favorable geographical conditions may, for example, reduce the amount of energy to be devoted to matters of security, so that greater efforts can be allocated for matters of prosperity or other requirements.

The most important factor and the one most difficult to assess is the people themselves. Mere number of population is a highly significant matter. Usually a large population is an asset; but overpopulation—that is, too many people as compared with the available means of subsistence—may be a weakness, as is indicated by a country like India.[17] To what extent size of population will count in future war-machinery is, however, a moot point. It is conceivable that quality—skill and morale, and social cohesion—may become increasingly important as the role of science and technology grows. Even those who are engaged in providing supplies for the so-called conventional weapons are actually now front-line targets. And that brings us to the question of production.

Not even the most able and courageous people can do much without the necessary tools. The ability of a nation to produce the various articles needed for war and peace is, therefore, a vital element of capability. An evaluation of this ability will include such basic items as food, construction materials, energy producers, production and transportation apparatus, and scientific,

---

[15] Some interesting examples from various ages of the importance of geography in military affairs are given by Nicholas J. Spykman in the article, "Geography and Foreign Policy," *The American Political Science Review*, Vol. XXXII (1938).

[16] Oskar Niedermayer, *Wehrgeographie*, Berlin, 1942.

[17] Cf. Harold and Margaret Sprout, *Foundations of National Power*, New York, 1951, pp. 111—118 and pp. 135—137.

technological and administrative competence.[18] In our day it is becoming increasingly important whether the industrial plants can be protected. Another important aspect of the problem of defence is that mechanized, or we may, perhaps, say scientific warfare requires increasingly great industrial capacity. There are actually very few powers which are strong enough to participate in the race for better mass-destruction media like guided missiles and atomic weapons. But of course, it may still be highly essential to assess correctly the strength of the smaller combatants, which in a given situation may tip the scale.

Political, economic and social organization is also a matter of considerable significance.[19] Each of the advanced political systems seems to have its drawbacks and advantages as seen from the point of view of ability to organize for strength. It is conceivable that a system which works well with one people may be less suitable for another, which has different traditions and other national characteristics. Ability to organize for conflict is, to a large extent, a question of whether the established institutions are easily adaptable, because in times of emergency it is usually necessary to improvise and organize according to changing circumstances. On the whole, it may be said that recent historical experience proves that wartime conditions require increased centralization and governmental control. This is true also of states which in peacetime try to maintain a liberal economy. Great Britain during World War II may be a good illustration of this tendency.

The immediate striking power of a state is naturally best indicated by its military forces. And in spite of strict security measures, the rivals in world politics are usually fairly well informed of each other's military strength, although fatal mistakes are frequently made also in this field. It may suffice to mention how the Allied Powers miscalculated the strength of the Germans during the initial phase of World War II, and how the German leaders underestimated the war potential of Russia. There will always be some highly intangible factors in

---

[18] *Ibid.*, pp. 118—135.
[19] *Ibid.*, pp. 137—150.

intelligence.[20] Even if the size of a state's military forces can be fairly accurately estimated, there may still remain some uncertainty about its quality. It may be sufficient to draw attention to the difficulty involved in assessing the morale of a foreign fighting force.

Finally it should be mentioned that a great power is rarely isolated in international politics. There are, as a rule, a varying number of allies. In assessing the capability of a state in international struggle it is, therefore, necessary also to consider its diplomatic position. It must be taken into account whether it receives or may receive under given conditions substantial assistance from other quarters, whether other powers are likely to line up with it or oppose it in a certain situation, and what the character and extent of this assistance or opposition may be like. This fact indicates that not even the capability of states can be studied on a strictly national basis, but must be evaluated against the background of the whole political pattern of power in world affairs.[21]

The Process of Policy Formulation

The process by which foreign policies are formed may, to some extent, influence their character. It also affects the speed and resolution with which action can be taken; and this is a matter of notable importance in our day, when vital security measures may have to be taken at very short notice.

Since the process by which foreign policy decisions are made depends on the political organization and social structure, there may be considerable variation from one state to another. The course of action may be determined by a dictator who is, at most, assisted by a few expert advisers, or it may, at the other extreme, be decided upon as a result of referendum

---

[20] Sherman Kent, *Strategic Intelligence*, Princeton, 1949.

[21] For a penetrating study of capability see Klaus Knorr, *The War Potential of Nations*, Princeton, 1956.

to the electorate. The more effective the democratic control, the more thoroughly is the policy likely to be debated. Personal biases are then likely to have their scope of action reduced, and it must be presumed that the chances of reaching a sound conclusion are heightened. But long-drawn constitutional proceedings may naturally entail waste of time and occasionally frustrate sound initiatives.[22] In any case the actual economic and strategic interests of the country must be taken care of irrespective of the character of the political system.[23]

The process of policy-making extends, as a rule, far beyond the constitutional organs, no matter how wide and democratic they may be. A political move may originate in the national assembly, the party head organs, the government offices, or other planning and coordinating organs at government level; but even so it may be exposed to modifying forces from other quarters before a definite line of policy is agreed on.

Usually a government is dependent on the support, or at least the acquiescence, of a major section of the population. Even authoritarian regimes must pay some attention to the attitude of the people. Since, however, the policy-forming process reflects variations in social structure and political system, the sections of the population on which the government is primarily dependent may differ considerably. Generally speaking, it may be said that regard has to be given to business circles, trade unions and other organized interests and, occasionally, also the services.[24] Trends of feelings and climates of opinion must be carefully considered, especially in democratic countries. Particularly important are the opinion-forming organs, notably the press. The various economic regions may have conflicting interests which must be weighed against each other; and in

---

[22] Cf. William Yandell Elliot and others, *United States Foreign Policy, Its Organization and Control*, New York, 1952.

[23] There is now a fairly rich literature on foreign policy-making in the individual states, but concise comparative studies are still rare. Mention may be made of Kurt London, *How Foreign Policy is Made*, New York, 1949.

[24] Gordon A. Craig, *The Politics of the Prussian Army 1640—1945*, Oxford, 1955. The political role of the armed forces is particularly outstanding in areas like the Middle East and South America.

some cases, like the United States, even the national affinities of ethnic groups must be taken into consideration.

Sometimes the idea of a political move may originate within any of the above-mentioned interest groups. It may then be forwarded by the press, or representatives of the interests in question may bring pressure to bear directly upon the relevant constitutional organs. And it is often difficult even for an observer with very good contacts to find out where a policy originates and what interests are actually behind it.

Since international politics are, by necessity, reciprocal, action is quite often taken in response to requests, proposals, or challenges of other countries. Then the procedure is naturally different, and other problems enter into the picture. Dispatches from embassies and intelligence reports must be carefully examined. The opponent's intentions and ability to carry them out must be assessed in the light of one's own resources and ability to deal adequately with the situation. And interests and feelings at home, which have a bearing upon the matter, must be duly considered. Particular difficulties are usually encountered in dealings with authoritarian states, since they veil their preparations and intentions in secrecy to a much greater extent than do the democracies. The leaders can take decisive action quickly and without reference to the public, and the instruments of propaganda can immediately be mobilized to bring public opinion in line with the course of action decided upon.

A line of foreign policy may be carefully planned, and various contingencies and alternative courses of action taken into account. Sometimes broad principles or doctrines may be stated, which are adhered to for many decades. This procedure has been practiced to a considerable degree by the United States; but the meaning of such doctrines is often interpreted according to the changing needs of the relevant country.[25] On the other hand, actions may be improvised as needs may arise. British foreign policy is said to be strongly characterized by this kind of 'muddling along'. However, the foreign policy

---

[25] Percy E. Corbett, "National Interests, International Organization and American Foreign Policy," *World Politics*, Vol. V, No. 1 (1952).

of every country comprises long-range objectives which can be enduringly pursued, while tactics are changed according to circumstances. This is supposed to be the case in particular with the Soviet Union.

It is a fallacy to believe that a sharp line of division can be drawn between domestic and foreign policy. The situation is rather that almost any important political decision has internal as well as external implications. This is particularly obvious in many kinds of economic measures. It may suffice to mention tariff policy. And it is, by the nature of things, also true of some political steps affecting the capability of a country: for example, a decision to give preference to heavy industry, or to concentrate on the development of nuclear weapons.

Policy formulation is, of course, a subjective process in the sense that the actors may not know all the factors involved, or they may miscalculate the situation both at home and abroad.[26] This problem seems to involve imponderable matters which the scholar is hardly able to classify at the present state of our knowledge. It is, however, a major task of social science to reduce the scope of such contingencies.

It may be a matter of opinion how far the student of international relations should try to penetrate into the wide and complicated subject matter suggested above. There are, as a rule, no natural borders separating the social sciences. Usually he will have to rely heavily upon the findings of specialists in the field. But it seems, nevertheless, clear that he will have to acquire good general knowledge of the processes and techniques of policy-making and of the interplay between foreign and domestic affairs.

Instruments and Techniques

It is not merely accidental that the instruments and techiques of foreign policy have become a central theme of the new science of international relations. There has previously been a serious gap in our knowledge of these important matters, which

---

[26] Cf. E. S. Furniss Jr. and R. C. Snyder, *An Introduction to American Foreign Policy*, New York, 1955, introductory chapter.

had to be covered in one way or another. International relations has already remedied this shortcoming to a considerable extent, and it may actually claim that this field is a legitimate part of its subject matter.

In their endeavor to achieve their foreign policy objectives, the states apply several types of instruments and various kinds of techniques. There is considerable difference from one state to another, which may reflect variations in social and political structure. But there is, in any case, sufficient similarity to justify a general study of these matters. It also seems reasonable to examine the various kinds of techniques and instruments together, since they are interdependent in the sense that the highest effect can, as a rule, be achieved only when they are so coordinated that they are brought to bear on the opponent simultaneously. Thus *diplomacy*, for instance, is likely to obtain the best results when it is backed by economic and military strength[27] and assisted by the facilities of international communication and intelligence.

Some kinds of consular and diplomatic agents, as well as treaty-making conferences were occasionally applied even in ancient times. The Greek city-states developed a fairly elaborate kind of diplomacy.[28] But it is usual to trace the history of diplomacy only back to the Italian city-states, which carried on an extensive trade and made notable progress in the application of envoys abroad. However, the foreign service of the states was only slowly developed. As late as 1790, the staff of the Foreign Office in London consisted merely of a permanent under-secretary, twelve clerks, a Latin secretary, and a so-called decipherer of letters.[29]

During the past decades, diplomacy has undergone great changes. The personnel has become more democratic. The proceedings are far more public. The foreign ministry has had to share policy-making with several other institutions. And

---

[27] It is, for example, generally assumed that the bargaining power of the United States as against the Soviet Union was seriously impaired by the demobilization after World War II.

[28] Cf. Thucydides' remarkable *History of the Peloponnesian War*.

[29] Harold Nicolson, *Diplomacy*, London, 1952, p. 203.

the development of easy travel has favored conference diplomacy, which, together with improved communications, has tended to reduce the functions of the diplomatic agents almost to those of messengers. All these changes naturally reflect the technological, social and political developments which have taken place during the past hundred years.[30]

It may be said that the basic functions of diplomacy are, firstly, to advocate the policy and views of one's government, and, secondly, to report home the state of affairs abroad. For these duties are employed what may be called members of the diplomatic service proper. But the staff of the embassies has been strengthened by an increasing number of experts on military and economic affairs, and recently also by specialists on information and cultural affairs. In fact, there are many examples to indicate that even persons who are partly or wholly engaged in something like espionage and subversive activity have been included in the staff. The personnel of the embassies of the great powers has, in some cases, been increased to the extent that small states, being honored with visitors of this kind, have looked upon them with mixed pleasure. The embassies, particularly those of the great powers, are institutions not only of diplomacy proper but of all the instruments of foreign policy.

The machinery and practices of diplomacy, including the techniques of treaty-making and the pacific political settlement of disputes, are being adequately dealt with by diplomatic history. But a careful analysis of all the instruments and techniques of foreign policy within the study of international relations must naturally include also this subject. The student will be fortunate to have a rich literature produced by diplomatic history at his disposal.[31]

Economic means have, since olden times, been used in various ways to obtain foreign policy objectives. The increasing economic integration of the world has widened the scope for the

---

[30] For an interesting study of these kinds of problems see Gordon A. Craig and Felix Gilbert (eds.), *The Diplomats, 1919—1939*, Princeton, 1953.

[31] The standard work on diplomatic practice is *Guide to Diplomacy* by Sir Ernest Satow, revised edition by H. Ritchie.

application of this medium, to which apparently most states have become more vulnerable. Usually, economic gain may be sufficient explanation for business practices. But the ties which connect the economy of one power with those of others may be manipulated in many ways also for the purpose of attaining political and military advantages. In fact, the borderline between political and economic activity is often hard to distinguish. This is particularly true when the economy of a state is geared for wartime purposes.

It may at this point, moreover, be stressed that the science of international relations includes not only political but also purely economic aspects of interstate affairs. Every state endeavors to manipulate its economic relations with other states in such a manner that it can derive a maximum of benefit from them. External economic ties are instruments by which a state administers to its welfare. This has become all the more so with the increase in state control over foreign trade, which, in varying degree, has taken place practically everywhere.

The use of economic means as instruments of foreign policy is especially evident in wartime. The most widely used, and apparently the most effective, method is blockade. But numerous other ingenious techniques have been tried out; and it has, in fact, become usual to speak of economic warfare.[32] It may, however, be added that this kind of warfare never really ceases, although it changes character.

Various kinds of economic inducement have been practiced since time immemorial.[33] Gifts to statesmen and leaders are mentioned almost as far back as written record goes, and the practice still exists. Economic bribery was previously used in many forms.

Of older organizational devices must in particular be mentioned the trading company or government corporation. We cannot understand the history of colonial expansion without

---

[32] David L. Gordon and Royden Dangerfield, *The Hidden Weapon. The Story of Economic Warfare*, New York, 1947.

[33] C. C. Abbot, "Economic Penetration and Power Politics," *Harvard Business Review*, 1948.

taking its activity into account. It had economic purposes of its own, that is true; but it was largely developed as a means for acquisition of overseas territories.

Particularly in the late nineteenth and early twentieth centuries, loans and foreign investments became highly important instruments in the struggle among the national states, and they were largely used in the service of power politics. Governments endeavored to direct capital to those purposes which were likely to strengthen the position of the lending power and increase its chances of extended domination; it was withheld from potential enemies and urged or commanded into the service of allies.[34] Loans are still used extensively in the service of politics, but fortunately in somewhat different forms than earlier.

Legislation is, of course, an old medium for affecting international economic relations. Tariff regulations, for example, are frequently used as a bargaining lever in international politics in our own day also. A more drastic method is the integration of the economy of weaker countries with that of economically dominating powers. A frequently given example from recent years is the German economic policy in the Balkans during the 1930's. But it has apparently been dwarfed by Russian practices in the years after World War II.[35]

In recent years economic means have, in fact, been used in international politics on an enormous scale and in ways which seem somewhat strange as compared with former methods. It may suffice to mention the Marshall Aid Program and the Point Four Program. It is interesting to note that in regions where the economic resources have been indiscriminately exploited for centuries by the colonial powers, the leading rivals in world affairs are practically outbidding each other in economic assistance and welfare programs.

---

[34] The standard work on this subject is Herbert Feis, *Europe, the World's Banker 1870—1914. An Account of European Foreign Investment and the Connection of World Finance with Diplomacy before the War*, New York, 1930. See particularly Part II.

[35] *White Book on Aggressive Activities by the Governments of the USSR, Poland, Czechoslovakia, Hungary, Rumania, Bulgaria and Albania towards Yugoslavia*, Ministry of Foreign Affairs of the Federal People's Republic of Yugoslavia, Beograd, 1951, p. 283 ff.

Non-governmental arrangements for the interchange of patents and other results of scientific research, as well as the practices of cartels, may not be without political implications. And sometimes business arrangements of this kind may run contrary to the policy of the government.[36]

Application of *propaganda* with a view to affecting attitude and morale for political and military purposes is an old device used particularly in time of war.[37] As people became more politically minded, the audience which could be exposed to this procedure increased. Equally important was the rapid improvement of mass media for communication of information or propaganda. Opportunities offered by the use of printed matter have become better as literacy has increased; but this advantage has, particularly in recent years, been largely offset by government restrictions, which can be even more effectively applied against film. Experience proves, however, that limited quantities of printed matter can, as a rule, be brought into a territory in spite of vigilant control. But by far the best opportunities are offered by the remarkable progress made in broadcasting, although the techniques of disturbing transmissions have been much improved. It will be interesting to see what use can be made of television when this invention has been further improved, and production costs have been reduced so it can become more universal.

The role of the agitator is sometimes overlooked. But it is still very important, particularly in backward territories where the literacy is low or non-existent, and where very few have radios. Especially the propaganda services of the communist states are, therefore, making extensive use of this old and well-tried technique.

An entirely different and, on the whole, very wholesome aspect of the postwar information offensive, is the exchange of scholars, since it may promote mutual understanding and

---

[36] Cf. below, p. 153 ff.

[37] Alfred Sturminger, *Politische Propaganda in Weltgeschichte: Beispiele vom Altertum bis in die Gegenwart*, Vienna, 1938. See also Maurice Megret, *La Guerre Psychologique*, Paris, 1956. B. L. Smith and C. M. Smith, *International Communication and Political Opinion: A Guide to the Literature*, Princeton, 1957.

affect favorably the advance of science. The increasing practice of exchanging delegations for the purpose of disseminating information may also be looked upon with satisfaction.

Techniques by which the minds and feelings of people could be affected were rapidly developed or improved during the World Wars, and the term *psychological warfare* is now being widely used. It seems, however, as if the greatest effects can be obtained by spiritual movements of universal appeal. This situation was demonstrated by the Catholic Church in the Middle Ages, and confirmed during the French Revolution. But it was the Soviet Union which, primarily through the medium of the Comintern, developed propaganda into a major peacetime instrument of foreign policy. This fact explains, to a considerable extent, our concern with ideology in international affairs during the past decades.

During and after World War II, all the great powers developed large organs managed from government level for this new tool of foreign policy implementation and engaged great staffs of specialists to run them.[38] But historical experience indicates that it is not merely a question of having ingenious tools and elaborate techniques; what is required is, above all, an idea which appeals to the latent spiritual strength of man.[39]

Since knowledge of the opponent's capability and aspirations is a prerequisite to careful planning and effective action, *intelligence* is bound to play an important part in international politics. In fact, it has always been an important duty of the diplomatic agent to provide information of the country to which he was accredited. Intelligence is largely a matter of noting, relating, and evaluating the vast amount of information readily available.[40] Secret intelligence or spying is used to provide information otherwise not accessible. Unfortunately, this activity too has increased in our time, and in many cases taken a disgusting form.

---

[38] Public Opinion Ouarterly, Vol. XVI (1952—53).

[39] E. H. Carr, Propaganda and Power, *Yale Review*, Vol. XLII (1952), 1—9.

[40] Roger Hilsman, Jr., *Strategic Intelligence and National Decision*, Glencoe (Ill.) 1956.

Several circumstances have contributed to the tremendous increase in intelligence activity. The authoritarian movements, particularly international communism, have developed the use of underground tactics to an unbelievable extent.[41] And their opponents have eventually had recourse to similar techniques. In some countries the inclination to organize spying and other forms of clandestine activity seems to be partly due to the experience obtained in the underground movements during the war. But this can hardly be done without seriously impairing the democratic way of life, and, in fact, contaminating the very life-blood of democracy. The development in military techniques has, likewise, played its part in increasing the role of intelligence. The danger of surprise attack, especially since the invention of nuclear weapons and long-range airplanes, not to speak of guided missiles, has made it imperative to maintain the highest degree of vigilance, and to provide up-to-date information about rivals in world affairs. Technology and science have apparently also increased the chances of doing large-scale sabotage. But in spite of all this, our time seems too much obsessed with the role of secret intelligence in international politics. No matter how essential espionage may be, it cannot substitute for straightforward dealings among honest men with common interests.

In addition to the vast propaganda activity, very subtle underground tactics have been developed for the exploitation of disappointed peoples and potentially subversive elements of the population. Although *subversive interference* in rival states has been practiced since time immemorial, the extent and intensity of this kind of activity has, undoubtly, increased greatly in recent decades.[42] Particularly important is the development of carefully trained political elites, who, in given situations, are able to seize control of government with only a handful

---

[41] *White Book on Aggressive Activities by the Governments of the USSR, Poland etc., towards Yugoslavia*, issued by the Yugoslav Ministry of Foreign Affairs, Beograd, 1951, p. 351 ff. See also D. J. Dallin, *Soviet Espionage*, New York, 1955.

[42] Sigmund Neuman, "The International CivilWar", *World Politics*, Vol. I, (1949).

of men.[43] They are very well suited to serve as a spearhead for the new type of *pénétration pacifique*. We still know too little about this important matter.[44]

Adherents to a political movement or social model like the communist society will naturally feel attached to the great power where this kind of regime is most elaborate and will look to it for support. This situation can be exploited by the great power. When such a political group has gained power and feels that it is strong enough to manage its own affairs, it may become a less obedient ally. The extent to which an ideology or a social model appeals to the people naturally depends on the social and political conditions.

Most, if not all, of the above-mentioned instruments are more or less consistently used with varying strength, different combinations, and a variety of techniques. The *military instrument* is in a somewhat different position. For the greater part of the time, its influence is merely indirect.

The supreme importance of armed forces as an instrument of foreign policy implementation is due to the fact that in the world society, major problems may, in the final resort, be decided by the striking power of the interested parties. A change in the relative strength of the powers must, therefore, have far-reaching political repercussions.

In so-called time of peace, the military instrument is directly employed only for intelligence activity and the display of force, like military parades, naval visits, and parades or exhibitions of aircrafts, which are often accompanied by boasting speeches. The military forces are usually disposed in accordance with strategic plans which are calculated to provide the highest degree of preparedness to meet or launch an attack.

Display of force is intended to strengthen the indirect influence of the military instrument. By its very existence, it

---

[43] Philip Selznick, *The Organizational Weapon*, New York, 1952. This book deals only with communist tactics, but it should be remembered that the organizational weapon is used also by others, although apparently less skillfully.

[44] S. D. Kertesz, "The Methods of Communist Conquest: Hungary, 1944—1947," *World Politics*, Vol. II (1950), p. 20 ff.; Louis de Jong, *The German Fifth Column in the Second World War*, London, 1956.

works as a determinant of action—as a deterrent or an encouragement, as the case may be.[45] And even if it is not in direct action, it must be constantly adapted in strength to that of rival powers. If a decision cannot otherwise be reached, recourse may be had to armed force for actual physical coercion or annihilation;[46] this is a dreary prospect, but one which political leaders cannot disregard. The transformation of the international society from peacetime to wartime conditions changes so profoundly most aspects of social life that we may speak of the sociology of war. However, the development of mass-destruction media of colossal effect has created a new situation which as yet cannot be properly surveyed.[47]

Strategies

It has been pointed out that the social environment in which states operate is subject to continuous evolution, and so are the instruments of foreign policy. Foreign policy strategies are, therefore, also bound to change to a certain extent. Yet diplomatic history suggests that they are more stable and uniform than one might expect.

Choice of strategies must naturally be based on an estimation of the relative capability of the combatants. One power may be capable of expansion, another may have reached a point where it lacks inner strength to expand, or even finds it difficult to keep what it has already acquired. Some states carry so little weight in power politics that they can wield only slight influence beyond their borders. The choice of strategy will, moreover, have to be made under consideration of a number of factors: geographical, political, social, military, and economic. And such intangible matters as the ideas and morality of those exercising power will naturally enter into the picture. A comparison between the strategies of the United States and

---

[45] As an example may be mentioned the influence which the existence of the great military forces of the Soviet Union has on the morale of communist spearheads in non-communist countries.

[46] J. T. Shotwell, *War as an Instrument of National Policy*, New York, 1929.

[47] Sir John Slessor, *Strategy of the West*, London, 1954, pp. 7—13.

the Soviet Union may illustrate these assumptions. In any case, it seems essential that the strategies be chosen according to the facilities available for their implementation, and that they be based on a sound estimation of the capability of the states concerned. However, history indicates that even great leaders have occasionally failed on this point, because the various factors involved are, as a rule, very difficult to appraise.

The forming of alliances may be regarded as a basic method, and the techniques used have remained much the same for centuries. To form an alliance is the easiest way of obtaining changes in the existing pattern of power, and this method is used for offensive as well as for defensive purposes. Many kinds of regional arrangements are practiced to increase the strength and welfare of the participating states, and even to prevent their turning against one another. But the principle of the balance of power[48] is hard to apply in its old form on a world-wide basis, since the bi-polarization of power entails that there is really no third party strong enough to keep the balance. The world is divided in two major blocs which are engaged in an armaments race to balance or surpass each other. How this race is to be terminated, nobody knows. It is an interesting characteristic of alliance-making that it is, in a way, reciprocal. Alliances beget counteralliances, and armaments are met by armaments. This is an unavoidable consequence of the struggle to achieve superiority of strength or at least to maintain an equilibrium.

The old *divide et impera* principle also is hard to practice in the present groupings of powers. The minor states of the great alliances are geared to the superpowers by economic and military ties. Particularly important is the fact that the smaller powers are becoming increasingly unable to keep up-to-date in the production of military equipment, and therefore they are becoming more and more dependent on their greater partners. And, in fact, partial absorption or exploitation of weaker allies is not yet a wholly obsolete method.

---

[48] Alfred Vagts, "The Balance of Power: Growth of an Idea," *World Politics* Vol. I (1948), p. 82 ff.; Ludwig Dehio, *Gleichgewicht oder Hegemonie*, Krefeld, 1948.

Strategies of expansion have changed considerably during the past decades. The practices of older imperialism, which consisted mainly in acquisition of supremacy over culturally poorly developed regions either by direct military conquest, conquest after *pénétration pacifique*, or by sham agreements with native chiefs, have been almost abandoned. The expansion practiced by Germany and Japan in the 1930's was characterized by conquest of adjoining territories. The so-called fifth columns were used to the greatest extent possible; and the policy of the *fait accompli* was tried whenever the situation offered a chance of success.

Communist expansion is characterized by persistent underground fighting and *coup d'états* staged by political elites backed by Soviet assistance. When a communist elite has taken power in this way, it will depend on the Soviet Union for support for a long time. Direct military conquest is rare. By this method the communist ability in subversive techniques is exploited. The United States must, for obvious reasons, proceed along different lines. The strategy of a world-wide system of bases applied by this country reflects its superiority in some kinds of military technique as well as in industrial capacity, and it is adapted to obtain maximum advantage from geographical factors.[49]

Strategies of seclusion from power politics have been somewhat discredited since the United States abandoned its policy of isolation. But some minor states in Europe have, in spite of all, been able to remain neutral in both World Wars. And Asiatic states which have won their independence in recent years seem inclined to pursue a policy of neutrality to the greatest extent possible. Nor has the idea of buffer zones been entirely dropped in world politics. But the progress made in military techniques naturally entails that small and weak states are really poor buffers.

Economic strategies will usually depend on the economic structure and strength of the country concerned. Free trade

---

[49] E. H. Earle et al., *Makers of Modern Strategy*, Princeton, 1943; E. J. Kingston-McCloughry, *Global Strategy*.

has been preferred by industrially and economically strong states, while weaker ones have had to protect their industry. It seems less a question of what system is generally best than which one is applicable in each individual case,[50] although free trade may be looked upon as a more or less attainable ideal in a politically partitioned world.

Highly significant is the change in attitude toward poorly developed regions. Previously the economic development of these parts of the world was prompted primarily by the profit motive. To some extent this may still be true. But now they are also given extensive help. The motive is, in some cases, mainly humanitarian. But this assistance to underdeveloped regions is also, to a large degree, part of the struggle between the major rival blocs in world affairs, and the aim is to prevent an undesirable social and political development. We may in fact speak about strategies of assistance.

Almost any course adopted in international politics is said to serve the cause of peace. There are, however, some lines of policy which really deserve to be called peace strategies. First to be mentioned in this category is collective security, which in our day takes the form of supporting international institutions capable of providing—or promising to provide—facilities for peaceful settlement of disputes.

After World War I, it was increasingly realized that no single power was strong enough to secure its interests in the existing anarchical condition of the world, and that the only solution was to establish some system of law and order. By supporting this course, the leading European powers hoped to merge their own security in a general system of security for the world.[51] The objection was, however, made to the League of Nations arrangement that collective security was combined with plans for preserving status quo, thus favoring unduly

---

[50] For a brief discussion of assumptions about international trade, reference may be made to C. H. Carr, *The Twenty Years Crisis 1919—1939*, second edition, pp. 54—62.

[51] Royal Institute of International Affairs, *Political and Strategic Interests of the United Kingdom*, London, 1939, pp. IX—X.

the so-called satisfied states, particularly Great Britain and France.

In this respect, the new system of collective security which was established after World War II has been decisively improved upon. However, the fact that its ability to function satisfactorily is largely dependent upon agreement between the great powers is naturally a fundamental weakness. ·

Policies of disarmament also belong to this class of political contrivances. For ages, statesmen and scholars alike have elaborated ingenious plans for the reduction of armaments, not only as a means of securing peace, but also to diminish the economic burdens which armament races involve. The progress made during the early part of the interwar period was highly encouraging, but the method proved to be entirely incompatible with the policies of expansion later pursued by the totalitarian states. And since World War II lengthy discussions about disarmament have again been undertaken, but with little more success than before.

The welfare policies, which are gaining increasing popularity, whether they are carried out by the agencies of the United Nations or by individual governments, certainly also deserve to be classified with peace strategies. There is every reason to look at this tendency with sympathy and hope, although the progress obtained by the method seems slow.[52]

---

[52] For an interesting definition of the foreign policy strategies of a superpower see the article written by Secretary of State John Foster Dulles in *Foreign Affairs* vol. XXXVI (1957) pp. 25—43.

CHAPTER XII

THE ROLE OF ACTORS OTHER THAN STATES

Besides the states, there are, in international affairs, a number of important actors, who are rarely dealt with in textbooks on international relations.[1] A major reason for this omission may be that they do not fit very well into the subject matter when the state system or the international society of states is chosen as the framework of the study. But they cannot reasonably be left out of a study which is based on the world society concept. These groups differ basically from states in that they have no territory.[2] They operate on the territory of two or more states, usually having a sub-group in each state.[3] They have, with rare exceptions,[4] nothing like a diplomatic service to take care of their interests in the various parts of the world. They differ greatly in character and size. Their basis may be mainly religious, economic, or political.

It is often very difficult to find out who is really wielding power in politics, and this is usually all the more so in inter-national politics than in national politics. The kinds of actors with whom we are dealing here are particularly difficult, because they operate, as a rule, merely indirectly in politics. They can influence opinion, and, in some cases, they have great economic

---

[1] Among the few exceptions to this rule, mention may be made of G. Schwartz-enberger, *Power Politics*, which has a chapter on "Minor Members of the International Caste."

[2] It may be added that the Vatican has a territory of 109 acres.

[3] A group existing only within the boundaries of one state will ordinarily be represented by that state. In this chapter we will deal only with transboundary groups, which with greater justification can be looked upon as independent actors in the world society.

[4] Here again the Roman Catholic Church may be given as an exception.

forces at their disposal; but perhaps more important still, through a network of contacts, they can indirectly use the power of states by influencing groups and individuals who are exercising government. Many of them are in a position to carry on extensive information and propaganda activity, and through these media wield a quite noteworthy influence.

Religious Groups

More than one-third of mankind has one form or another of Christianity as its religion. Among the groups which make their influence felt in international politics to any noteworthy degree, the Roman Catholic Church is, undoubtedly, the most important one. It derives its strength partly from spiritual sources, partly from an extensive administrative structure. It considers itself the guardian of the law of God on earth; and it has at its disposal a more than thousand-year-old closely-knit hierarchical organization, whose head decides, with the aid of the College of Cardinals, in all important matters with authoritarian power. By means of a modern information and communication network and through an obedient, highly educated, and disciplined priesthood, it is able to influence the political opinions of some 400 million peoples scattered over a great part of the world. And today, the Vatican maintains a considerable diplomatic service.[5] Representatives of the Roman Catholic Church have often been requested to take part in the meetings of international organizations. The Vatican has sent observers to OFA and UNESCO, and the idea has even been discussed whether the Vatican should be a member of the United Nations.

Usually, the Roman Catholic Church takes a stand on all major political issues. Since it recognizes the Christian principle of equality, its attitude is, in some ways, democratic, and its influence on racial problems is, as a rule, favorable. However,

---

[5] It has diplomatic representatives in 42 states, and representatives without diplomatic character in another 23 states; and 41 states maintain at present diplomatic representation at the Vatican. Cf. Erwin von Kienitz, "Der Katholizismus als Weltkirche," *Europa Archiv*, 3. Jahrgang, 3. Folge, p. 1231 ff. Cf. also Humphrey J. T. Johnson, *Vatican Diplomacy in the World War*, Oxford, 1933.

being itself a great landowner and controller of many industrial enterprises, it tends to advocate the right of private property, and this circumstance tends to increase its leaning to the right. Its policies and methods are rather flexible, and, to a large extent, adapted to regional variations in social and political conditions, but, on the whole, it can be said without qualification that its attitude towards the major spiritual and material issues of our age makes it an important ally of the Western coalition in the global struggle between the communist and the non-communist world. Its tactics are always subtle and careful, but it is likely to be more or less involved in many, if not most, of the major issues of international politics.[6]

The role of the Protestant section of Christianity is different. It is split up into so many churches that it cannot easily maintain a world-wide organization. Some of the churches are also so closely connected with the state that they rarely advocate a strong line of foreign policy different from that of the state concerned. There is, however, no doubt that some of the Protestant Churches also may wield considerable influence in various problems of international affairs, but it is, as a rule, rather difficult to distinguish.[7]

When we turn to the great religions of the East, the problem is even more difficult.[8] Buddhism is the religion and philosophy of more than one-fourth of mankind; it is interesting particularly because of its tolerance towards other religions and ways of life. In some countries, especially Tibet, its political influence is very strong. But it has no central organization comparable to that of the Roman Catholic Church, and it is, on the whole, rather aloof from practical political issues.

Islam has long ago ceased to be a centrally organized warlike group. It is hard to say whether any sense of solidarity at all is felt among its fairly widely scattered 250 million adherents. But we are occasionally reminded of its political significance, as, for instance, recently in Egypt and Arabia. And like its rival in India, Brahmanism, it is so bound up with almost every

---

[6] Guido Gonella, *The Papacy and World Peace*, London, 1945.

[7] Max Weber, *The Protestant Ethic and the Spirit of Capitalism*, New York, 1930.

[8] Sarvepalli Radhakrishnan, *Eastern Religions and Western Thought*, Oxford, 1939.

aspect of the life of its followers that it cannot fail to be of far-reaching political importance. However, since the abolition of the Caliphate, there is a lack of central institutions for Islam as an international religion.[9] In recent years, there have been signs of increasing desire in the Moslem countries to act as a bloc within the world society.[10] But this neo pan-Islamism has not yet taken any clear-cut shape.

It is true that very few can become authorities on these complicated social and religious bodies, but it may be essential for the student of world politics to keep in mind their possible influence. In any case, the world society can hardly be understood without taking them into consideration.[11]

Political Movements

It is probably correct that international political movements can, as a rule, attain real strength only when they have a great power as a nucleus, for which they serve as an instrument of foreign policy. They can, therefore, rarely be considered as independent actors. Some of them may, nevertheless, deserve a brief discussion. An important aspect of the matter is the fact that political movements tend to have a certain section of society or class as their social basis. This circumstance may increase their integration and homogeneity as a social body.

Since the establishment of the First International in the 1860's, repeated and determined attempts have been made to unify the labor parties of the world into one political organization. And although the ambitious aims set have never been reached, the International has been able to play an important role in world politics.[12] Its character was, however, changed to a considerable extent by the Russian revolution, after which it

---

[9] Edwin E. Calverley, "The Fundamental Structure of Islam," *The Moslem World*, Vol. XXIX (1939), pp. 364—84.

[10] Majid Khadduri, *War and Peace in the Law of Islam*, Baltimore, 1955.

[11] Early students of sociology were keenly aware of the necessity of understanding the role played by the great religions, as is indicated by the writings of Max Weber.

[12] Lewis L. Lorwin, *Labor and Internationalism*, New York, 1929.

was split into two major fractions on the old issue of democracy versus dictatorship. The Third International or Comintern, which was created by the communists, became so intimately connected with the government of the Soviet Union that it actually had to be looked upon as primarily an instrument of Russian foreign policy,[13] although it purported to represent international labor. The same was still more true of its successor, the Cominform. It has recently been abolished, and the publication of its periodicals has ceased. But it is conceivable that some other organ will be created to take over its functions.

The Socialist International which was established in the 1920's was badly broken up during the following decade by the advance of fascism in Europe. Since World War II, its machinery for administration and exchange of information has been much improved, and its formal reinstitution in 1951 may herald a new and more vigorous line of policy. Unlike its communist counterpart, the Socialist International is not primarily the instrument of any single great power.[14]

Right wing movements are, at present, very hard to depict. Their existence and importance cannot, however, be ignored by the student of international relations. There seems to exist an international fascist movement, more or less underground. But it is, at least for the time being, handicapped by having no strong power as a mainstay. Conservative democracy can be identified as a social and political type,[15] which may reveal some cohesion.[16] But it is not a properly organized international political movement. The Liberal International which was established in 1947[17] includes many highly distinguished persons among its members, but its activity seems, so far, to have been somewhat restricted. International capitalism is a frequently

---

[13] Jane Degras (ed.), *The Communist International 1919—1943. Documents*, London, 1956. So far only volume I has appeared.

[14] Julius Braunthal (ed.), *Yearbook of the International Socialist Labor Movement 1956—1957*, London, 1957.

[15] Cf. W. Friedmann, *An Introduction to World Politics*, London, 1951, p. 93 ff.

[16] Cf. above, p. 125.

[17] Deryck Abel, "Liberal International," *Contemporary Review*, Vol. 178 (Oct. 1950), pp. 228—232.

used term in the political vocabulary, but it is one of the rather evasive political concepts. A particularly noteworthy movement is Zionism, because it is unique in the sense that it has never been in a position to benefit from being the ideology of any power. It has, nevertheless, been able to carry considerable influence and achieve great objectives, especially since the establishment of the Jewish Agency as a kind of executive organ.[18]

Business Institutions

Usually, a great business undertaking will identify its foreign policy interests with those of the state to which it belongs, and the state will identify its interests with those of the business undertaking. The government may use it as an instrument to pursue a policy which it advocates, or the business concern may itself call on the government for support of its foreing interests. The Baghdad Railway project may be a good example of an enterprise originally undertaken by business interests, and then encouraged and strongly supported by the government to serve its political purposes. Hardly any type of business undertaking has played a more conspicuous political role than the chartered company, which was frequently used during the early part of the European colonial expansion; the best known example is the English East India Company. But the chartered company cannot always be considered as an independent actor. It must often be looked upon rather as an instrument used by the colonial powers to achieve their foreign policy objectives.

However, large international business enterprises, notably of the type called cartels,[19] have sometimes pursued independent purposes at variance with the interests of the states to which

---

[18] Chaim Weizmann, *Trial and Error, The Autobiography of Chaim Weizmann*, London, 1949.

[19] Put very simply, a cartel may be defined as a kind of institution which is created when a corporation in one country makes an agreement with a similar corporation in another country for the division of the markets, with a view towards eliminating competition and stifling competitive enterprises in the field, thus obtaining artificially high prices.

they belonged. There are some examples which indicate that parties to cartels have carried on business practices that have been harmful to their country of origin, while they have bene-fited rival, or even enemy countries. In unfavorable cases, their activity may be prompted by business interests and considera-tions of profits which may run contrary to national interests. Although it may be hard to examine by the scholar, their influ-ence in international affairs may sometimes be rather peculiar.[20]

The largest corporations have developed something amount-ing to a foreign service; and some of them have even taken the trouble to have reports prepared for them about diplomatic officials of their country, rating them according to their useful-ness in advancing the interests of the companies.[21] On the other hand, it should be added that great corporations with world-wide contacts may be able to offer the government valuable services, for instance, in the field of intelligence. How the great internationally operating corporations and cartels will adapt their activity to the conditions of our changing world is a matter of great interest indeed.

In our time, oil is probably the kind of raw material which creates the greatest political problems,[22] and the leading oil concerns are apparently wielding a considerable influence in world affairs. Usually, though not always, their political interests are shared by the states to which they belong. In some cases it may be said with few qualifications, that they are largely instruments of the government.[23] Particularly in the Near

---

[20] Wendell Berge, *Challenge to a Free World*, Washington, 1944. See also George Gurvitch, "Social Structure of Pre-War France," *American Journal of Sociology*, Vol. XLVIII (1943), p. 535 ff.

[21] Adolf A. Berle Jr., *The 20th Century Capitalist Revolution*, New York, 1954, p. 131.

The author of this book looks at the problems from a somewhat different point of view than does Mr. Berge. These two authors, therefore, supplement each other. On the whole, surprisingly little has been written on this most important matter.

[22] Wallace E. Pratt and Dorothy Good, eds., *World Geography of Petroleum*, New York, 1950.

[23] It may be mentioned that the state holds the majority of shares in the Anglo-Iranian Oil Company, which in turn holds shares in the Iraq Oil Company. Thus the British government is able to exercise considerable control over the oil industry.

East, the oil deposits complicate the international scene. While oil is the largest source of revenue, it also impedes the progress towards real political independence of some countries of this region and complicates the foreign policy of others. Nearly the entire oil production of the non-communist world is shared among only seven great companies; and objections have been raised against their marketing arrangements.

Various Other Organizations

Repeated attempts have been made to unite trade unions all over the world, but the success has hardly been much better than in the case of politically organized labor. International trade unionism is torn by the opposing forces of nationalism and internationalism, democracy and dictatorship, the Western alliance and the communist bloc. And it is at present too much geared to the policies of the states to which the individual unions belong to be able to wield any significant influence in world affairs as an independent international actor.

The establishment of the World Federation of Trade Unions in 1945, in which both communist and socialist oriented unions took part, seemed promising. But it soon became clear that the organ was too much under communist sway; and in 1949 trade unions in democratic countries, notably the United States and Great Britain, had to establish their own organ, which was given the name of International Confederation of Free Trade Unions.[24]

However, in spite of present disintegration and antagonism, trade unionism has great forces at its disposal, which can also be used to play a role in international affairs. Occasionally we are reminded of this fact when the unions display their willingness to give economic assistance to fellow organizations abroad.

It seems natural to include under this heading the 'trade union' of international business. The International Chamber of

---

[24] Arthur Deakin, "The International Trade Union Movement," *Internationa Affairs*, Vol. XXVI (1950), p. 167 ff.

Commerce has, since its foundation in 1919, displayed a quite significant activity in international affairs.[25] Through its special committees and biennial congresses, it has encouraged many measures to facilitate international trade; and it maintains a considerable information service. Perhaps more important still is the fact that through its powerful contacts it may be in a position to influence foreign policy issues in many countries.

There have, in recent years, been created a considerable number of international professional organizations.[26] Their immediate political influence is apparently very slight. But in the long run, it may prove to be of more than professional importance that such bodies are established and developed.

It has already been pointed out that there is a rapidly increasing number of international organizations having universal political and humanitarian objectives. As an example may be given the World Association of World Federalists.[27] Some of these organizations have extensive facilities for information and propaganda activity, and their political influence can certainly not be disregarded.

On the whole, it may be said that the role of the above-mentioned international bodies is insignificant as compared with that of states, and it is also very difficult to ascertain. Yet there has taken place during the last decades a development which indicates clearly that the student of international relations can no longer ignore these actors on the international scene.

---

[25] Lyman C. White, *The Structure of Private International Organizations*, Philadelphia, 1933.

[26] Most of them are listed in the *International Yearbook* and *Statesmen's Who's Who*.

[27] *World Federalism, 10th Anniversary Congress*, The Hague, August, 1957.

CHAPTER XIII

THE PROBLEM OF VIOLENCE

There is a continuous struggle going on between the major rivals in world affairs. It may vary with regard to severity and techniques used from one region to another and over time within the same area, but it hardly ever ceases entirely. Each one will try to improve his own position by a variety of means. Every conceivable chance to change the pattern of power to one's own benefit is exploited. An incessant rivalry goes on to achieve predominance in science and technology, economy and organizing ability, as well as in military strength. Ingenious efforts are made to win the sympathy of other peoples, while rivals are discredited and their reputation undermined. In achieving these ends, all the instruments of foreign policy may be used with differing strength and techniques. But a drastic increase in the severity of the struggle occurs when interstate relations change from peacetime conditions to war, and the full use is made of all the means of destruction.

The Anthropologist's View

The most appalling and tragic phenomenon of the whole subject matter of international relations—and one which fundamentally affects the very nature of international affairs —is the large-scale use of violence and destruction as a means of settling disagreements among sovereign political units. So old and widespread is this practice that many serious scholars have been induced to ask whether vindication of interests by means of violence and war does not really emanate from a warlike instinct or disposition of man. And some of them have reached the conclusion that history answers this question in the affirmative.

The question of whether the inclination to wage war is, so to speak, inherent in man, or whether it has been acquired at some stage in his cultural development, naturally came to focus attention on the state of affairs among primitive peoples. If they were primarily peaceful it might be concluded that war as a social phenomenon had come into being during man's cultural progress, and the warlike spirit was at least no more than an acquired drive which could be reduced or possibly even removed.

Unfortunately, the answers which the authorities are in a position to give vary greatly and seem far from conclusive. Some anthropologists, particularly of the older school, maintain that relations among primitive peoples are, and apparently always have been, to a considerable extent characterized by war.[1] A few of them have even gone so far as to maintain that the original forms for exchange of goods were little more than piracy, from which various types of barter later developed.[2] They agree that armed clashes are, as a rule, very limited, being often little more than shouting and attempts to terrify the opponent. But this fact may largely be explained by the small size of the groups and the low technical culture of hunting, fishing, and gathering societies, which actually preclude large and well-organized operations.

In recent years, somewhat different views have been maintained. Some students of preliterate cultures have come to stress more the peaceful relations among primitive peoples. They suppose that savages rarely avail themselves of war as a method of looting, and permanent conquest is even less frequently attempted. But many tribes wage war to settle disputes and avenge wrongs, real or imagined, inflicted upon

---

[1] Cf. M. R. Davie, *The Evolution of War*, New Haven, 1929.

[2] F. Müller-Lyer, *Phasen der Kultur und Richtungslinien des Fortschritts*, München, 1908, p. 264. For a somewhat less extreme view, reference may be made to E. E. Hoyt, *Primitive Trade, Its Psychology and Economics*, London, 1926.

them;[3] and even carefully planned raids have been observed among some peoples. It is, however, assumed that primitive peoples have, in many cases, been corrupted by contacts with advanced nations, which have introduced arms and disrupted their social organization, and, in various ways, engendered a militant character in the native.

The findings of anthropology are certainly not without interest to the student of international relations. It may be useful and suggestive to study the world in which we live in the light of social evolution. However, the variations from one primitive people to another are often considerable, and there are, undoubtedly, many qualifying factors which complicate the matter, and render it extremely difficult to arrive at tenable general conclusions which are applicable to our own civilization.

War as the Evil of an Unintegrated Society

In spite of all that has been said, the fact remains that armed conflicts between autonomous groups have occurred as far back as written records go. The basic motives of war seem, on the whole, fairly stable. There is apparently some similarity between the looting raids of the nomadic tribes of ancient civilizations and the modern wars for raw materials; and a line may perhaps be drawn from the expansion of early Teutonic tribes to the European conquest of the continents more than a thousand years later. Religious intolerance has almost ceased to be a cause of war, but the question is whether it is being superseded by ideological intolerance. Dynastic wars have ceased to exist, but dictators are frequently involved in the game.

The causes of war are, as a rule, deep-rooted and very complicated, often interrelated, and sometimes even contradictory. They are really very difficult to disclose by empirical research; this is particularly true of psychological causes. The immediate cause may be only the spark which sets off the explosion; it may even be staged. As the progress in military tech-

---

[3] R. Numelin, *The Beginnings of Diplomacy*, Copenhagen, 1950, pp. 103—107.

niques has favored the attacker, the danger of a sudden outburst of war without any preceding incident has increased.[4]

Above all, it is important to disclose self-deception on the part of political leaders as well as cunning attempts to obscure the real issue. It has not been unusual to rationalize the real motives of armed conflict into moral slogans like preservation of law and order, or the liberation of oppressed peoples; in recent decades, the protection of small nations against some brutal aggressor has been a favorite pretense for unprovoked intervention.[5] On the other hand, we are not entitled to strip all nations and their leaders of moral principles to the extent that we exclude the possibility of such motives being additional determinants of action together with more fundamental causes.

It is interesting to note that repeated clashes and political incidents have usually occurred in periods prior to war. On the one hand, they tend to increase antagonism and social tension, while on the other, the fact that they occur repeatedly may blunt people's attention to the danger of which they are indicative.

It may be argued that economic antagonism and intense social tension are common also in well-organized societies, and here they can be settled without the use of violence. This fact seems to indicate that large-scale use of violence is characteristic of unintegrated societies, and that armed conflict can largely be explained by the social setting in which it occurs. It seems safe to predict that in a dynamic and more or less unintegrated world society, serious armed clashes of interests will take place. The balance of power is being disrupted by the decline and growth within states, and changes in the international pattern of power are bound to occur from time to time. All attempts to preserve status quo by international arrangements have proved abortive in the face of social dynamics. Some peaceful adjustment can, as a rule, be achieved at international conferences.

---

[4] There is already a vast literature on the causes of war, among which may be mentioned *Conference on the Cause and Cure of War, Report,* Washington, 1925; Arthur Porrit (ed.), *The Causes of War,* London, 1932. For some special aspects of the subject, reference may be made to H. C. Engelbrecht and F. C. Hanighen, *Merchants of Death,* London, 1935.

[5] L. L. Bernard, *War and Its Causes,* New York, 1946, chapter 12.

But great changes in the pattern of power rarely occur entirely peacefully. When states consider their position endangered, their vital interests being encroached upon, and feel that time is against them, they may prepare for war even if they earnestly want peace. There are some interests for which even a peace-loving nation is ready to fight; otherwise it would make little sense to carry the economic burden of great armaments.[6] To put it this way looks, however, like starting at the wrong end. It seems more logical to argue that the danger really emanates from the hungry states, which want a place in the sun. There are periods of expansion in the lives of nations when their own territory seems to offer insufficient scope for their activity;[7] and in a society which lacks a central authority to act as a supervisor and controller, the adjustment of needs and interests cannot easily take place peacefully.

It is, of course, not necessary to assume that all peoples are warlike, or to introduce the hypothesis of an incurable fighting instinct. Peaceful relations can be interrupted in the world society, as well as in any other society, if there are a few people who are prepared to use violence, unless the social environment provides sufficiently strong restraining forces; and it is highly significant that such people frequently miscalculate the chances of success.

All powers declare that the sole purpose of maintaining great military forces is to deter an aggressor. The logic of this reasoning is basically similar to that underlying the systems of law and order in well-organized societies. But the principle does not work well without a sufficiently strong central authority, and even then serious eruptions may occur unless the system is properly adapted to the forces of social dynamics.[8]

---

[6] Cf. *Political and Strategic Interests of the United Kingdom*, London, 1940, p. x.

[7] Interesting, but somewhat extreme and simplified views on this matter, are given by Friedrich Ratzel in the article, "Die Gesetze des räumlichen Wachstums der Staaten," *Petermanns Geographische Mitteilungen*, Vol. 42 (1896), 97 ff.

[8] "No society can function harmoniously if its institutions are not equipped to provide for the adaption of its legal framework to the dynamic forces which irresistibly dominate it. A moment is reached when, behind the formal equilibrium of legality, vital forces give rise to new necessities. And adjustment then becomes necessary. If it is not made by the application of regular procedures, there is a risk that it will be

If, however, we assume that war is largely a result of political and social disorder, and that man is quite able to abstain from large-scale use of violence in a reasonably well-integrated and properly managed society, it is natural to hope that continued integration and institutionalization of the world society will bring about improvement in the present state of affairs. The increase in the size of the states means that larger parts of the world are being brought under the rule of law. In many regions, where only a few hundred years ago local chiefs waged war against each other, the idea of using violence as a means of settling political and social questions seems today utterly remote. In fact, when we view the development of world institutions in a historical perspective, we are bound to agree that progress has, after all, been considerable during the past decades. There has also occurred a change in attitude towards the importance and prospects of world institutions, which it would be foolish to ignore. The possibility of establishing institutions of sufficient strength to control peaceful changes and adjustment is today, in spite of serious setbacks, no longer regarded as wholly utopian.

This kind of reasoning should, of course, not lead to a sort of social determinism, which entails that we adopt an attitude of helplessness, and leave it to a seemingly irresistible and uncontrollable social integration to bring peace. Man is not, to that extent, the slave of his social environment. He is, in our time, able to destroy life in large parts of the world; and he can, on the other hand, definitely shorten and smooth the road to more settled political conditions in the world.

Encouraging progress in the direction of supranational institutions cannot blind us to the fact that there is still much to do. As long as the world society retains its anarchical character, the problem of violence in international politics remains un-

---

carried out by violence. Within a state, when the legal system loses its elasticity and opposes too obstinate a resistance to the pressure of facts, it may collapse amid the uproar of revolution. On the international level, a similar phenomenon occurs, with the difference that in this case war takes the place of revolution."—Maurice Bourquin, "Introductory Reports," in the volume, *Peaceful Change*, issued by the International Studies Conference, Paris, 1938, p. 18.

solved. And we have rightly been warned against the danger that our civilization may spend so much on armaments that its resources will not suffice for a satisfactory development of the more creative aspects of social life.[9] The enduring preoccupation with armaments and the danger of war may divert our civilization unduly in the direction of destructive technology to the detriment of achievements promoting general welfare. The strong emphasis on technical education[10] may be significant in this respect, although it need not necessarily be an ominous sign, since technical knowledge can be used for good as well as bad ends. In fact, the progress made in the physical sciences may *per se* be highly appreciated. What is questionable is the great discrepancy between the progress made in this field and that made in the social sciences. Perhaps we should have learned to reduce the use of large-scale violence in international politics before we invented the hydrogen bomb. But any great change in this situation can hardly be expected as long as superpowers are matched against each other.

On the other hand, it is interesting to note that there has been a favorable change in the attitude toward war.[11] While previously the concept of war as a normal or even necessary social phenomenon was fairly common, most people today dread the horrors of armed conflict and look upon it as sheer madness.

The problem of violence in international politics has been widely studied, but it appears as if relatively little attention is being paid to it in some university curricula and textbooks.[12] The idea of introducing this subject into the study of international relations is by no means to make prefabricated or easy solutions to international conflicts, but, in particular, to strip the matter of all such garbs as glory, mystery, and undue fear, and to make it plain that this is the greatest political problem of man, and one which intimately concerns all of us.

---

[9] Arnold J. Toynbee, *War and Civilization*, London, 1951.

[10] P. M. S. Blackett, *Atomic Weapons and East-West Relations*, Cambridge, 1956, pp. 61—63.

[11] L. L. Bernard, *War and Its Causes*, p. 115 ff.

[12] Among the textbooks which contain suggestive chapters on this matter may be mentioned Norman Hill, *Contemporary World Politics*, New York, 1956, Chapters 17—18.

PART III

NOTES ON RESEARCH

INTRODUCTION

Research may be said to be the first link in the academic process of acquainting ourselves with the world. It provides knowledge to be given in education, although there is, in fact, a circular movement insofar as education usually, though not always, prepares the research scholar for his work. The researcher in international relations will generally profit by having wide knowledge. And the increasing tendency in some social sciences, particularly sociology, to inform the beginning student about the techniques used in the collecting of data, in composition, and in verification, may be very useful in this new field too. It appears, however, that the really great research scholars are men of special gifts rather than men of special education. It has been pointed out that ingenious basic research, like the creative arts, is the product of the experience of a peculiarly sensitive mind,[1] although patience and hard work are certainly important factors also.

The primary motives for engaging in research seem to be intellectual curiosity and desire to know, explain, and create.[2] Prospects of social prestige and a moderate economic gain may also enter into the picture as encouraging factors. But, unfor-

---

[1] Quincy Wright, *The Study of International Relations*, p. 79. Professor Wright goes on to say that the essence of research is the perception of unobserved likenesses and differences, classes and entities, sequences, processes, associations and relationships, causes and consequences, means and ends. And he believes that the peculiar ability to do primary research is as likely to be blunted as it is to be sharpened by education. *Ibid.*, pp. 79—80.

[2] An interesting analysis of this matter is given by Thorstein Veblen in his penetrating work, *The Place of Science in Modern Civilization*, New York, 1932.

tunately, the history of the greatest intellectual achievements has, from ancient times, too often also been the history of struggle against poverty and the fanaticism of ignorance. It should, however, be admitted that the conditions under which the research scholar in the social sciences works and the facilities placed at his disposal change notably, not merely over periods of time, but also from one country to another—apparently even more than is the case for his colleagues in the natural sciences.

It must be clearly pointed out at the outset of this discussion on problems of research that we are actually dealing both with international affairs in the wider sense of the term as defined on page one, and with international relations as a special subject. In chapter XIV, we are concerned with the organization of research in international affairs in the wider sense. Our field of operation is, then, all human behavior which originates on one side of a state border and affects human behavior on the other side of that border. Several disciplines are, as we have already seen, engaged in exploring this wide subject; and there may be, in some cases, fairly great differences in their techniques of research. It may suffice to compare the techniques of diplomatic history, for instance, with those of social psychology or international communication. But it may be possible to coordinate, by means of certain types of organization, the work of the specialists in various fields.

However, it certainly exceeds the scope of this study to deal with the processes of research for all the disciplines which have a bearing upon international affairs; in the following chapters, the field must, therefore, be very much reduced. What we will do is simply to make some reflections as to which techniques may be applicable to the kind of subject matter which has been outlined in part two of this volume, or, in other words, we will discuss the processes of research for international relations as a special discipline. Even this task would be wide enough if the subject could be treated in detail. But it goes without saying that a detailed description can hardly be given for a discipline merely in the making. Since, however, some techniques are basically the same for several sciences, it is already possible to base our work on a considerable amount of experience. As further progress is made, new techniques peculiar to international relations may be developed, in addition to what can be borrowed and elaborated from kindred disciplines. Finally, it may be mentioned that most of what is said in this part seems relevant to the study of contemporary affairs in general. To avoid any misunderstanding as to the aim of these chapters on research it must be repeated that we will not endeavor to make any suggestions for the improvement of the various techniques dealt with; our sole purpose is to show what kinds of techniques and source materials are available to the research scholar who tries to cope with the kind of subject matter outlined in the model of analysis.

CHAPTER XIV

THE ORGANIZATION OF RESEARCH

Individual and Collective Research

From olden days, research has been primarily an individual undertaking. It is, to a large extent, combined with teaching in higher institutions of learning. Previously it has, as a rule, been done as an off-time job, but it is becoming increasingly common to grant educators leave with pay, either from their own institution or from foundations or publishing firms, so that they can concentrate exclusively on their research work. Many universities, particularly in the United States, are now setting up large research projects, where several members of the faculty are engaged for long periods of time.

Research also goes on in the preparation of graduate theses, which, since the Middle Ages, have been regarded as the highest tests of able scholarship. However, the variation in standard is great from one country to another and even from one university to another. In some countries the greater part of this kind of research is rather uninteresting and remains unpublished.

During the past decades, the number of people exclusively engaged in research has increased rapidly in the biological and physical sciences. In recent years, a similar increase has taken place also in some of the social sciences. Not only are a greater number of university employees engaged in research as a full-time job, but research is being done on an increasing scale in government offices and other official institutions. Particularly important is the rapid development of research institutes.

By far the greater part of all research in the social sciences is done as individual work. But various forms of teamwork have been practiced in recent years, and this kind of research is becoming increasingly popular, notably in the field of international affairs. The major reason for this development is that research in international affairs is often faced with great and rather heterogeneous projects, and it may be an advantage, or even a necessity, to share the work among specialists in several fields in order to have the various aspects of the subject properly dealt with. Group research, moreover, makes it possible to collect more material than could be done by a single person, and that is important, particularly in a vast field like international affairs. There seems, in our time, to be an increasing demand for empirical research—for a more careful examination of the sources. Some authorities even go so far as to look upon philosophical contemplation as a sort of armchair research of very moderate value.

Individual research can, of course, be penetrating and ingenious in its conclusions; in fact, there are some scholars who believe that the very nature of several social sciences is such that group work can have only a moderate success; but, on the other hand, it cannot be denied that there is, in a complicated and wide field like international affairs, often a danger that individual research may be one-sided and erratic.

It is also of the greatest importance to create a professional milieu. Discussions with colleagues may be suggestive and broaden the mind.[1] And as a rule, scientific achievements can be properly assessed only by authorities in the field, although it naturally happens that jealousy and competition or animosity, for one reason or another, may be an obstacle to fair judgement.

Institutes

The development of institutes has been of fundamental importance to the study of international affairs. The economic resources available have been substantially increased during the past fifty years, and various types of institutions, from small

---

[1] The present Director of the Institute of Advanced Study at Princeton, Dr. Robert Oppenheimer, is quoted as having said that gossip is the lifeblood of physics. See Goode and Hatt, *Methods in Social Research*, p. 23.

study groups to large associations with great funds at their disposal, have been organized to facilitate the work. Some of them are societies largely concerned with the education and information of their members. Most of these institutions carry on a considerable information service. At present, the tendency seems to be away from popular dissemination of knowledge and to concentrate on 'teaching the teachers' and leave it to them to pass on the knowledge to a wider public.[2] It may be noted that it is an important aspect of the institutes that they are well qualified to make the findings of science known to those responsible for shaping policy and public opinion, not only by means of publications, but also by discussion meetings. The institutes maintain, as a rule, large collections of documents, and, in some cases, also considerable numbers of press-clippings, which are essential for the information and reference service as well as for research; and nearly all of them have a reference library, which naturally varies much in size from one institute to another. This collection of special source materials, without which research in international affairs is difficult, is a primary function and *raison d'étre* of the institutes.[3] And it reflects the scientific temper of our time, which tends to favor empirical, at the expense of merely contemplative, research, although it seems obvious that the two forms are not conflicting, but actually supplementary to each other.

The establishment of the great peace foundations in the beginning of this century was a milestone in the development of the study of international affairs.[4] They were not really

---

[2] *Institutes and Their Publics*, New York, 1953, pp. 91, 97—98.

[3] "First of all, we must maintain and develop the services which the research worker and advanced student in this field must have at his command if he is to do his best work." This is the opinion of the Director-General of the Royal Institute of International Affairs in London. Ivison S. MacAdam, "The Purpose and Accomplishments of Institutes of World Affairs," *Institutes and Their Publics*, pp. 91—92.

[4] In 1910, the Carnegie Endowment for International Peace was founded in Washington, D. C. Particularly important from the point of view of research are the Division of Economics and History and the Division of International Law. The World Peace Foundation, which was founded in Boston the same year, did not really become a research and documentation center until after World War I. Cf. Carnegie Endowment for International Peace, *Institutes of International Affairs*, New York, 1953, pp. 12—16.

dispassionate academic workshops. Their function was to further the chances of peaceful relations among nations. But since it was believed that better enlightenment and information about other people would pave the way for more tolerance and increase the chances of peace, they naturally supported the study of international affairs, although, in the beginning, their activity was, perhaps, characterized more by missionary zeal than by careful empirical research. And the great economic resources which they placed at the disposal of the scholar opened up opportunities rarely enjoyed before. Gradually, the belief gained ground that they could better serve the cause of international peace by inquiring into the complex nature of international affairs and disseminating accurate information than by the moral propaganda originally practiced.

In the years following World War I, much progress was made. Already during the war interest in international affairs had been much stimulated by the discussions going on in most Western countries about the creation of a League of Nations.[5] An important stimulus came also from another quarter. The statesmen working at the Paris Peace Conference felt very strongly the impact of public opinion, and it became increasingly clear to them that the progress of democracy would make the governments more dependent on the support of their citizens also in matters of foreign affairs. It was realized that the creation of an informed public opinion on international affairs was a task which no longer could be neglected.

Delegates from the British Commonwealth and the United States entertained the idea of setting up a joint British-American institute of international affairs. This original plan was discarded, but the idea was carried further. Soon after the war, institutions for the study of international affairs were established

---

[5] Among the many institutions established to promote international cooperation must be mentioned the Foreign Policy Association, which was set up in New York in 1918. In addition to notable research, it has carried on an excellent information service on international affairs. Cf. *Institutes of International Affairs*, pp. 60—62.

in both London[6] and New York.[7] They were actually kinds of associations with several hundred members, recruited mainly from the leaders in politics and business who could improve their knowledge of international affairs by means of the services of the associations; but they soon undertook vast projects of research. It is because of this activity that they have become known all over the world. Institutes affiliated with that in London have been established in the Dominions; and the institutes established in other European countries[8] during the past twenty years have, to a large extent, been modeled on Chatham House in London.

This kind of institution is financed by membership subscription, grants, endowments, and revenue from publications.

Their activity includes the study of the history of international affairs, and surveys are issued to provide the reader with as up-to-date materials as scholarly considerations permit.[9] No less important are their efforts to explain major current problems of international affairs by individual or concerted research made by the foremost specialists in the field. They collect and publish documents, maintain a press clipping service, have reference libraries of considerable scope, and publish periodicals of the highest scholarly standard.[10]

---

[6] The London Institute, which was later given the name of Royal Institute of International Affairs, was founded in 1920. It is a non-political and unofficial body governed by a council. Membership is confined to British subjects. There have been established affiliated institutes in Canada, Australia, New Zealand, South Africa and Pakistan.

[7] By a fusion between the group organized by delegates returning from Paris and a group set up in New York during the war, the Council on Foreign Relations was created.

[8] The largest of these is Centre d'Etudes de Politique Etrangère, founded in Paris in 1935. Cf. *Institutes of International Affairs*, pp. 51—54. Among its publications must be mentioned *Ouvrages d'Information*. The Italian counterpart, Istituto per gli Studi di Politica Internazionale, had a more modest start in Milan in 1933, but it has issued an impressive number of publications, among which may be mentioned *Annali di politica internazionale*.

[9] At the Royal Institute of International Affairs is prepared the well-known *Survey of International Affairs*, which has been planned to appear annually since 1920. The Council on Foreign Relations prepares the annual publication, *Survey of American Foreign Relations*.

[10] For a brief description of other functions, such as lectures or dinner meetings, see *Institutes of International Affairs*, pp. 55—59, and 102—111.

Institutes have also been established with the purpose of studying the problems of a particular area. Most remarkable are the efforts made to study and interpret the thoughts, cultures, and institutions of the Pacific countries with a view to improving their mutual relations. Affiliated with the international secretariat in New York, there are eleven autonomous national councils,[11] which are engaged in this kind of work.

More common still are those whose purpose is to study a particular topic, like international law or international trade and finance. To this category belong nearly all of the older university institutes.[12] The foreign policy of the institute's country of origin is occasionally chosen as the major field of study. Another favorite topic is international organizations.

Institutes organized as part of, or affiliated with, a university were extant in Europe before World War I.[13] This type is becoming increasingly common in most countries; but in Europe they are, as a rule, small institutes connected with a department, and lack the necessary resources to undertake larger projects. In the United States, the situation is somewhat different. Some of the university institutes there are quite large; and they may often be inter-disciplinary in the sense that they engage specialists from a variety of fields, who are doing research as a full-time job. Such institutes are well suited to undertake the study of large projects in international affairs.[14] Usually there is an advisory council composed partly of faculty members and partly of persons from outside the university, who approve the program of work.

---

[11] The Institute of Pacific Relations has national councils in the United States, Australia, Canada, France, India, Indonesia, Japan, New Zealand, Pakistan, the Philippines, and Great Britain. As examples of other institutes studying particular areas may be mentioned Südost-Institut at München or the Russian Institute at Columbia University in New York.

[12] As an example may be mentioned Institut für Weltwirtschaft und Seeverkehr an der Universität Kiel, which was founded as early as 1914.

[13] Cf. Handbook of Institutions for Scientific Study of International Relations, compiled by the League of Nations' Institute of Intellectual Co-operation, Paris, 1929.

[14] Cf., for instance, Center of International Studies, connected with the Woodrow Wilson School of Public and International Affairs at Princeton University.

Interest in institutes of international affairs has increased in recent years. This development is due largely to the fact that several countries which have previously pursued a policy of neutrality have become more involved in international politics and, therefore, felt the need to stimulate and broaden interest in and knowledge of foreign affairs. This is particularly the case in the United States, but it is also true of some minor countries like Belgium and The Netherlands.

On the whole, an increasing number of small states have found it useful and possible to establish institutes.[15] Significant is the development in the East, where the increasing role in international affairs of the new Asiatic states is heralded by intensified study and the establishment of institutes for research and education.[16]

Finally, it may be mentioned that recovery after the war in Germany, where the practice of institutes is of long standing, is beginning to bring this country in line with the leading states in the field,[17] and a similar situation is to be found in other countries like Italy.

Research by Public Institutions

The natural sciences have been greatly furthered by the research done in institutes and laboratories connected with larger industrial concerns.[18] In this respect, the social sciences

---

[15] In Sweden, Utrikespolitiska Institutet was established in the late 1930's with a desire to sponsor and contribute to popular education in international affairs.

Schweizerisches Institut für Auslandsforschung was established in 1944. It has a rather strongly academic character.

Shortly after World War II, Institut des Relations Internationales was set up in Belgium, and Nederlanshe Genootschap voor Internationale Zaken in The Netherlands. Both are modeled, to some extent, on Chatham House in London.

[16] There are the Burma Council of World Affairs, the Indian Council on World Affairs, and the Indonesian Institute of World Affairs.

[17] Institut für Europäische Politik und Wirtschaft in Frankfurt am Main seems to have become a leading institution as a research center for Deutsche Gesellschaft für auswärtige Politik. In some ways, it resembles Chatham House.

[18] As an example may be mentioned the well-known Kaiser-Wilhelms-Institut für Physikalische Chemie und Elektrochemie in Berlin, where Professor Albert Einstein worked for several years.

are naturally in a less favorable position, although there are some branches which have been stimulated by commercial demands.[19]

The social sciences are better off when it comes to research carried out by public institutions. As far as international affairs are concerned, it may be mentioned that the foreign offices of the larger states have, for several decades, maintained research departments, and this activity has, in most states, been substantially increased during the last few years. However, this kind of research is being viewed with mixed feelings by many scholars. It is, by the nature of things, usually marked by the rivalry among the states, and things are looked at from the point of view of national interests and advantage; but, although it is practical in character, and deals almost exclusively with immediate problems and is little concerned with fundamental generalizations, it does have a great effect upon the development of science. It may suffice to refer to the great influence which research in international propaganda has had on the development of the study of communication. In this respect, the social sciences resemble the natural sciences, which have often made much progress under the impact of wartime needs.

Important is the fact that those in charge of public research projects often have access to source materials which are unavailable to privately working scholars. And for this reason their publications may be interesting, even though essential aspects of the subject in question frequently have to be omitted because of the regulations for the publication of political and diplomatic documents.

Research done on behalf of international institutions also tends to increase,[20] and there is much to say in favor of this development. Scholars from various parts of the world can here be brought together, bringing their special knowledge and possibly regional views to bear on the problems to be dealt with. The fact that it is necessary to tread very warily

---

[19] Cf. the influence of commercial audience research on the development of the study of communication in the United States.

[20] Cf. "University Teaching of International Relations," *International Social Science Bulletin*, Vol. I (1950); and "Education for the World Community," *ibid.*, Vol. IV (1954).

to avoid adversely affecting national feelings in the member states may conceivably work both ways and have a positive as well as a negative effect.

To all public research, whether national or international, it may perhaps be objected that it neglects basic problems of importance to science. A considerable amount of the energy spent in scientific work must be devoted to the regeneration and promotion of science itself. This is apparently most true of the physical sciences, where theory has so far played a greater role than in the social sciences. But the latter cannot by any means afford to disregard the study of methods and techniques, or to neglect the search for higher generalizations; nor can they ignore a task because its immediate importance is hard to define in terms of material comfort.

Types of Research

We have seen that the institutes have several functions. They are centers for source materials, and collect documents, press clippings, and professional literature. They publish documents, periodicals, pamphlets, and scientific books. They arrange lectures, meetings, and discussion groups. Most of them also do extensive research. We are primarily interested in the last mentioned function, although it should be stressed that the opportunities of doing research are entirely dependent on the availability of source materials.

The establishment of institutes or research centers has opened up new opportunities for teamwork and made it possible to embark upon larger projects. Here scholars, statesmen, administrators, businessmen, and military experts can conveniently come together and exchange views and experiences. Much has been done to exploit these opportunities, and considerable ingenuity has been revealed in developing new types of research.[21] However, in spite of this fact, individual research may

---

[21] The Royal Institute of International Affairs in London has probably carried out more experimentation in this field than any other institution. Cf. *The Future of Chatham House, Report of a Planning Committee of the Council of the Royal Institute of International Affairs*, London, 1946. See also above p. 170 ff.

very often be preferable or even necessary. Whether individual or team work should be applied depends upon the nature of the subject. When the project is fairly well defined, not too vast, and reasonably homogeneous, individual research may prove to be best. A large and heterogeneous project, on the other hand, may with great advantage be dealt with by a team composed of scholars trained in different fields. The lone-working scholar runs, in this case, a greater risk of looking upon the subject too narrowly, or even from the wrong point of view. This shortcoming can, however, be avoided to a great extent if colleagues are willing to comment on the manuscript. This is an old method which is very much practiced, particularly in the field of international affairs.[22] But it may happen that a project is so specialized that it is difficult to find well-qualified critics. In many cases there is also a question of economic resources, since some forms of group work are more expensive than is individual research. Several of the larger institutions have research committees which set up the program, but practically anybody may hand in a proposal to be considered by the committee. So-called 'pilot projects' are being practiced, particularly in the United States. It means that exploratory research is done to clarify the problems involved and to provide suggestions for the further planning of the work.

Various degrees of cooperation can be distinguished. Some types of research are actually a combination of individual study and team work. The making of a symposium involves a very moderate degree of cooperation. Several authorities are merely requested to prepare reports on the same subject[23] or on the same subject from different points of view. An old and well-tried procedure, which involves a higher degree of cooperation, is to share

---

[22] A common practice is that the members of an institute meet at regular intervals to discuss their manuscripts, even if they do not form part of an integrated program. Since several disciplines may be represented at such institutions, it may be possible to have the works examined from many points of view. This method is practiced at, for instance, The Center of International Studies at Princeton University.

[23] Cf. *Democracy in a World of Tensions*, a symposium prepared by UNESCO and edited by Richard McKeon, with the assistance of Stein Rokkan, Paris, 1951. This work is interesting, as it contains a concluding survey analyzing the various papers with a view towards pointing out agreements and disagreements.

a project among a number of more or less individually working scholars, who are, as a rule, chosen from different disciplines. The members of the research team may meet at regular intervals to discuss the manuscripts and the progress of the work. This method has proved to be very applicable in the study of international affairs, and it is much used, especially in the United States, since in this field the projects tend to be large and rather heterogeneous.[24]

Another, less frequently applied method, is to entrust the project to a single editor, who is assisted by a full-time research staff and, in addition, may choose specialist assistance from outside contributors. This method requires a fairly large and financially strong institution, which can keep a considerable permanent staff carrying on continuous research.[25] A variation of this type is to appoint an authority in the field to take over the whole project. He is, then, entitled to engage at will qualified persons to assist him in special parts of the work, or to take over whatever parts he is unable to do himself.[26]

The second main category is the study group proper. Several variations of this method have been developed, each having its special merits or weaknesses. Which one should be chosen depends upon the subject to be studied and the resources at the disposal of the sponsoring institution. In some cases, the study group can be used to great advantage, but there are many subjects which would hardly lend themselves to this kind of research.

Basically, the procedure consists of inviting carefully selected experts to discuss, at a round table conference, a subject which is suited for this type of study, and a rapporteur writes down the conclusions reached by the participants. The rapporteur's job is really a very difficult one, and much depends on whether it is possible to find a qualified person to undertake this part of the process. After being carefully examined by the members

---

[24] Cf. *The Future of Chatham House*.

[25] This method has been used in the well-known *Survey of International Affairs*, edited by Professor Arnold J. Toynbee.

[26] As an example may be given the Chatham House project, *The African Survey*. Actually this method is frequently used for historical surveys.

of the group, and amended, the final manuscript is published under the name of the group or on its collective responsibility. This method is useful particularly for subjects about which written information is not easily accessible, but, to some extent, can be contributed from the personal knowledge of the members of the study group.[27] However, reports produced in this way are, as a rule, vague and sometimes ambiguous. This shortcoming is particularly evident in abstract subjects, which are, in fact, rarely suited for this kind of research.[28]

The third main category of teamwork may be called conference study. The most comprehensive use of this technique was made by the International Studies Conference, which, in the 1930's, arranged several series of study meetings. An editorial committee, headed by a general rapporteur, prepared the report, which contained papers presented at the meetings, as well as the records of the discussion.[29] Universities and other institutions may also sponsor conferences on suitable subjects, at which papers are read and discussed. The papers, together with a record of the discussion, may then by published as a kind of symposium.[30] In some cases reports have been prepared by committees and then submitted for discussion in plenary sessions.[31]

This is obviously an expensive way of studying a subject, and quite often the quantity of written materials produced seems rather small as compared with the money spent. But it makes it possible to examine a wide and complicated subject from many points of view within a very short time. The second

---

[27] "One of the most important contributions the institutes have made—and can continue to make—is that they constitute a meeting place for men with expert knowledge, but drawn from diverse milieux."—John Goormaghtigh, "Commentary on the Theme," *Institutes and Their Publics*, p. 106.

[28] As to the experience gained with this type of study at Chatham House, where it has been much used, see *The Future of Chatham House*.

[29] Reference may be made to the eleventh session of the International Studies Conference held at Prague in 1938, which dealt with university teaching of international relations.

[30] Cf. Quincy Wright (ed.), *The World Community*, Chicago, 1948.

[31] Cf. August Schou, *Western Democracies and World Problems, Report on the Norwegian Nobel Institute's Conference in Oslo, June 13—30, 1955*, Oslo, 1955.

of the variations mentioned above may, in most cases, be the best. It requires, however, that a sufficient number of qualified persons be willing to prepare papers for discussion. And it is usually preferable to distribute copies of the papers to the members a few days before they are read at the conference, so that the members can appear somewhat prepared at the discussion.[32]

International Cooperation

In the study of international affairs, extensive transboundary cooperation is undoubtedly indispensable. The very nature of the subject requires that some of the data must be looked for abroad or in foreign source materials. The student must always be aware of the achievements made by his colleagues in other countries. The field is so wide that only by international collaboration is it possible to arrive at syntheses based on empirical research. Actually, there is, in all branches of learning, a certain amount of fruitful cross-fertilization of ideas over the political borders. And the increasing interdependence of the nations naturally accentuates the need for international cooperation and distribution of works. But it seems obvious that in no other branch of study is there a greater need for broadening out to a world-wide scale the basis of research.[33]

During the last decades of the nineteenth and the beginning of the twentieth centuries, there was a distinctly growing interest in other peoples' ways of life. The usual media for this kind of study were history and geography, on which increasing emphasis was placed. The activity of international news agencies was much expanded, and the greater newspapers sent more and better correspondents abroad. As a consequence, the space allotted to foreign reports by the newspapers was much increased. In a field like international law, considerable efforts were made to establish organized cooperation among the students in the various countries, but not until the late 1920's

---

[32] For some further comments on the matter of research see *Institutes and Their Publics*, pp. 98—100.

[33] Cf. above, p. 53 ff.

did a similar development take place in the study of international affairs in general.

The initiative came, as we have already seen, from the International Institute of Intellectual Co-operation. In the beginning, the work was almost exclusively concentrated on the development of an international machinery of liaison and coordination among national institutions concerned with the study of international affairs. Coordination within the different countries was also stimulated, and national coordinating committees for international studies were formed for that purpose. It was decided that in all countries where such studies were carried on in more than one institution, participation in the work of the International Studies Conference could be affected only through national coordinating centers. This centralization was considered necessary to avoid confusion and undue overlapping of functions. By means of these centers the Conference sought to lay the foundations of a comprehensive international system of technical cooperation among the various national groups and institutions.

This system of cooperation was successfully used for the compilation of international handbooks of information[34] and bibliographies, and it proved very useful for the exchange of surplus publications and professional information. In the 1930's, national institutions also made a practice of using the administrative services of the International Institute of Intellectual Co-operation in Paris for the purpose of obtaining information from one another and of making arrangements for collaboration in carrying out specific programs of study.[35]

Unfortunately, this machinery of international cooperation has not been maintained since World War II at the same level as in the inter-war period. However, meetings of The International Studies Conference have been held, and although The International Institute of Intellectual Cooperation has not resumed

---

[34] Of special interest for the development of the machinery of cooperation was the compilation of the handbook, *Centers of Reference for International Affairs*, published by the International Institute of Intellectual Co-operation, Paris, 1931.

[35] International Institute, *The International Studies Conference*, Paris, 1937, pp. 11—18.

its pre-war activity, there is reason to expect some progress in the field. The service of UNESCO is important, if not essential. It has encouraged more systematic teaching in international affairs,[36] sponsored the study of some highly important problems in international politics, and arranged several successful round table conferences. The work of some other branches of the United Nations, notably the preparation of statistics and social reports, is also of the greatest value. Various agencies publish abstracts of research done in the different countries,[37] but this activity is still inadequate. As far as bibliographies are concerned, the situation is somewhat better.[38] On the whole, it has become much easier to get hold of essential source materials, not only because of the fact that the governments are more willing to publish official documents, but also because of the increasing information service of the institutes. Especially noteworthy is the publishing of information about research projects in progress,[39] which should help to avoid wasteful overlapping of work. But, in spite of considerable advance, there is much need for improvement in the fields mentioned above, and it seems especially that better coordination of work would be useful.

An interesting development is the increasing tendency by institutes to maintain direct liaison with analogous institutions abroad. This practice facilitates a rewarding exchange of views and reduces the risk of needless overlapping in research. The old and highly useful practice of exchanging publications among institutes in various parts of the world has benefited

---

[36] Cf. *International Relations*, edited by C. A.W. Manning in the series *Teaching in the Social Sciences*.

[37] The International Political Science Association prepares, in cooperation with the International Committee for Social Science Documentation, *International Political Science Abstracts*, a quarterly publication containing abstracts of articles; and several excellent periodicals devote much space for reviews. Cf. *International Affairs*, published quarterly.

[38] Cf. *The Foreign Affairs Bibliography*, prepared by the Council on Foreign Relations in New York.

[39] For some years the Carnegie Endowment of International Peace has published a series called *Current Research in International Affairs*. It includes, however, only institutions in the United States and the British Commonwealth.

from the rapid improvement in transport;[40] and it is becoming increasingly common that institutes assist scholars who are doing research abroad. Some of the top-ranking ones, in fact, used to invite distinguished scholars from all parts of the globe to take part in their projects.[41] It appears that these opportunities for a cross-fertilization of ideas are particularly important in the study of international affairs, where, at the moment, great efforts are being made to improve the techniques of research and arrive at new points of view.

The advantage of travel to the student of international affairs has long been realized. Although man's capacity to observe may often be rather limited as compared with the task before him, it is true that a stay of reasonable duration abroad may increase one's knowledge and add a touch of realism to one's appreciation of other peoples' ways of life. And visits to foreign institutions of learning and personal contact with colleagues abroad are, undoubtedly, very useful. An increasing number of large research institutes have opened up new opportunities in this field. The largest obstacle to this kind of international cooperation and contact is, as a rule, the economic problem. However, the scholar has benefited very much from the great emphasis which, since World War II, has been placed on intellectual contact between nations. And the fact that many states are now making agreements about cultural affairs, granting fairly large sums of money, and setting up administrative organs to deal with this kind of matter, is a significant indication of further progress.[42]

---

[40] For some currency problems involved in the exchange of publications, see *Institutes and Their Publics*, pp. 100—102.

[41] In this respect mention may be made of the activity of the Institute for Advanced Study in Princeton, New Jersey.

[42] Cf. above p. 89. Particularly important was the decision made by the United States that aid given under the Lend Lease agreements be repaid in the form of grants for study. This arrangement has been supplemented by large American grants like he Smith-Mundt grant.

CHAPTER XV

THE APPROACH

Subject Matter and Technique

In order to discuss what research methods should be used, it is necessary to have an idea of what is to be studied, since it seems reasonable to choose, adapt, or develop tools and techniques according to the kind of subject matter and problems to be dealt with. In accordance with the points of view maintained in part two of this study, we may say that the broader field of international relations is the structure and functioning of the world society, as human society is the broader field of sociology, and the past that of history in general.

It seems, however, as if every social science, for the purpose of effective operation, has to abstract from the broader field some relevant objects of study, or it may observe some objects from a particular point of view, while other disciplines observe the same objects from other angles. In this way, the work of science can be reduced to manageable proportions.

Fortunately, the techniques of research are not strictly confined to the individual disciplines. The main types of research are based on such techniques as documentary examination, interview, use of statistical and geographical data, and field observation, which can be more or less used by all of the social sciences with some adaptation for the special needs of the individual ones. The methods of documentary research, for example, can perfectly well be, and, in fact, must be used by the practitioners of most disciplines, although they appear to have been primarily developed by the historian. The same may be said about most of the techniques which have been developed by the economist and the sociologist. But the scientific examination of new social phenomena may require new techniques.

It seems to follow from the nature of most social sciences that they are, to a large extent, descriptive. Unlike that of the biological and natural sciences, the subject matter of the social sciences is such that the trial and error or laboratory method can only rarely be used; and the role of hypothesis is limited as compared with the situation in the natural sciences; it simply cannot be easily tested.

Because international relations is a general subject, it is necessary to rely very much upon secondary sources. When the primary sources must be studied, considerable difficulties are often encountered, because the field is so vast that distance and linguistic problems may be serious obstacles, and because the subject matter is so new that it is frequently affected by regulations for secrecy.

Planning of Projects

Already the planning of projects may deserve a few comments. Some aspects of this matter are, however, more or less common to all kinds of research and need not be included in this brief survey. To this category belongs the fact that it often is a long and painstaking job to carry out a major research project, and may require more perseverance and patience than is generally realized.

It may be mentioned that projects on contemporary problems frequently turn out to be far greater and involve more expenditure than orginally calculated. To consider carefully the economic side of a project is certainly an important matter. It may be true that the greatest achievements in the history of learning have often been made under very unfavorable conditions, and have been mainly prompted by an irresistible interest on the part of the student; but that may require too great sacrifices.

The student of international relations has a truly great amount of source materials at his disposal, but that does not mean that they cover every conceivable aspect of the subject. There are, in fact, many highly interesting problems which cannot be dealt with at all because the necessary source material cannot be provided. The old rule, that one of the first things for the research scholar to do is to find out whether the essential raw material is available, holds good in this field, too.

When a project is to be dealt with by an institute, it will usually be carefully examined by the research committee or a special committee set up for that particular purpose. The committee makes comments about whether the proposed project is suitable for research, and if accepted, what form it should be given, how it should be delimited, what type of research should be used, and in case of teamwork, how it should be divided among the various participants.

It is becoming increasingly common to undertake a pilot study[1] to clarify the project and to find out what technique can best be used. This method is much practiced, particularly by sociologists. But it can be done in any field. In fact, it is probably practiced more or less systematically by every careful scholar. It is not always sufficient merely to read some of the relevant literature and to consult experts. A little experimental research may be highly useful before the project is given its shape. And often it has to be considerably modified as the research proceeds.

The belief seems common that the work on a thesis should begin by propounding an assumption or hypothesis, in a somewhat similar manner as the forming of a hypothesis may initiate research in the natural sciences. This notion may be partly due to imitation of the physical sciences. But in the physical sciences, a hypothesis can often be fairly easily tested in a laboratory. The procedure in the social sciences is, as a rule, very different. To test a hypothesis may be a rather laborious task, if possible at all; and to work on a wrong assumption at any length may lead far astray; it is, therefore, necessary to practice this technique with caution.

In some cases the research scholar in the social sciences can do little more than collect scraps of information on the subject and see what the mosaic is becoming like. This happens

---

[1] Goode and Hatt, *Methods in Social Research*, p. 145 ff.

particularly in historical and other descriptive studies. In this case, even questions raised at the outset must usually be of a rather general character; and the research scholar can hardly form clearcut and relevant hypotheses before he has obtained a fairly good over-all view of the subject.[2]

This does not mean that the project should not be as relevant and well-delimited as possible, or that it is unimportant to raise questions in an ingenious and wise manner. On the contrary, it may sometimes be useful to raise pertinent questions or point out new tasks, even if they cannot be conclusively dealt with at once. To focus attention on such matters may be an important initial step, which eventually leads to applicable solutions. Science is a pyramid on which many architects are engaged.

On the whole, general rules are naturally hard to give. The various parts of a discipline, like that outlined in the previous chapters, may require somewhat different techniques. A study, for instance, of trends in the world society may require methods different from those needed for the study of motive forces of political action in a given state or for the analysis of international propaganda.

Dynamic Analysis

The dynamic nature of the world society has already been pointed out. The fact that the subject matter is in a state of flux confronts the student of international relations with many highly difficult problems. The ranking of the powers and the political pattern are consistently exposed to forces tending to bring about alterations, even though it may appear as if the changes are taking place abruptly. The instruments used for the implementation of foreign policy objectives are changing. The climates of opinion have only a moderate stability. The rulers are in power merely for short periods of time, and even the peoples themselves change. On the whole, the forces of stability seem hopelessly outmatched by those of change.

---

[2] Cf. what is said of pilot project on the preceding page.

Because of this situation, the most common way of treating a subject is to describe it over a period of time and analyze the cause and effect relationships in time and in space.[3] Actually this approach, which is generally called the historical method, must, to a greater or lesser extent, be used by all the social sciences, since the subject matter with which they are concerned has many changing elements that hardly lend themselves to a static analysis. In this respect, the social scientist is in a rather unfortunate position as compared with his colleagues in the physical sciences, who can deal largely with static and inanimate subject matter. They can isolate the individual phenomena through laboratory experiments and test the effect produced by varying a single factor while holding all others constant.

The dynamic analysis makes it possible to view a subject in a time perspective, which may reveal how the existing situation has come to be what it actually is. It further enables us to evaluate with some reliability the motives and actions of persons. There are, indeed, many subjects in international relations which we can understand only when we study them in this way. Not only may we be in a position to find out how and why a certain phenomenon has come into being, or how it has functioned in the past, but we may also, under particularly favorable circumstances, be able to discover whether a phenomenon is partly or wholly recurring under given conditions, and to see whether certain types of phenomena are prevailing over long periods of time.

Naturally, the application of this approach requires techniques developed particularly for this kind of research: that is, techniques for examining the past by means of various kinds of remnants, the most common of which are documents. These techniques have been elaborated primarily by historians, therefore they are largely intended for the study of older historical epochs. The study of contemporary history involves, to some extent, different problems, to which, so far, inadequate atten-

---

[3] It falls beyond the scope of this study to enter into detail with regard to the logic of historical analysis; but reference may be made to studies like Patrick Gardiner, *The Nature of Historical Explanation*, Oxford, 1952, and Feigl & Brodbeck, *Readings in the Philosophy of Science*, New York, 1953.

tion has been paid. There is reason to expect that an elaboration of the research techniques of international relations will prove to be of distinct value for the entire field of contemporary history.

One of the most characteristic types of dynamic approach is trend analysis. It has been maintained that the study of the development of the world society and the trends towards its integration, disintegration and transformation are major tasks of the student of international relations.[4] If so, trend analysis and its techniques are highly relevant. It is a method which has already been tried to a considerable extent.[5] It may, in fact, be asserted that the depiction of social trends is more or less implicitly done in many studies of history. The method has been more explicitly applied in some other branches of learning, notably economics[6] and demography. It may further be mentioned that attention has been paid to the possibility of a correlation existing between certain technological phenomena on the one hand and the increase in the size of states[7] and in the cohesion of communities on the other hand. Some interesting beginnings have also been made to investigate trends in international tension.[8]

The applicability of this method naturally depends very much on whether the social trends to be studied can be reasonably well defined and delimited, and whether the factors influencing them can be determined. It seems likely that if success can be achieved on a small scale, it might be possible to coordinate

---

[4] G. Schwartzenberger, *Power Politics*, second edition, p. 8.

[5] Cf. *Recent Social Trends in the United States. Report of the President's Research Committee on Social Trends*, New York, 1932.

[6] For a recent example of the application of trend analysis in economics, see *International Trade 1955*, issued by GATT, Geneva, 1956. Sources and methods are commented on in an appendix.

[7] Hornell Hart, "Technology and the Growth of Political Areas," *Technology and International Relations*, edited by W. F. Ogburn.

[8] Ithel de Sola Pool, *Symbols of Internationalism*, Stanford, 1951.

This study is part of a comprehensive research project on war, revolution, and peace set up at Stanford University. The aim of this project is "to make available to historical scholars a body of trend data concerning what is variously called ideology, public opinion, Zeitgeist, public attention, public attitudes, class analysis, elite analysis, social affiliations, and the like." — Harold D. Lasswell, *The Revolution of Our Time*, Stanford, 1951, p. IV.

the findings of several areas of study. Thus, the necessary over-all view may be obtained. There appear to be many weak points in this method, but it may, nevertheless, provide aid in a field where we need it very much.

Static Analysis

Since the study of international relations is largely concerned with the present, it would seem convenient if the phenomena could be analyzed as if they were static. To some extent, this can be done, because the social and political change is sufficiently slow to allow for a static approach. Even though it may be said that the entire subject matter of international relations changes, some elements, like the politically relevant aspects of the natural environment, do it so slowly that it is rarely necessary to study them in a historical manner. Geographical studies often use this kind of approach and describe the subject matter as if it were static. This geography may do simply because it has to; otherwise, it might be very difficult to reduce the subject matter to manageable proportions.

Geographical, economic, social, political, and military phenomena can be analyzed by means of the latest data without being viewed in a time sequence. Subjects like the capability of wielding power in international affairs, the instruments of international politics, as well as foreign policy interests can be studied in this way. But they may be better understood if they are analyzed over a period of time. And it is always necessary for the student of international relations to bear in mind the greater or lesser dynamics of the subject matter with which he is concerned.[9] Even though it may be possible to describe on the

---

[9] The situation may be illustrated by the following statement by President Eisenhower: "Every single day things change in this world, and any staff or other group of leaders doing his job is re-examining the world situation, geographic and otherwise, of our country and of others, to see what it is that we now need most to insure our security and our peaceful existence. You cannot possibly say that the kind of unit and organization that I took over across the Channel in 1944 would have any usefulness today whatsoever. . . . What would two atomic bombs have done to the whole thing?" *Senate Report No. 1627*, Washington, 1954, pp. 17—18.

basis of available data what a subject was like a year ago, it must also be taken into account that it may be different today.

It is interesting to note that governments reveal an increasing tendency to prepare plans for their activity for several years to come; this is particularly the case with state-regulated societies. This practice enables the social scientist, as well as the statesman, to eliminate, to a considerable extent, the disturbing influence of social dynamics. Such government plans affect, to a large degree, the subject matter of international relations. In many cases, the student is in position not only to know what a subject is like today, but also what it is planned to be in four or five years. But, of course, it is always necessary to take into account that projects may have to be altered.

CHAPTER XVI

BASIC TYPES OF STUDY

When we examine research work done in the field of international relations, we find that three basic types of study are prevailing. The research scholar may prefer to focus his attention on the acts of people and describe more or less chronologically those events which he considers to have sufficient international implications. Another alternative is to study the character and functions of one or several social phenomena; this method is being increasingly practiced in the new field which we have called international relations. Finally, the research scholar may select a geographical region as his subject, trying to explain its role in international affairs. These three types may be called study of events, topical study, and regional study.

Some, probably most, research projects involve the use of only one of these methods. But sometimes all three types of study have to be applied; and occasionally there may be doubt as to which method should be selected. If we examine textbooks on international relations, we are also likely to find that two, and sometimes even all, of these types are used to a greater or lesser extent.

These basic methods are by no means peculiar to the study of international affairs. It may be said that the first type is normally practiced in the study of political history; the second type is characteristic of such subjects as cultural history, cultural sociology, and, in particular, economics; the third type compares more or less to what is now being called area study, and it is usually practiced in the study of geography. Nor is it peculiar for works on international relations to contain more than one of these three types of study; that is true of some works in other fields, too—for example, geography and economics.

It seems, however, as if relatively little attention is being paid to the character and applicability of the various types. It may, therefore, be worth-while to discuss them briefly from the point of view of international relations. This is all the more so since these methods are frequently referred to in the literature, although there is apparently some uncertainty with regard to their character. In a new and still poorly integrated discipline like international relations, it seems particularly useful to pay attention to these kinds of methodological issues. It may not only lead to a better understanding of these phenomena, but also stimulate a more competent criticism.

Study of Events

In its simplest form, this type of study may become merely a dull recording of events. At a more scholarly level, it consists, not only in describing, so to speak, the flow of events or in reconstructing what has actually happened, but endeavors are made also to subject the events, the motives and actions of people to examination and discussion, and the scholar may try to explain the causal relationships. The method is characteristic of most forms of history, and so familiar that further comments on it seem needless.[1]

A historical survey of the foreign policy of a power tends to take this form. In fact, nearly all empirical research in international politics is to a greater or lesser extent a study of events, whether the subject be the forming of an alliance, the solution of a particular problem, or any other event in the area of international politics. It can, as a rule, be based on an examination of documents; but when several powers are involved in the matter, the research scholar may have some difficulty in getting access to the necessary source material, even if it is released for study; to rely only upon the information disseminated by the ordinary news services can rarely be recommended.

---

[1] This method can be studied in most of the volumes in the series, *Survey of International Affairs*, which we may probably be entitled to call the greatest of all historical studies of international politics.

To what extent this type of study should be used in international relations depends, naturally, on what kind of subject matter we agree to include in this discipline. Any student of international affairs needs some knowledge of 'what has happened before', of how things have come to be what they are today. This knowledge can, however, best be obtained by the study of general history. It would be a fatal mistake to believe that international relations as a special subject can or should obviate the traditional historical study of international affairs; but it can supplement it in a most useful way. It has, however, become usual to deal, in courses on international relations, more or less thoroughly with the foreign policy of the great powers, and even to give a brief survey of recent international politics on a world-wide basis; and this dynamic subject matter can, of course, not be properly explained without studying the flow of events.

A study of events must naturally be delimited in space; it cannot take place in a social vacuum. It is not sufficient to fix an event merely in time; it must also be located in space. There are almost endless possibilities for spatial delimitation. An event may occur in a small community, and it may have the entire world as its scene of action. However, a general historical study of international politics in the twentieth century tends to sprawl out over the greater part of the globe, and this fact confronts the student with great methodological problems, notably problems of composition.[2]

Topical Study

There are some important, and previously somewhat neglected, aspects of international affairs, which can be described and explained by a more generalizing method than the so-called study of events. The economist has, for a long time,

---

[2] As an example of a well-composed study of this kind may be mentioned volume six of *Histoire des Relations Internationales*, *Le XIXe Siècle*, by Pierre Renouvin. For the epoch dealt with by this study, it is probably correct to see world politics largely from a European point of view; but in our time there is the danger that this tendency may be too strong.

used it in the study of international economic relations; and some works in this field[3] are, from the methodological point of view, highly interesting to the student of international relations. Obviously, the method can be applied to other kinds of international relations than economic ones; and it can be used, for example, both in the study of the instruments of international politics and in the study of standards of conduct in the world society. It will be noted that the study of elements of international relations outlined in part two of this volume is based, to a large extent, on this method.

A topical study is characteristic of disciplines which tend to take a generalizing rather than a purely descriptive form. The method makes it possible to reduce and simplify the subject to more easily manageable proportions; and that is extremely important in the study of world affairs; but it assumes some degree of uniformity of subject matter from one region to another. In any case, it ought to be carefully founded on reliable data; there is always the danger that this kind of study may become too theoretical and unreal.[4]

A special variety of topical study is the so-called *functional analysis*. It is often useful, if not necessary, to inquire about, and examine the functions of a social phenomenon.[5] This method, which is already of long standing in several fields, seems applicable to the study of international relations to a far greater extent than is the case today. We may ask, for example, what the functions of international propaganda and information service are; and we may even inquire what functions the state has as a social group in the world society.

It is conceivable that social functions are more stable than generally realized; a functional analysis can, therefore, sometimes be done in a more or less static manner. However, a

---

[3] As an example of a study which seems neither too overburdened with historical details nor too theoretical may be mentioned J. B. Condliffe, *The Commerce of Nations*, London, 1951.

[4] Some studies particularly in economics and sociology seem actually to be partly guesswork; even if a conclusion seems logical, there may be no proof that it is in conformity with the hard facts of life.

[5] Cf. above Chapters IX—X.

historical or dynamic analysis is, as a rule, likely to be more rewarding, but naturally more laborious, since it may not only indicate what the functions of a given social phenomenon — for example, the diplomatic service or the instruments of war — are at a certain point of time, but also reveal in what direction they have been developing during the last decades, and, hence, suggest what they may be like in the immediate future.

Regional Study

It has been stated that a certain degree of spatial uniformity is essential for the successful application of topical analysis; and it may often be doubted whether this condition is adequately covered. It may be asked, for example, whether the functions of armed forces do not vary substantially from a country like Switzerland to a superpower like the Soviet Union; or whether the diplomatic service of the United Kingdom does not differ from that of Communist China. It seems that the only way of dealing with this problem is to study the phenomena more or less regionally.[6] We thus see that these three types of study in a way supplement each other.

A topical study can be underpinned not only by examples from the past, but also by contemporary cases from various parts of the world. In this way, regional similarities, as well as variations, can be demonstrated. But if regional peculiarities are to be properly described and explained, the student of international relations may select a certain region as a subject of study, in a somewhat similar way as the geographer does. This method has been stimulated by the prevailing interest in area study since World War II.

Problems of international affairs are usually more or less regional in origin, even though their implications today may

---

[6] If we examine, for example, Harold Nicolson's excellent book, *Diplomacy*, we find that diplomacy is, in some chapters, dealt with in a general topical way, while in other chapters a more regional point of view is adopted. See particularly Chapters III, IV and VI.

be world-wide. Their background can, therefore, be largely explained by the geography and history of the region in question; and, consequently, we find that regional studies are, as a rule, a mixture of historical and geographical analysis.[7] This kind of presentation may be well suited for the compilation of general surveys, particularly if they can be done as teamwork in which persons having special knowledge of the various aspects of society take part.[8]

---

[7] Cf. Charles P. Schleicher, *Introduction to International Relations*, Part II.

[8] As examples may be mentioned *The Scandinavian States and Finland. A Political and Economic Survey*, London, 1951; and *The Middle East. A Political and Economic Survey*, London, 1954, which are both done as teamwork at the Royal Institute of International Affairs in London.

CHAPTER XVII

COLLECTION OF DATA

On proceeding further in the research process, the student is confronted with such questions as what kind of data does he need, what can he get, and how can he get it? How reliable is the available source material, and what does it really tell him? Since international relations as a distinct discipline has not yet developed any technique of its own, the first thing to do is to select what is useful from the practices of older related sciences. This is all the more natural since several social sciences use, to a large extent, the same kinds of source material.

On the whole, international politics is more secret than is domestic politics; but in spite of that, there is a vast amount of source material available. There are, nevertheless, many stumbling blocks to be aware of. Much of the source material that exists is unreliable. This is particularly true of the information disseminated by the ordinary news services. Much of it may also be difficult to obtain because it is scattered widely apart in many places, since the subject matter, by its very nature, covers geographically wide areas. It seems safe to conclude that the study of international relations must be primarily based upon documentary research, although there are a number of what may be called auxiliary techniques.

Documentary Research

Documents and other kinds of materials containing written statements are still the most important sources of data, although an increasing number of other sorts of source materials have become available to the student of social science. Documents have always been the major raw material for history-writing. The historian has, therefore, been much concerned with problems involved in their use, and has drawn attention to many pitfalls.[1] Materials have been classified according to the degree of reliability, and historians and archivists have paid much attention to methods for checking the authenticity of documents.[2] The findings of the historians, although far from exhaustive, are, naturally, of the greatest interest to any student of international affairs.

If he uses the traditional method of the historian and concentrates on diplomatic documents, the student of international relations may occasionally be disappointed. Although regulations for the publication of diplomatic documents have, in most countries, tended to become increasingly favorable to the research scholar, he may still find that the documents in which he is particularly interested are stamped 'secret' and locked up in the safes of the Foreign Ministry. And any 'pushfulness' on his part to get information about their content may result in unpleasant consequences. The period for which diplomatic documents are kept secret varies, from one country to another, between ten and fifty years. But even ten years may be too long, because during that lapse of time the international situation may change so much that conclusions drawn from historical evidence may be of reduced value for the study of current affairs.

The most reliable written sources are, as a rule, conventions, treaties, and other diplomatic agreements. There is, however, quite often disagreement as to the interpretation of their content and stipulations. A realistic assessment of their importance must, moreover, take into account the fact that such agreements are frequently broken under one pretext or another. It may be regretted, but history provides countless examples to prove this assertion. During the past decades secret treaties have become

---

[1] Practically all writers on methodology in history-writing, like E. Bernheim, Wilhelm Bauer, Charles Seignobos, and G. J. Renier, give very useful information for the student of international relations.

[2] Cf. G. J. Lacey, "Questioned Documents," *The American Archivist*, October, 1946.

increasingly rare, and this tendency is generally appreciated by both politicans and scholars. Doctrines or statements of political principles are also of considerable interest, even though they may, within certain limits, be interpreted according to circumstance.

For a full understanding of international affairs, it is necessary to pay due attention to the dealings of foreign ministries and other agencies in charge of foreign policy. But a high percentage of the files in their archives is of little or no interest to the scholar. Publications containing selected documents may, therefore, facilitate considerably the research work. But it may, to some extent, always be a matter of opinion as to what documents are important and, therefore, should be published, even though there is no intention of hiding anything.

During the past thirty years, there have appeared a considerable number of very useful document publications. The endeavors of the great powers to explain their actions or minimize their responsibility for the outbreak of World War I stimulated this practice. The motives for the preparation of these works might implicitly undermine their reputation, but they are, in fact, very good.[3] There have also been cases like that of the Soviet Union, where the archives of the old regime have been thrown open to students by the new masters. However, the theories of the evils of secret diplomacy have largely been abandoned in recent years by these countries. Since World War II new collections of documents have been placed at the disposal of the historian, as materials captured in enemy archives have been published.

In addition to these sporadic publications, some foreign ministries regularly issue collections of documents on international affairs.[4] The same is true of many institutes.[5] There are also a number of more privately-prepared collections, which are

---

[3] The major publications are *British Documents on the Origin of the War, 1898—1914; Die Grosse Politik der Europäischen Kabinette 1871—1914; Documents Diplomatiques Françaises 1871—1914.*

[4] Cf. works like *The Foreign Relations of the United States.*

[5] See above, p. 174.

primarily intended for educational purposes.[6] And the quantity of documents poured out by the various organs of the United Nations is actually so overwhelming that the student has difficulty in finding his way through them.

Changes in diplomatic practices[7] and in the management of external affairs have had some interesting consequences with regard to source materials. Since the competence of the national assembly to deal with foreign affairs has been increased in most countries, and the development of conference diplomacy offers members of national assemblies and party leaders, to say nothing of cabinet ministers, a greater opportunity to participate in diplomatic affairs, documents of interest to the research scholar have not only become more abundant, but also more easily available. The records of the national assemblies, including the proceedings of committees on foreign affairs, as well as the archives of the political parties are today of primary importance, although, as a rule,the files of the foreign ministries are still the most important source.

It should also be mentioned that there is vast and highly useful source material in the archives of great institutions like international banking concerns and other large enterprises, which has, so far, been inadequately examined, mainly because such archives have been inaccessible to research scholars. A further study of this kind of source material is certain not only to increase our knowledge of the nature of international affairs, but, in particular, to provide much-needed information about the role of what we have called actors other than states.[8]

The social upheaval in several countries after World War I drove many leading statesmen into exile. They produced a very important emigrant literature, which included memoirs

---

[6] For a list of document collections, reference may be made to Normand D. Palmer and Howard C. Perkins, *International Relations*, London, 1954, p. 1233 ff.

New document publications are currently listed in the chapter, "Source Materials," in the quarterly, *International Affairs*, issued by Royal Institute of International Affairs in London.

[7] Lord Vansittart, "The Decline of Diplomacy," *Foreign Affairs*, Vol. 28, (1950), p. 177 ff.

[8] Cf. Chapter XII.

of comparatively high standard. Since World War II, there has appeared a similar literature.[9] It has also become increasingly common for retired statesmen to write memoirs of their political activity.

It is obvious that this kind of literature may have serious limitations as source material. Even if the memoirs are based on carefully written diaries, the possibility of personal biases and partiality must be taken into consideration. If they are written merely by memory many years after the events dealt with happened, it goes without saying that they may be misleading, even though the punctiliousness of the author is unquestionable. It is conceivable that historians have sometimes been inclined to overestimate the documentary value of memoir literature.[10]

The increase in periodicals and newspapers has provided the research scholar with truly vast, but somewhat unreliable, sources of materials. The information given in these sources must, as a rule, be used with great care in reconstructing a sequence of events or in forming an over-all picture of political and social conditions. This precaution seems all the more necessary in the study of international politics, where the machiavellian recipes for lighthearted eluding of veracity are rather frequently observed. Another difficulty with which the student of international relations is confronted is the fact that the character of the press may vary substantially from one country to another. However, public opinion, attitudes, and trends of feeling may, at least in highly developed democracies, be fairly well registered by the press.

Periodicals and newspapers frequently present interviews with political leaders. But even if the statements of the interviewed person are correctly rendered, which is often far from the case, the information given must sometimes be received with scepticism, since it may be formulated with a view towards favorably influencing public opinion. The same may be said of public speeches given by top-ranking statesmen,

---

[9] Nils Ahnlund, *Document och Vittnesbörd till vår tids historia*, Stockholm, 1950.

[10] The value of memoir literature as source material has been somewhat inadequately examined. For a brief discussion see E. Wiskeman, "Memoirs as a Source of Recent History," *The Times Literary Supplement*, 1950, No. 2545.

both at home and at international conferences. The possibility cannot be disregarded that they are propaganda maneuvers rather than reliable descriptions of the existing states of affairs or statements of policies actually to be adhered to.

On the whole, periodicals differ so greatly in quality and purpose that general comments can hardly be made on them. Some of them must, of course, be classified rather with learned books than with newspapers.

Unfortunately, scholarly studies of the press as source material for research are still far too few. There are, obviously, many pitfalls. It seems, however, that specialists in the field of communications are likely to provide the student of international relations with much useful information about the techniques of disseminating news and about the reliability of the various sources of information. The establishment of press archives at various institutes for the study of international affairs has led to increasing use of these kinds of sources,[11] and their merits and limitations must be given more attention than has so far been the case. This requires, however, further study of the press as a social phenomenon in general.[12]

---

[11] The largest one is that at the Royal Institute of International Affairs in London. Here they also have a speaker's index for all important speeches given since 1931. A reference to the press archives is filed under the name of the speaker. The archives, which have press cuttings from 1916 on, are being used by Members of Parliament, government departments—notably the Foreign Office—the press, advanced students, and especially the research section of Chatham House. They have been widely used for the great series, *Survey of International Affairs;* and useful experience has been gained with regard to the value and limitations of the press as source material for research.

Even smaller institutes, such as Utrikespolitiska Institutet in Stockholm and Nederlandsche Genootschap voor Internationale Zaken in The Hague, have good press archives.

[12] Of activity in this field may be mentioned the research done at Deutsches Institut für Zeitungskunde at Berlin University in the interwar period. Cf. Paul F. Douglas and Karl Böhmer, "The Press as a Factor in International Relations," *The Annals of the American Academy of Political and Social Science*, Vol. 162 (1932), p. 241 ff.

Since World War II The International Press Institute in Zürich has done highly important work to increase our knowledge of the press. Useful information can be found in the proceedings of its annual assemblies and in the *IPI Surveys*. Mention must also be made of the publication, *The Flow of News*, Zürich, 1953.

It seems possible to include statistics also under this heading and regard the use of statistical publications as a special kind of documentary research, although there might be good reasons for treating them as a special topic. Statistics have come to be the basic research tool of the economist, and they are being used increasingly by research scholars in practically all of the social sciences. National statistics, including reliable information on foreign trade and the international economic position in general, have for a long time been prepared by most of the major countries; they contain highly important data also for the student of international affairs.

Of particular interest is the admirable work done by the agencies of the United Nations in collecting data from practically all parts of the world. Attention is being paid to a variety of political, social, and economic aspects. A continuation and improvement of this activity is, in fact, a prerequisite to the study of the kind of subject matter outlined in part II of this volume.[13] It goes without saying that there are still many loopholes. A society must reach a certain stage of cultural development before reliable statistics can be easily obtained. However, good progress has been made in most parts of the world during the past years.

Statistics have, because of their very nature, notable shortcomings and pitfalls of which it is better to be aware.[14] The publications prepared by the United Nations have, as a rule, important explanatory notes on the interpretation of the information given.

There is now also a vast literature giving encyclopedic information and biographical data. Most well-equipped libraries will

---

[13] Among the many useful statistical publications prepared by the agencies of the United Nations may be mentioned, in particular, the *Statistical Yearbook*, which has been issued since 1948.

Of interest also is *Balance of Payment Yearbook*, prepared by the International Monetary Fund, although this publication seems to be more intended for the professional economist.

[14] W. F. Ogburn, "Limitations of Statistics," *The American Journal of Sociology*, Vol. XL (1934—35), pp. 12—35.

be able to offer satisfactory service.[15] Naturally, not all such information can be accepted without criticism; but it is, as a rule, fairly reliable. The more common types of publications which the student of international relations will find useful are the large reference books like yearbooks and bibliographical dictionaries.[16]

Interview and Questionnaire

The interview and the questionnaire are research tools primarily developed by the sociologist; they have now become his most important means of collecting data for major sections of his field; and they are, undoubtedly, very useful for the study of contemporary affairs in general, although they appear to have certain shortcomings.[17]

The interview, and somewhat less frequently the questionnaire, can be used with definite advantage when written sources are lacking or too scanty; and since the student of international affairs is largely concerned with the present, this situation occurs rather frequently. It may, then, be necessary to draw on the memory of statesmen and other persons playing an important role in international affairs, simply because this may be the only means of obtaining the necessary data.

These research tools can be useful even in cases where document collections are too vast for the research scholar to get through within a reasonable period of time. This may be the case, for example, with the vast amount of documents issued by the agencies of the United Nations.

[15] Josef S. Komidar, "Use of the Library," *Methods In Social Research*, by Goode and Hatt. This chapter is, however, primarily concerned with American literature. In particular, mention must be made of Helen F. Conover, *A Guide to Bibliographic Tools for Research in Foreign Affairs*, Washington, 1956.

[16] As examples may be mentioned *Statesman's Yearbook*, issued since 1864; *World Almanac*, which has appeared since 1868; in addition, *Political Handbook of the World*, *World Biography*, and the many variations of national biographies like *Who's Who*, as well as professional biographies like *American Men in Government*.

[17] Some of which are touched on in the next chapter.

There are several studies about the use of these media, which may be read with considerable advantage.[18] However, rigid rules can hardly be given. It seems that each situation must be dealt with more or less according to circumstances. The newspaper man has practiced the interview technique in a rather informal and flexible manner for decades. The scholar may find some of his methods useful.

A commendable way of obtaining a high degree of objectivity is to ask the person in question to write down all he knows of the subject to be studied, and then supplement his report by asking some questions. However, a statesman or other important person is rarely willing to do that; he is usually at most willing to answer a few clear-cut questions.

Geographical Data

It appears to be frequently forgotten that elementary tools such as an atlas[19] or a school globe are almost indispensable for anyone trying to obtain a realistic view of international affairs. The globe is particularly useful for high latitudes, where many maps convey illusions about geographical relations, because of the methods for projecting a spherical area on a flat surface.[20] This shortcoming of maps has even been exploited in international propaganda.[21] There is all the more reason to be aware of this matter since the polar regions are playing an increasing role in world politics.

Much essential information can be read directly from maps without having recourse to any other source of information.[22]

[18] Goode and Hatt, *Methods in Social Research*, p. 132 ff.; see also bibliography on p. 208.

[19] A frequent disadvantage of atlases is that they use too much space on the country in which they are issued, while some other areas are almost neglected.

[20] Nicholas J. Spykman, *The Geography of Peace*, New York, 1944.

[21] S. W. Boggs, "Carthypnosis," *Department of State Bulletin*, Vol. XV (1946), 1119 ff.

[22] For an introduction to cartography, reference may be made to Erwin Raisz, *General Cartography*, New York, 1938; mention may also be made of *Atlas of Global Geography*, New York, 1944, prepared by the same author.

A mountain range or a sea may have political, economic, and directly military importance. Several factors may be involved in determining the significance of such geographical phenomena, which may require experience to understand. General geographical knowledge and some experience in using maps are needed to take full advantage of the opportunities which they offer.

Geographical data can be obtained from a large number of reference books.[23] In some cases, it may be useful or even necessary to use geographical handbooks, particularly on political and economic geography. New and highly useful sources of information are the reports made by special commissions set up by the United Nations for investigation of poorly developed areas.[24] And the statistical publications prepared by the agencies of the United Nations[25] provide the most reliable data obtainable on demographic, economic, and social affairs, which, combined with general geographic information, will convey a fairly good conception of the various regions of the world and of trends in the world society as a whole.

Observation

Observation in the field is, so as to speak, an inherent ability of man, and has naturally been practiced since the dawn of civilization. But it can be done in a more or less effective way.[26]

The application of this technique in the field of international affairs may meet with many obstacles. It takes time and money to cover sufficiently large areas to give the student a reasonably wide personal knowledge of his subject. And even if these problems could be overcome, the political problems

[23] John Kirtland Wright and Elizabeth T. Platt, *Aids to Geographical Research*, New York, 1947.

[24] Economic and Social Council, *Reports on the World Social Situation*, New York, 1952, (E/CN. 5/267).

[25] Notably, *Statistical Yearbook* and *Demographic Yearbook*.

[26] For some useful suggestions as to the technique of observing, see Goode and Hatt, *Methods in Social Research*, p. 119 ff.

involved might be still more difficult. However, observation has been the basic technique of the geographer, and, to some extent, it is essential also for the student of international relations. And it should not be forgotten that even a good documentary film may add a touch of realism to knowledge obtained merely from written sources.

Ordinarily, the information provided by broadcasting will not be of much use to the scholar. He can just as easily obtain the same thing from the press. Occasionally, however, qualified commentators may provide him with useful background information. And it may be more suggestive to listen to a speech by a statesman than to read the comment in the press.

Since the student of international relations endeavors to include as much of the present in his field as possible, it follows that he is eager to exploit all the means of modern communication insofar as this is compatible with the requirements of scholarly reliability. But this is hardly a task for the lonely working social scientist; and, therefore, the greater institutes have established information departments to take care of this matter.

CHAPTER XVIII

PROBLEMS OF PRESENTATION

Professional Terms and Concepts

Each academic discipline must develop, to a greater or lesser degree, its own conceptual tools—adequate terms and concepts for communicating its findings. When properly elaborated, each concept communicates to those who understand it a considerable amount of clarified experience and cognition. But the use of such concepts varies greatly from one discipline to another. A descriptive science, such as geography, develops relatively few concepts of its own, while generalizing sciences, like physics, tend to develop many more. And, some of the social sciences, like economics and sociology, have, particularly in countries where they have been rather theoretical, included extensive and somewhat indigestible sections on definitions. But as the sciences have progressed and penetrated deeper into the subject matter, these sections on definitions have taken a less abstract shape.[1]

The development of such conceptual tools is an important process, which seems to need more attention than has so far been given. In some cases where it has been allowed to proceed haphazardly, the results have been controversial indeed. Many studies in, for instance, philosophy of history are fraught with undefined and almost unintelligible terms.

The still poorly developed discipline of international relations has naturally not yet proceeded very far in this respect; and to avoid from the outset an undue ambiguity of terms would be a distinct service to the newcomer. The danger of confusion

---

[1] J. R. Hicks, *The Social Framework*, Oxford, 1942, p. VI.

is increased by the fact that the proponents of the new subject have been educated in different fields. One may have had his university training in philosophy and law, another in history and geography, and a third in economics or sociology.

In the United States, in particular, the influence upon international relations of social sciences prone to beget their own language is already considerable; the new subject is borrowing an increasing number of technical terms and notions from kindred disciplines like sociology.[2] It has also made a start in developing its own concepts. In Europe, where the contours of the infant science have emerged only in one or two countries, the development of professional terms and concepts is somewhat less, but there, too, a good many words have been created, which may sound rather strange in the ear of the uninitiated.[3]

Sociologists and economists have for years paid much attention to the problems of definition, and the student of international relations is likely to profit by examining their experience. As theoretical constructs are being developed, the use of new concepts is bound to increase. It seems, therefore, important to pay due attention to this matter from the beginning, since ambiguity of terms confuses the thinking, encumbers fruitful communication of ideas among scholars, and retards the attainment of valid conclusions.

Interpretation and Evaluation

Problems of interpretation and evaluation have so far been rather inadequately examined from the point of view of international affairs, but increasing attention is being paid to the matter. Actually, the subject matter of international relations presents some highly interesting problems in this respect, although they are apparently not unique. The historian is confronted with somewhat similar problems when he is analyzing former civilizations, as is the student of international relations

---

[2] It will be noticed that many terms and concepts from related disciplines, particularly from sociology, have also crept into the present work.

[3] Cf. C. A. W. Manning, *International Relations*.

when he is studying political and social affairs in parts of the world which have a civilization different from his own.

Both when we form our ideas by means of other peoples' statements—in the terminology of the philosopher, it may be called by means of symbols—and when we are in a position to make personal observations on the spot, we are confronted with questions of interpretation and evaluation which are not only of an academic or theoretical, but also of a practical interest. They concern statesmen and scholars alike, and, in particular, those who are engaged in information and propaganda activity. In fact, there is reason to hope that the progressing study of international communications will provide the student of international relations with much useful information about the processes of interpretation and conception.

The persons who in the beginning of this century donated large sums of money for the promotion of peace realized the value of traveling abroad and learning about other peoples' ways of life. But even if we have the opportunity to live among foreign peoples for quite a long time, it may be difficult to become well acqainted with their manners, mores, and customs and to understand the ways in which they look at the basic problems of life, particularly if their civilization is very different from that of the observer. And it goes without saying that we cannot always interpret without qualifications their peculiarities in terms of the standards of our own society, although that is frequently done. Motives are interpreted and social phenomena are evaluated in the light of values and standards prevailing in our own society, but which may be more or less absent in that concerned. It is not unusual that the propaganda of the Western great powers advocates values for which the upper classes of the Western societies have developed, so to speak, an acquired drive, but which mean practically nothing to people who scarcely have the opportunity to satisfy their most elementary biological needs, such as the minimum of food required for remaining alive.[4]

---

[4] For a brief discussion of this kind of problem, see Bruce L. Smith, "Communication Research on Non-Industrial Countries," *The Public Opinion Quarterly*, XVI (1952—53), pp. 527—538.

Especially difficult is the problem of interpretation when the ideas must be formed merely on the basis of statements.[5] A person's interpretation naturally depends on his ability and ways of conceiving, which in turn depend on his intelligence, education, and experience. Words denoting social and political phenomena may have a local connotation. They may stand for phenomena which are lacking or entirely different in other societies. When they are used to describe or explain foreign societies, they may convey a rather distorted picture.[6] However, this difficulty may be partly offset by the fact that the vocabulary of an advanced society offers a wide variety of opportunities for detailed description of social phenomena which seem strange. And it may, perhaps, be added that this is one of the situations in which even a good documentary film can do valuable service.

A student of international relations can hardly abstain from making evaluations. And even if he could, he would have to accept the fact that values and value scales are important ingredients of the subject matter of his study, and that they decisively affect the life and behavior of all nations.

Evaluations can be made only on the basis of some value system, and value systems may vary to some extent from one society to another. They are part of a cultural configuration and can be properly understood only when regarded as such. In some cases, the influence of economic and social conditions upon morality and value hierarchy is very clear. Mention may be made of the horrible practice of female infanticide in barren and bleak regions like Tibet and parts of the Arctic, where primitive subsistence economy and a high death rate of males make it desirable. Patriotism is another force which makes its influence felt, consciously or unconsciously, upon value judgements.

---

[5] Felix Kaufmann, *Methodology of the Social Sciences*, New York, 1944, p. 166 ff.

[6] The American sociologist, Charles Y. Glock, gives as an example a Turkish worker who lives in a small one-room hut together with a couple of other families and suffers from the frequent quarreling. He is horrified when he sees a picture of a New York skyscraper where a thousand families live, because he visualizes all the fighting which may develop among all these families which have to 'live together'. *The Public Opinion Quarterly*, XVI, pp. 521—22.

The situation is further complicated by the fact that the value hierarchy may vary from one social group to another within the same society. An action which is regarded as right and proper within one social group may be looked upon as wrong and improper within another. This is particularly evident in societies where there is a strong class animosity. There is usually a fair chance that personal interests of various kinds, notably economic interest and social status, affect, more or less, this tendency. Finally, it must be mentioned that the value hierarchy of one person may vary from that of another within the same subgroup.[7] This line of reasoning should, however, not be pursued to the extent that we forget the fact that people everywhere also have quite a few basic values in common.[8]

The reasons for these variations from one nation to another, from one social class to another, and from one person to another are many and complicated. But whatever the differences may be due to, it is obvious that peoples having more or less different moral codes, dissimilar patterns of behavior, and different, if not irreconcilable, political, social and religious views, will have difficulty in arriving at similar opinions and evaluations of international political problems.

It may be added that this is a matter of far-reaching political significance. Particularly in the interwar period, much reliance was placed upon what was called world opinion, and in recent years statesmen have increasingly referred to this social force. It may, however, be questioned whether such a thing as world opinion really exists at all, since it is difficult for peoples with partly different value scales, conflicting interests, and very different political views to form similar opinions of political conditions and events. However, the propaganda services of the great powers, as well as the fact that political leaders frequently form their speeches with a view towards influencing public

---

[7] It may be mentioned that the philosophy of Plato has an interesting bearing on the ranking of values in the conceptions of the "three lives" expounded most fully in the *Republic:* The life of the philosopher devoted to the attainment of wisdom, that of the man of action devoted to the attainment of distinction, and that of the votary of enjoyment, who seeks gratification for his appetites.

[8] Cf. above, pp. 72—73.

opinion in the greatest possible number of states, indicate the political importance of opinion also at the international level. Even if we cannot yet speak of world opinion, we may be entitled to speak of international opinion, which may have great, although not easily defined, political implications.[9]

As global integration is progressing and the information services are being improved, our concern with and knowledge of events in remote parts of the world are being increased, and world opinion may become a reality. This matter seems to be of particular importance to the small states, which cannot rely upon their armed strength. The great difficulty for the time being appears to be that peoples in different parts of the world receive different or even entirely contradictory descriptions and interpretations of political phenomena. This difference is particularly evident between the communist and the non–communist world. Progress in broadcasting techniques can only partly reduce this problem. Information disseminated from one great power into a rival nation tends to be regarded merely as propaganda.

Human values and evaluations are undoubtedly among the most evasive topics of the whole subject matter of social science. A scientific proposition can be empirically demonstrated as correct or incorrect. This cannot be done to value judgements. But an action can be proved to be in conformity with agreed standards of behavior, and it may be demonstrated that it produces desired values. And it is, for obvious reasons, necessary, as many authors have pointed out,[10] to distinguish clearly between statements of facts as conceived by a person and his personal evaluation of a phenomenon.

Some of the problems of evaluation may be due to the fact that the student of international relations tends to concentrate attention largely on our own time. It is widely agreed that a relatively unbiased study of contemporary affairs is more difficult than is a study of older historical epochs. In the latter

---

[9] The spontaneous reaction in the greater part of the world to the events in Hungary in November, 1956, is a striking example.

[10] Felix Kaufmann, *Methodoloy of the Social Sciences*, p. 199 ff.

case, the phenomena can be viewed in a time perspective and, perhaps, evaluated somewhat more dispassionately, but this view may be questionable.[11]

Pitfalls of Composition

The problems of composition with which the student of international relations is confronted resemble, to a large degree, those of the student of general history, although the element of art may be greater in general history than it is in international relations. They change with the character of the 'picture' to be drawn and the source material available. Sometimes the subject may be fairly homogeneous and clearly delimited. In this case the composition may be relatively easy. But frequently the subject will be vague and comprehensive; then it is naturally more essential to plan the project carefully and to make sure to begin on the right track.

In composing his work, an artist may sometimes endeavor to conjure up moods and feelings; and to obtain the desired artistic effects, he may purposely distort reality as he sees it. But it follows from the very nature of his profession that a serious scientist is primarily, if not exclusively, concerned with obtaining as 'true' a presentation of the aspects of reality with which he is dealing as possible.

Life is, in fact, far too rich to find full expression in documents and other kinds of source materials; and it frequently happens that the information most needed cannot be obtained. Constructive imagination, though apparently less essential than in the study of ancient history, where reliable data are very scarce, is, undoubtedly, important also in this field. When we are dealing with the present, personal experience and observation can be drawn upon extensively, but this advantage is offset to a considerable degree by the vastness of the field of international relations.

---

[11] Percy E. Corbett, "Objectivity in the Study of International Relations," *World Affairs*, Vol. IV (1950), pp. 257—263.

Like the historian in general, the student of international relations needs not only creative imagination and the capacity to construct, but he must also have the ability to make wise selections. He is describing and studying vast social phenomena, and rarely indeed is his subject so small and manageable that it is possible to treat it in detail. Actually, some aspects of the subject matter are so immense that they require the greatest ability to abstract what is considered to be their most characteristic traits. It may suffice to mention the study of trends. Or perhaps a still more illustrative example: The history of world politics since World War I could easily be made to fill ten large volumes, but it might, for practical purposes, be necessary to give it in only one by selecting what seems most important and leaving out the rest.

It seems as if any such choice may, by the nature of things, be somewhat subjective. It depends to a large extent on the character of the student—his knowledge, intellect, feelings and idiosyncracies—what he regards as important or interesting and, therefore, finds worthy of presentation or emphasis, and what should be left out. This circumstance seems to be one of the reasons why history must be rewritten over and over again. And it makes it difficult to do accumulative research in the social sciences; that is to say, a kind of research where it is possible to rely on previous findings, because the conclusions arrived at are final and represent the only correct solution, so that it is unnecessary to deal with the same problems repeatedly.

The rapid development of the means of transportation has made it increasingly easy to make observations on the spot, although political obstacles have, in some parts of the world, impeded the progress. It has been pointed out that in the study of the world society, it is essential to make use of this technique. There are, however, some dangerous pitfalls of which one had better be aware. When we are collecting our data by observation on the spot, or when the information is obtained by the interview technique, we are, as a rule, confronted with very difficult problems of composition. What in particular attracts the attention of a person traveling in a foreign country, or what questions a person raises in an interview, or what he puts on a questionnaire, depends, naturally, more or less on his intelligence, interests, experience in the field, and so on; or, put in other words, it depends to a large extent upon subjective qualities of the observer or interviewer himself.

If the observer is to study a region or a country, he will usually be able to cover, within a reasonable period of time, merely parts of it. And he may be deliberately guided to places which reveal only one or a few aspects of the society in question, and which may, in fact, convey a wholly misleading impression of the generally existing state of affairs. This happens frequently to delegations invited by the regime in power to visit a country.

Especially noteworthy are educational and professional biases. The mind may be so firmly directed towards certain aspects of the phenomena to be observed that other ones are almost disregarded and, in extreme cases, practically overlooked entirely.[12] Occasionally, it also happens that departmental chauvinism and academic jealousy engender the attitude that only what belongs to one's own field or discipline is regarded as really significant. Even within the same discipline there may be great variations; what one person considers interesting and important and therefore gives much attention and space, another may regard as dull and insignificant, and consequently leaves it out almost entirely. It thus appears that interpretation and, in particular, evaluation influence, to a large extent, the problems of composition.

The situation is an entirely different one when the source material is restricted, as it often may be in documentary research, and usually is when statistics must be relied upon. It is, then, less a question of selection than of balance and constructive imagination. If it is forgotten that the source material may cover merely some aspects of the subject while other, perhaps more important ones, are not represented at all, the picture may be unduly simplified and wrongly composed.[13] There is,

---

[12] J. B. Conant, *On Understanding Science*, New Haven, 1947.

[13] "La recherche historique oscille toujours entre deux écueils: rester trop strictement liée à une documentation apparemment solide et incontestable, mais risquer

in fact, always the danger that those aspects which are well represented by the source material may be given too much space, while those which are inadequately covered by the sources may be too poorly treated. This may be the case particularly when statistics are used, since this kind of source is, on the whole, less capable of conveying ideas and conceptions than are words.

In all kinds of research, it is necessary to have recourse to what is called introspection.[14] The precise character of this mental activity is not quite clear. It appears that it involves the treatment by logic of knowledge obtained in various ways during the course of life. Thus, the personal knowledge of the student constitutes, in a way, the source materials.

Actually, we all practice this technique, more or less, in everyday life. However, when carried to an extreme as a scientific method, it may result in merely a twisting of words which hardly produces any findings of real value, since this kind of source material, too, is limited. Sociology has had a great conflict about the relative merits of intuitive and empirical research. It has now died down, and it has been realized that the two forms of scientific procedure are not opposing, but rather complementary.

Non-Scientific Obstacles

In most countries we have, for a long time now, been used to regard freedom of scientific inquiry as a foregone conclusion. And it is generally believed that a maximum of freedom from political control and interference is necessary to achieve the greatest advance in the social sciences. However, this is a rather complicated matter. A thorough examination might prove that illusions on this subject are more often entertained than is generally

---

d'ignorer l'essentiel; ou bien regarder au-delà de ces documents, en se contentant de données fragiles, dont l'interprétation laisse trop de place à des hypothèses séduisantes."
Pierre Renouvin, *Le XIXe Siècle*. Deuxième partie. De 1871 a 1914, Paris, 1955, p. 3.

[14] This practice is characteristic of philosophy also in dealing with international affairs. Cf. Quincy Wright, *The Study of International Relations*, p. 104.

realized. There are many ways of bringing pressure to bear on a scholar, and it is not always easy to say what forces may support a supposedly objective study of a given social phenomenon and what forces may oppose it.

Since the social sciences explore social and political phenomena, their findings are likely to have political implications which cannot easily be predicted. Historians and sociologists, as well as economists, have occasionally had unpleasant experiences,[15] not only in the more or less totalitarian countries, but also in societies usually regarded as having a high degree of personal liberty.

Unfortunately, the past decades have witnessed a tendency to encroach upon the liberty of scholars in countries where the ideal of freedom has been most vociferously expounded. And the world-wide antagonism in the political field is likely to stimulate this phenomenon. The increasing emphasis on power politics and the bi-polarization of world power entail a tendency to bring implicit pressure to bear on the scholar to make him abstain from his irritating inquiries and present his findings in terms of the policy of the country or political bloc to which he belongs.[16] At the same time, the increasing emphasis on ideology has tended to strengthen the demand that the phenomena be explained in accordance with prevailing political dogmas.

On the other hand, cultural progress in previously backward and totalitarian states seems to open up new opportunities for a wider and better study of international affairs. But the subject matter with which the student of international relations has to

---

[15] This highly important matter has, in most countries, been surprisingly poorly explored. A sociologist put it this way: "If his [the scientist's] speciality is the study of a geological formation, for example, his deviance from prevailing beliefs on the subject is no longer fraught with much personal danger. If his speciality is the study of some aspect of human relationships, however, his deviance may place him at odds with powerful vested authorities—political, economic, ecclesiastical, and familiar."- Alfred M. Lee (editor), *Readings in Sociology*, New York, 1951, pp. 1—2.

[16] Edward C. Kirkland, "Do Anti-Subversive Efforts Threaten Academic Freedom?" *The Annals of the American Academy of Political and Social Science*, Vol. 275 (1951), p. 132 ff.

deal is such that it may frequently bring him in opposition to national, economic, political, and even ecclesiastical interests which would like a different explanation of the phenomena from the one he has attained.[17]

Ignorance and indifference may, under certain circumstances, be no less discouraging. A research scholar frequently needs, particularly for economic reasons, the support of more influential colleagues or circles wielding some political or economic influence.[18] However, the fact that a social scientist can benefit by being the advocate of politically or economically influential quarters may, from a strictly scientific point of view, naturally involve a danger.

International affairs is, in fact, a far too important field to be dealt with in a non-scientific manner. It is essential to be aware of any undue encroachment upon the prerequisites of a strictly scientific examination. If the foci of interest are moving from historical case studies in the direction of more general problems—as they actually appear to be—political and social obstacles of the kind mentioned above may be somewhat reduced. But in any case, the demand of the student can be nothing less than full liberty to conduct his work in accordance with the highest standards of scientific procedure.

[17] C. A. W. Manning, *International Relations*, Chapter III.

[18] Not only individual researchers, but also institutes are confronted with this kind of problem. Cf. *Institutes and Their Publics*, pp. 97, 106—107.

CHAPTER XIX

ON THE USE OF RESEARCH

It is usually difficult to appreciate scientific work. There may be doubt as to what value system on which to base an evaluation. A scientist, particularly in the natural sciences, may feel inclined to value a work on the basis of its contribution to the advance of science, e.g., its improvement of theoretical constructs and higher generalizations, or on the degree to which it extends the field of human knowledge.[1] A layman, on the other hand, may place emphasis on the immediate utility. In either case, some uncertain factors are involved, because it is, as a rule, difficult to foresee the importance or consequences of scientific work, even by those who are doing it. Science can be used for a variety of purposes, as is clearly indicated by inventions in the physical sciences.

Work in the social sciences is probably even more difficult to evaluate than in the physical sciences. Here emphasis may be placed merely on the entertaining merits—on whether a study is interesting or pleasant to read, or on the thrill of logic which it produces. Appreciation on such bases may be made almost automatically and without further reflections, even by highly respected authorities.

There is much confusion as to the functions of the social sciences, and doubt as to whether they can be defined at all.[2] Nor is it easy to form an opinion about the capability of science —as to what can be explained, and what cannot, within a

---

[1] "This science, in which we are all interested, is a dynamic process aiming at the extension of our field of cognition. In other words, it derives from a need for extending our knowledge."—Gutorm Gjessing, *Socio-Culture*, Oslo, 1956, p. 14.

[2] Cf. Robert S. Lynd, *Knowledge for What? The Place of Social Science in American Culture*. Princeton, 1945, Chapter IV.

given area of social life at a given stage of scientific perfection. Several scholars have maintained that there is a general tendency to overrate its ability. And science, too, is subject to social dynamics and change. On the whole, there may seem to be some discrepancy between efforts and achievements, but is this really true?

The Value of Descriptive Research

In this, as in so many other fields, it is almost impossible to express with any certainty an opinion of the value of the vast and patient descriptive research done. A variety of disciplines make their contribution, notably history and geography. For good or evil, research advances human knowledge directly by its achievements and indirectly by providing materials for education. By providing subject matter for university education, research in international affairs shares the responsibility for training the next generation of leaders in the various branches of society. And by providing information to government agencies as well as to non-governmental institutions, it plays a role in the handling of contemporary affairs.[3] In our field the greater part of this vast research activity has so far been descriptive. It goes without saying that before we can understand the characteristics of social phenomena, we must have them reasonably well described. Descriptive research may be regarded as the more elementary part of the process, but it is none the less essential.

It may be argued that we can observe the world in which we live, and that we can get much more information by means of the various media of communication like the press and radio, than we can ever make use of for practical purposes. This may be an illusion. The situation is rather that the full advantage of observation and the media of communication can be obtained only when the data or the information they provide can be duly arranged and placed into their proper context. And there

---

[3] This situation can be more easily observed in the great states than in the small ones.

are wide and essential areas of social life which only science can explain.

It is not merely a question of intellectual curiosity on the part of a few peculiar fellows. It is a practical and vital matter. In foreign affairs, as well as in internal politics, responsible, planned, and wise action requires knowledge.[4] The great social revolutions have been preceded and accompanied by intensive intellectual activity and progress, which, in many cases, have largely taken the form of catching up with the advances made by other nations.[5]

A great part of the research in the social sciences must be descriptive. The data must be provided and the phenomena described. That is, in any case, essential. To what extent it is possible to proceed further and make more or less reliable generalizations is a far less obvious matter. But because of the vastness of the subject, the task is probably more difficult in international relations than in most other fields. Descriptive research falls, because of its very nature, into many unrelated parts. It cannot, therefore, easily provide the general view needed. To find some sort of solution to this problem is a major and urgent task for the young science. It is undoubtedly possible to coordinate descriptive research in the various parts of the world to a far greater extent than is the case today. In this way, it may be possible to get a better global view of the existing state of affairs than we now have. It should not be impossible to reduce the scope of this work to manageable proportions. But, it must be stressed, this procedure would require world-wide scientific cooperation.[6]

---

[4] The development of the Arctic in our own day is an interesting example of how practical political, economic, and military measures are preceded and accompanied by descriptive and analytical research. Cf. George T. Kimble and Dorothy Good (eds.), *Geography of the Northlands*, New York, 1955, Preface.

[5] Gilbert Highet, *The Mind of Man*, London, 1954, p. 119 ff.

[6] As an example of this kind of cooperation in the historical sciences may be mentioned *Excerpta Historica Nordica*, edited by Povel Bagge and others, Vol. I, Copenhagen, 1955.

Considerable progress has already been made in preparing abstracts of articles. Cf. *International Political Science Abstracts*, and *Historical Abstracts 1775–1945*. However, some abstracts in these publications are so brief that their value is controversial.

Prediction on the Basis of Generalization

Few students of international relations have, so far, taken an interest in the technique of prediction. It is generally believed to be too difficult a matter to handle.[7] And it is, in fact, not surprising that a negative attitude is taken towards the problem of predicting the future. Indeed, there was a time when even contemporary affairs were regarded as an improper subject for a decent scholar.[8] But this view is disappearing. An increasing number of students have begun to wonder how the consequences of political action can be better foreseen than is generally the case today; and it is realized that the problem is particularly urgent in the field of international politics, where the phenomena to be predicted are, as a rule, complicated and extensive, and the matters involved of fundamental importance. It may well be argued that the use of research in this field should be measured by the extent to which it improves our ability to manage international politics; this means that we must aim at improving our ability to foresee the consequences of our own action, and to foresee the action and reaction of other relevant players in the game, and the consequences of such action and reaction. The main questions before us are, firstly, to find out how the technique of prediction is practiced today, and secondly, how science can improve it.

A certain ability to predict appears to be a prerequisite to organized social life, because without this ability we are hardly able to plan. Prediction is largely based on generalizations or 'laws'. We know that from situation A may, under given conditions, follow situation B. In a simple situation, prediction is made almost automatically. In complicated situations, like those frequently met in international politics, a prediction may

---

[7] "The argument usually runs about like this: Politics consists mainly of unique and imponderable phenomena; it is impossible, the argument continues, to predict with any certainty the specific actions and reactions of the specific persons who rule and are ruled." — Harold and Margaret Sprout, *Man-Milieu Relationship Hypotheses in the Context of International Relations*, p. 86.

[8] James T. Shotwell, "The Study of International Relations," *Institutes and Their Publics*, pp. 8—12.

have to be based on a number of generalizations, derived from the same or from different fields like psychology, economics, and geography. Prediction seems to be a subjective process in the sense that it depends on the conception or mental image which the predictor has of the situation in question.[9]

A somewhat similar technique is used in explaining the past when we are unable to provide detailed information about the subject; that is to say, we make our conclusions on the basis of generalizations about human affairs.[10] We conclude that what seems logical and natural is likely to have happened.

Any prediction involving human action is, by necessity, very complicated. Persons may alter their plans and their behavior when they become aware of the consequences of their action. The possibility of free choice, which is absent in inanimate matters, complicates the task of predicting to a very great extent. However, as already pointed out, some of the factors of politics may be fairly stable. And mere descriptive research improves our chances by providing information about the existing state of affairs. The better we know the factors involved in the situation to be dealt with, the better we can plan our action, and foresee its consequences. We can predict, to some extent, on the basis of numerous generalizations derived from education and personal experience, which make up part of the intellectual assets of every individual.[11]

Generalization is very difficult in international politics because the variables are so many and so complicated. This explains to a great extent why prediction is so hard to make. Yet, in assessing the various political situations which require action, statesmen and strategists do predict. They reason that if this is done, that result will follow. The question is not whether we can leave out prediction or treat it merely as an intellectual curiosity. International politics, as well as any other aspects of social life, requires that predictions be made. Un-

---

[9] It seems natural for psychology to extend our knowledge of these kinds of phenomena.

[10] Patrick Gardiner, *The Nature of Historical Explanation*, London, 1952.

[11] For a further discussion of this matter see Sprout, *Man-Milieu Relationship Hypotheses in the Context of International Politics*, p. 89 ff.

fortunately, the kind of prediction practiced in this field is often little more than guesswork—indeed a very unpleasant situation in view of the great matters at stake. The scale varies from choice made on the basis of mere guesswork to choice made on the basis of more or less scientifically verified predictions.

There are a large number of hypotheses on the basis of which we are inclined to explain the past and predict the future. But even if they may be valid for a period of time, social dynamics tends to render them obsolete.[12] It is really very hard to say whether any hypothesis involving human action has general validity irrespective of time and space, but it may be assumed.

Hypotheses about international affairs may originate in several ways. We do not know much about this matter. But it seems as if most of them have been induced from observations of historical events, particularly recent events. The concept of power politics may be cited as an example of this process. Sometimes they appear to be derived from social practices which have worked well under certain conditions. When they advocate the interests of great powers or leading social classes, they may be very tenacious of life. The concept of free trade· may be classified with this type. Some seem to be partly or wholly derived from prevailing systems of philosophy, or developed in reaction to such systems.

The function of political hypotheses as a basis for explanation of past and present events and for prediction of future developments is extremely important. This is true in particular when such explanations and predictions are used for the formulation

----

[12] "The legal and political theories of the nineteenth century were developed by men who looked at the facts of the world of the eighteenth and nineteenth century, but later thinkers drew their deductions from those nineteenth century theories and not looking at the changing world in which they lived. . . . We are paying a heavy penalty for this mischievous practice of theorizing from the theories of predecessors." — Linden A. Mander, *Foundations of Modern World Society*, pp. V—VI.

Some scholars seem to consider it more learned to study other students' 'theories' about social life, no matter how strange they are, than to study life itself. Perhaps this tendency is a kind of rationalization of the fact that it is, as a rule, more convenient to analyze books than to study life directly.

of policies and for aligning of the masses behind adopted policies. This is a well-known fact. But can we say that it has been properly studied? Belief in such 'political laws' tends to entail a firmness of conviction which seems to be a definite asset to political leaders. This kind of hypothesis is usually deterministic and offers a single factor or otherwise easy explanation of political problems; the developments which it predicts are generally regarded as inevitable. Nothing illustrates our subject better than some traditional Marxist 'theories'.[13] It seems essential to examine more carefully such phenomena before we can expect to bring about an improvement of the prevailing techniques of prediction. It holds good also in this case that a reliable diagnosis is a requisite to correct treatment.

The next question we must raise is whether further research can improve the reliability of prediction in international politics, or whether science can at least bring this fundamental human practice from a more or less metaphysical or prescientific level to a stage of more careful and reliable planning. It must be admitted that, at present, the social sciences cannot boast of great achievements. But if attention is focused on the subject some progress will, no doubt, be obtained.

It seems natural to concentrate on a search for constants and generalizations, or theories, if we prefer to call them that. The experimental method has produced remarkable results, notably in the physical sciences, and this success has also encouraged some social scientists. We regard international relations as a science, and it may be assumed that basic assumptions of science apply to it. Thus, it may be assumed that the phenomena of its subject matter are related causally; i.e., that events are related in such a way that under given conditions event B will follow from

---

[13] The prediction made after World War II by Soviet economists that the capitalist economy of the United States was bound to suffer a crack before long may be cited as an example of such Marxist predictions. Another example is Stalin's prediction that war between capitalist states was inevitable. According to his reasoning, capitalism was bound to lead to imperialism, and imperialism in turn to war; hence, the inevitability of war between capitalist states.

A careful analysis of predictions made by leading statesmen is likely to reveal highly interesting information on how this technique is practiced in the field of international politics.

event A; and it may further be assumed that this causal relationship occurs in time and in space. But, in spite of this, it is obvious that the subject matter of international relations is, on the whole, very different from that of the physical sciences. Part of it has a much higher degree of abstraction, since it deals with human beings—human thoughts, emotions and other psychological characteristics. It is generally also much more difficult to isolate the various elements of a complex to be studied. And perhaps most important of all, the greater part of the subject matter changes fairly rapidly. It has been maintained that it is possible to organize experimental research in the study of human affairs;[14] but at least in international affairs, it seems extremely difficult. It should, however, be added that prediction in international politics is made on generalizations derived from several fields; and it may well be that the experimental method is applicable to a greater or lesser extent in some of them.

It is frequently argued that the main reason for studying the past is to become better qualified to deal with the problems of the present. Whether that be true or not, the historical method is, for reasons which we have already explained,[15] the most common one in the social sciences. The question is whether it is applicable for the discovery of generalizations or theories and for ascertaining the extent of their validity. We cannot attempt to answer this formidable question conclusively; all we can do is to raise a few relevant points.

Some great statesmen have found the life cycle of the Roman Empire pleasant reading. And useful suggestions may apparently be obtained from the study of the rise and fall of civilizations. However, only some twenty civilizations have been established within the six to seven thousand years of which we have historical record, and reliable generalizations can hardly be made on the basis of this moderate number of cases.[16] More-

---

[14] F. Stuart Chapin, "The Experimental Method in the Study of Human Relations," *The Scientific Monthly*, Vol. 68 (1949), p. 132 ff.

[15] Cf. above, Chapters XV and XVI.

[16] Arnold J. Toynbee, "The Study of History in the Light of Current Development," *International Affairs*, Vol. XXIV (1948), p. 555 ff.

over, a civilization is rarely a clear-cut subject. General historical studies of this kind tend to be lacking in precision and reliability. Naturally, if there are many striking similarities and repetitions, attention certainly ought to be paid to them, although it is really very difficult to compare situations divided by several hundred, not to speak of thousands, of years.

It is not unusual to speak of the evidence of history and of historical truth. But it seems, on the whole, necessary to be critical of this sort of evidence. Sometimes it appears to be little more than preconceived opinions underpinned by a small number of historical cases.

This is by no means to say with Hegel that the one thing we can learn from history is that nobody ever learns anything from it. The simple trial and error method of learning is more or less effective for nations as well as for individuals. And there can hardly be any doubt that many, if not most, statesmen have drawn lessons from historical experience.[17] Even if the situations change, some of their aspects may recur. The future is not likely to be fundamentally different from the past in every respect. To what extent we can form scientifically applicable generalizations on the basis of historical observations is nevertheless a question. Yet this method seems to be the best we have, and it is not unlikely that we can improve it.

Trend Projection

It would be highly valuable for actors in international affairs to see some distance into the future and learn something about political, social, economic, and military developments. Actually, they have to make some reflections about future developments. And it has been wisely said that among the factors moulding the future are interpretations about the future.[18] The study of trends offers apparently one of the best opportunities for predicting future conditions, although we had

---

[17] For a discussion of the use of history in general, see A. L. Rowse, *The Use of History*, London, 1946.

[18] H. D. Lasswell, *The Revolution of Our Own Time*, Stanford, 1951, p. 5.

better be moderate in our expectations of this as well as any other method. Economic, political, and other kinds of trends can be followed, and their variations and intensity can be observed over a considerable period of time. And since it may be assumed that society tends to resist great and abrupt changes, it seems possible to project such trends some distance into the near future, although some unforeseeable variations must be expected.

Interpretation of future situations on the basis of trends has been practiced in an informal and prescientific manner since time immemorial in everyday life as well as in a wider context. In recent decades some of the social sciences, notably economics and demography, have tried to exploit this method. The so-called population forecasts have, in particular, attracted attention. On a limited scale and in fairly stable societies, it seems possible to make such forecasts with some accuracy. When, however, larger areas are involved, the number and extent of unpredictable variables are naturally considerable.[19] It may also be mentioned that such forecasts have had a favorable influence in leading to interesting reflections about such matters as the food resources of the world and the prospect of shortages in the near future.

The study of international relations can obviously benefit from the achievements made by related subjects like economics and demography, both with regard to method and useful data. And there is the possibility that this subject, too, can make a contribution of its own. The political pattern seems to be the legitimate field of operation for the student of international relations. We still know rather little about the forces which shape it, but here, too, we can benefit by the improvement of research facilities, notably the progress made in statistics. Some endeavors have already been made. Considerable attention has been paid, for example, to the increase in the size of states, and a few timid attempts have been made to project the discovered trends into the future.

---

[19] For an explanation of the technique used, reference may be made to Frank W. Notestein and others, *The Future Population of Europe and the Soviet Union. Population Projections 1940—1970*, Geneva, 1944, pp. 15—43 and appendix I—II.

The most outstanding phenomenon revealed by the political pattern today is the so-called bi-polarization of power. And there is good reason to wonder where this development will lead. The chances that a third party can become strong enough to act as a balance in a new system of power are already small. There have, however, recently appeared forces which tend to check the trend toward a further concentration of power in Moscow and Washington; and NATO and, in particular, the Warsaw Pact organization have met with considerable difficulty. On the other hand, the United Nations has become more universal; and there is, in spite of all, a strong desire to strengthen this institution. An interesting question is what role the weaker nations can play by rallying around it. As things have developed during recent years, they have apparently the least to lose and most to gain by supporting wholeheartedly the still very weak tendency to transform the United Nations from an international to a supranational institution. Although they carry little weight from the military point of view, they have together the greater part of the world's population. Perhaps we should turn our attention to educating cosmopolites in every country rather than to hope in vain for a lasting balance of power.

The reliability of trend projection may be reduced by variables which cannot be foreseen and taken into account; but it also depends very much on the quality and quantity of observations made. Predictions made on a limited number of observations can hardly claim to be more than conjecture. This is, therefore, still another instance where success depends on whether extensive international cooperation can be organized.

Most scholars probably take a delight in the hope—perhaps sometimes vain—that their work may be useful. Quite a few students in the field would, no doubt, like to see international relations deliberately made an applied science to a greater extent than has so far been the case. And it may well be argued that the main task before us is to make it a subject which enables the actors in international affairs to plan their action more wisely and justly and to foresee its consequences with greater accuracy.

CONCLUDING REFLECTIONS

At the end of this somewhat disconnected intellectual journey it seems worth while, so to speak, to sum up the ideas, and retrospectively make some reflections on the great problems encountered. It is possible to formulate some fairly clear-cut conclusions; but the character of the subject requires that substantial qualifications be made.

The Effect of the Great Changes of Our Age upon the Study

It is usual to speak of the revolution of our own time. What is meant by this term is not always clear. The confusion is largely due to the fact that it is very difficult to understand the nature and scope of contemporary social processes. But it is at least obvious to most of us that we are living in an age of great events and great changes. The accelerating speed of social evolution entails that we are confronted with ever new and perplexing phenomena; and the problems of world politics are being thrust so suddenly upon us that it takes foresight and a certain flexibility of mind to grasp the situation.

Within a lifetime far-reaching changes have taken place in the political pattern of the world, which have deprived Europe of her leadership in international affairs. About one fourth of mankind has advanced from a colonial status to a more or less effective political independence. One third of mankind has experienced the breakdown of the old social order and witnessed the bloody horrors of a communist revolution. Even in countries where the social continuity has been more or less retained the shift in political power and the social changes have been great indeed. The spiritual foundation of Western civilization has in many ways been severely shaken; and strange political creeds have had an amazing and alarming success.

When we look more closely into the matter, we easily realize the profound changes which have taken place in government practices and administration. The increase in mass production is amazing. The means of transport and communication have been elaborated to the extent that neither mountains nor oceans are frontiers any longer. World trade has been multiplied during the recent decades. But most impressive, and at the same time horrifying, is the progress in the art of war.

The global integration is a subtle process; yet it is becoming increasingly clear that we are all citizen of one world, whose welfare is inescapably bound together; in fact, it may well be argued that the progressing social unification of mankind is the most important phenomenon of our age. That international politics is global in our time of intercontinental rockets and hydrogen bombs is the main argument of this study, and it fundamentally affects the·views on how international affairs can best be analyzed.

The social and human sciences, whose primary objective is to explain the social world in which we live, are bound to be affected by changes in their subject matter. Such changes will naturally entail variations with respect to intensity and focus of attention as well as to methods of analysis; and viewed over a reasonably long span of time science reveals a tendency to aspire toward ever higher perfection.

We have briefly explained how the growing interdependence of the nations and the increasing effectiveness of the media of mass-destruction have stimulated interest in international politics, and pointed out that there is a pressing need for more accurate, more widespread, and above all for new kinds of knowledge. It is becoming ever more obvious that it is of vital importance to prepare man for the task of dealing adequately with the political and social problems of a rapidly integrating world.

It is, moreover, fairly certain that we shall not be able to obtain this knowledge unless we can elaborate better tools of research that will make us more qualified to cope with the kinds of subject matter and the kinds of problems with which we are confronted by the changing circumstances. Science is itself more or less subject to the vicissitudes of social dynamics, and in order to fulfill its social function it must be able to conform to the changing needs of man. The task of the scientist is far more difficult than is that of the demagogue. His role is not to stir the lurking drives of the animal *homo sapiens*, but to aid the rule of calm and tolerant wisdom.

Three Kinds of Reaction

The first reaction to the increasing demands for better knowledge of international affairs was naturally greater effort on the part of the old and firmly established disciplines. But their ability to respond to the challenge varied considerably from one subject to another. For the purpose of illustration we may divide the disciplines which have a bearing upon international affairs into special and general subjects. To the former belong disciplines like law and economics; to the latter history, sociology, anthropology and geography.

The contributions of economics and law are naturally essential. But they deal only with certain aspects of international affairs: the former with economic relations, the latter with the function of law in the world society. They are by their very nature unable to provide a general presentation of international affairs. Their contributions to our knowledge in this field are in a way specialized information. The opportunities of the disciplines which we have called general subjects are much wider; and it is necessary to pay more attention to their role.

To deal with international affairs as part of the study of history is not only possible but also absolutely necessary. Most aspects of human social life must be studied dynamically. History extends, so to speak, our knowledge in time. It enables us to look into the past and to get glimpses of the long walk of man. It reveals to us the continuity of social evolution as well as the convulsions of social dynamics. The tendency to regard the study of international affairs merely as a discussion of contemporary events is utterly untenable. We actually have to do with certain aspects of social life, which of course also have a history; and rarely indeed is it possible to understand the contemporary international problems without taking into account their historical background. We must have an idea of how things have come to be what they are today, before we can form a well-founded opinion of people's attitudes and behavior. How can we understand, for example, the Palestine question or the North African question or any other great international problem without looking back into history?

There are, however, several weak spots in the historical presentation of international affairs. "L'insuffisance de l'histoire diplomatique traditionelle et l'étroitesse de l'explication 'politique' qui borne son horizon à l'examen des actes ou des intentions de l'homme d'Etat ont été, de longue date, soulignées par nombre d'historiens."[1] As already pointed out, the tendency has, however, in recent years been to give a more inclusive presentation of the subject. The importance of economic and demographic factors has in particular been stressed; and even an analysis of the influence of mass pscychology has been tried.[2]

There are also other formidable methodological problems. The past decades' preoccupation with the nation has tended to narrow the horizon of historical study.[3] This development has been particularly unfavorable to the study of international affairs, which in fact requires at least the involvement of two states to become intelligible. The choice of the state as a kind of 'self-sufficient unit' has led to a rather unrealistic unilateral analysis of international affairs, and a wider scope must be adopted.

If, however, our assumption that international politics can best be analysed in a global framework holds good, the histor-

---

[1] Pierre Renouvin, "L'histoire contemporaine des relations internationales. Orientation de recherches," *Revue historique*, Vol. 211 (1954), p. 233.

[2] Cf. Pierre Renouvin, *Le XIXe Siècle*, Deuxième partie. See particularly Chapter VIII.

[3] For a discussion of this matter see Arnold J. Toynbee, *A Study of History*, Vol. I.

ical study of international affairs is confronted with rather difficult problems of selection and composition. How much are we to include in the subject, and what are we to leave out? A reasonably detailed study may easily become too comprehensive and unmanageable. If we follow the other direction to the extreme, and drop too much, the subject tends to take the form of a philosophy of history. Even if we succeed in finding a satisfactory balance between these opposing tendencies,[4] it seems necessary to supplement the traditional study of events by a somewhat more topical and functional analysis of certain aspects of international affairs.

Sociology is in a way the widest of all the social sciences, since its scope is society in general. It seems a promising procedure for the study of world affairs, and we have seen that its contributions to this subject are essential both with regard to factual information and useful concepts. It is possible to conceive of the study of international affairs as the study of world sociology, and to think of interstate relations as group interaction. Sociology is, moreover, concerned with the structure of societies; and it analyses the character of the various groups of which societies consist as well as the functions of social phenomena. It also endeavors to explain on a theoretical basis the processes of social change.

The objection may be made that the sociologist has remained too much in the realm of unverified hypotheses, and that the student of international affairs must proceed to a more detailed and empirical analysis of the subject matter. But in spite of that, all the above-mentioned concepts and methods are directly applicable to the study of international affairs.

Notably in the interwar period the idea of studying international affairs as a kind of world sociology gained much ground in Europe. Unfortunately the trend has been away from this view during recent years. In any case, the fact remains that sociology has not yet produced any complex of ideas or

---

[4] As an example of a well-composed but mainly event-recording course of the history of international politics from 1914 to 1945 may be mentioned that given at the Institut d'Etudes Politiques of the University of Paris. Cf. C. A. W. Manning, *International Relations*, p. 92.

sub-discipline which can claim to provide anything like a satisfactory general presentation of international affairs.

The name *geography* may be translated as description of the earth. This discipline is by its very nature global. Some of its aspects, like climate, can be understood only when analysed in a topical and global manner, and the kind of mental training which it provides is excellent for the student of international affairs. We have seen that the study of geography has been fairly easily able to adapt its modes of analysis to the requirements of global affairs.

In a somewhat similar way as history extends our knowledge in time, so geography extends our knowledge in space. The combatants in world politics do not operate in a vacuum. Geography provides us with information in particular about the physical environment in which man operates and about the relationships between man and nature. It also gives us a much needed impression of the variety of human social life. The fact that care should be taken in inferring conclusions merely from geographical data does not mean that they are unimportant. They form essential parts of social complexes which cannot be understood without taking geography into consideration.

Many international problems can largely be explained in terms of geography. It looks in fact as if every power bases its foreign policy more or less upon strategies which take the factors of geography into consideration. But there are a number of essential aspects of international affairs which it would seem quite unreasonable to include in the study of geography, and it is hardly possible to modify this discipline to the extent that it can provide a satisfactory analysis of international affairs in general.

Another answer to the increasing demand for a better understanding of international affairs is to bring new disciplines to bear upon the subject. Social phenomena tend to split into new branches as their scope of activity is expanding; this is true of science as well; and it has been briefly described in previous pages how this trend has made itself felt in the study of international affairs. Naturally, specialized studies are essential for a deeper penetration into the different parts of the subject matter. The difficulty is that not only specialized knowledge is needed, but also an over-all view of the field; and this is all the more so as the subject matter of international affairs is being divided among an increasing number of disciplines.

The most common educational solution of this problem is to make various arrangements for combining several disciplines, the most advanced of which is the school of international affairs. This method seems, however, to have some short-comings. There are administrative and pedagogical problems; and since each academic discipline tends to develop its own technique and concepts as well as its own way of looking at the phenomena, it is not easy to acquire a good working know-ledge of several subjects within a reasonable period of time. More important still, it appears as if such combinations, how-ever skilfully arranged, are not always able to provide a suffici-ently clear-cut and well-composed picture of international affairs.[5]

The confusion is equally great in the field of research. It is impossible to know what has been explored and what not, or what can possibly be examined with the source materials and techniques available to the research scholar today. Natur-ally, many of the problems involved are mainly due to the vastness of the field; but an improvement of the present state of affairs is surely possible.

The third reaction, the development of a new subject, seems in some ways to be the most promising solution, and it has therefore been made the principal theme of this study. It must, however, be stressed again that the idea of developing a general study of international affairs is by no means to obviate the special studies, but rather to supplement them in a useful

---

[5] In commenting upon the situation at an eminent institution of learning like Chicago University, Professor Quincy Wright says that the students have from time to time complained that, although the courses recommended had some relevance to what was called international relations, they were nevertheless not sure of what that subject was. It seemed to branch out into various directions, the ends of the branches being unrelated to one another. And the courses seemed sometimes to rest upon different assumptions and to reach divergent conclusions. Cf. *The Study of International Relations*, p. VII.

way by synthesizing otherwise isolated findings. The splitting up of the field into an increasing number of competitive disciplines tends to obscure the inherent connection between the phenomena.[6] A purely theoretical study may be in a position to ignore this interdependence, but a realistic analysis of world politics cannot leave it out. Nobody who has the slightest knowledge of the history of learning can be surprised that the growth of a subject of international relations has met, and will continue to meet, stiff opposition. It always happens when a new branch of learning emerges. There are still some practitioners of the time-honored disciplines who stubbornly refuse to recognize sociology as a respectable subject. But a new branch of learning is not created by whims and oddities, and a social creation for which there is no need whatever tends to be rather short-lived. The fact that consistent endeavors have been made for several decades to create a synthesizing and coordinating discipline dealing with the field of international affairs seems by itself to prove that there is a need for it.

We are entitled to expect some methodological merits from a science of international relations. It opens up new possibilities for forming theoretical constructions which may enable the research scholar to plan his work better. Such constructions may disclose more clearly the gaps in our knowledge and point to the most promising approaches in research. Even if only moderate expectations can be entertained with respect to the chances of forming higher generalizations and making trustworthy predictions, it is clear that reliable diagnosis is a prerequisite to successful prognosis. It cannot be denied that international politics, in spite of its fundamental importance, is frequently dealt with by the rule of the thumb. If the development of a synthesizing and coordinating branch of learning can improve, if only very slightly, upon this situation, it would mean a distinct service to mankind.

---

[6] "Such specialized study is desirable and beneficial, but unless a student is aware of other aspects of the subject, the specialization may lead to a warped and unreal picture of the field as a whole." — Frederick A. Middlebush and Chesney Hill, *Elements of International Relations*, New York, 1940, preface.

The Character of International Relations

The character of the subject of international relations is to a large extent determined at the outset; that is to say, by the framework chosen. This is a point where considerable difference of opinion exists. In the previous chapters it has been repeatedly stressed that the study of international affairs must adopt a global outlook in the second half of the twentieth century.

It can be historically demonstrated that international politics has actually developed from being regionally delimited to becoming world-wide. Of course, we are better acquainted with and more interested in those matters which are nearest to us in space and time; yet it is quite clear that today we may be plunged into a war by events in remote places. This situation is a natural consequence of the technological integration of the world. Mere attentive newspaper reading may confirm this assumption. The world has become divided into two major rivaling blocs with relatively small stretches of 'no man's land' between them. In this situation it seems inadequate, if not meaningless, to use, for instance, only the Western state system as the framework of the study, although the introduction of that concept in the early 1930's was a great step forward. International affairs in the age of jet propulsion and atomic fission can hardly be any better understood on a regional basis than can climatology.

Another basic assumption of this study is that the old concept of a society of states is inadequate. Endeavors have been made to prove that there are other actors in international politics than states which have to be taken into consideration, and that therefore the world society must be chosen as the framework. The applicability of the society concept as a basis of analysis has been demonstrated on several occasions.

The adoption of the world society as a framework of the study entails, however, great methodological problems. The subject matter must be reduced to manageable proportions; and the question must be raised what aspects of this vast body are relevant to the student of international relations. However, this is not a unique situation in social science. Several disciplines are confronted with similar problems of abstraction.

Somewhat unlike the traditional American practices, which tend to concentrate attention largely on the instruments, techniques, and strategies used for the implementation of foreign policy objectives, considerable emphasis is placed on the description of the environment in which international politics takes place. In this particular respect the outlined study appears to be more in accordance with British than American methods.

As it is supposed that the natural environment may substantially influence the behavior of the actors in international politics, it has been considered natural to begin the study by an analysis of this phenomenon. Fortunately, the progress made in human ecology and political geography during the past decades can be of considerable value in this respect.[7]

The social environment in which the actors in international politics operate resembles the natural environment in that it reveals a remarkable variety, but differs from it in that it is subject to a far more rapid change. It is considered essential for the student of international relations to be properly aware of the amazing variety of human social life, which makes for deep-rooted differences in outlook and interests. And it is equally important to remember that this subject matter is subject to continous change. In the beginning, an analysis of the structure of the world society within the general study of international relations is bound to be rather elementary, because we still know too little about this matter; but we may expect greater efficiency as increasing attention is being paid to this subject. The progress being made by the services which provide data for the social scientist makes it now easier also to observe the major trends of evolution in the world society, notably incipient changes in the pattern of power. It is believed that

---

[7] It may be mentioned that an increasing number of universities now require courses in geography as part of a concentration on international affairs. For instance, at Yale University, which until recently had no department of geography, the department of political science set up a course on political, economic, and social geography to meet the needs of students majoring in international relations. Cf. Grayson Kirk, *The Study of International Relations*, pp. 43—44.

to describe and explain these trends is a legitimate and most important task of historical science, and one which can be done with increasing efficiency.

It has been presumed that morality and law must be studied and evaluated on the basis of the society in which they function. The same applies to political, social, and economic institutions. The detailed study of these important phenomena is done by others. But the student of international relations cannot understand his field properly without asking what are the functions and efficiency of international law and morals as well as of international institutions.

The analysis of the behavior of states is bound to include areas where the student of international relations cannot claim to have detailed knowledge. He will have to draw largely on the findings of specialists. This is the natural consequence of the fact that international relations is a general subject, which endeavors to provide an over-all view rather than to penetrate deeply into small areas of social life.

It is supposed that the most logical and rewarding way of studying the subject is to start off with an analysis of motive forces, then go on to the capability of states and the processes by which policies are formulated. It is presumed that motivation and capability or war potential are interconnected in the sense that capability influences motivation;[8] and it is maintained that the constitutional processes by which policies are formed may determine to some extent their character. Then follow in logical sequence the tools and techniques which the powers use for the implementation of their foreign policy objectives; and finally the strategies which the states commonly practice are briefly discussed.

Actors other than states have so far been inadequately studied; this is true in particular of the great international economic enterprises; and much pioneering research will have to be done before reliable findings are readily available. It is, however, clear that social evolution moves in a direction which

---

[8] For an explanation of this matter see above, p. 123.

renders it necessary to pay more attention to this matter than has so far been the case.

It seems also essential to encourage a dispassionate study of the problem of violence in international politics. Because of its nature the study of this subject has frequently engaged the emotions and feelings too strongly; the immediate task is therefore to strip it of this shortcoming, and to make plain that this is a problem which intimately concerns every one of us.

The greatest difficulty encountered in undertaking an analysis of this kind is to give appropriate scope to the decision maker. In some ways man seems to be the most enduring element of the subject matter. The social environment changes, while basically human nature appears to be much the same as it has always been. But in spite of all that, man's action and interference seem unpredictable; this is all the more so since political leaders appear to be somewhat exceptional persons. It still remains to be seen whether progress in the so-called behavioral sciences can provide applicable generalizations about political behavior.

The Academic Arrangement of the Subject

We have suggested that many of the problems involved in a general study of international affairs can best be solved by continued development of the new subject which is commonly called international relations. The question then arises how this subject can be fitted into the curriculum of institutions of learning. It may be said that at present two methods are being practised.

A few higher institutions of learning have already established a department of international relations conceived as a distinct and homogeneous subject. The teaching may be shared among a number of educators, each of whom lectures on one or several aspects of the subject.[9] This advanced form of education is, however, still very rare. But a considerable number of chairs

---

[9] C. A. W. Manning, *International Relations*, p. 22.

have been established which may be regarded as the nucleus of a department of international relations. In this case the greatest problem is really no longer one of academic organization, but rather one of staffing; that is to say, the difficulty is to find persons who are qualified to occupy the chairs.[10] On the whole, it seems already safe to predict that international relations will develop in the direction of a distinct subject and that an increasing number of institutions will establish departments for this discipline.

A rapidly increasing number of universities are giving a subject variously called international politics or international relations in the department of political science. This method seems to work well in spite of the fact that there is hardly any organic connection between this subject and those previously given in political science. That international relations could develop so freely as a separate subject in the department of political science seems largely due to the fact that political science is a new and not too homogeneous discipline.[11] At larger institutions there may in fact be one or several professors who are specialists on international relations and lecture practically exclusively on this subject. As far as the teaching is concerned, there is in this case relatively little practical difference from the procedure followed in a university which has established a department of international relations. Particularly in the United States it has become increasingly common to deal with international relations as a sub-discipline of political science.

Various attempts have been made to plan the courses in the department of history so that they can satisfy the needs of students who want to concentrate on international affairs. These courses are frequently given the name of international relations; and in some cases they tend to take the form of a

---

[10] *Ibid.*, pp. 32—33.

[11] Usually political science includes the study of such different subjects as political theory, political institutions, parties and other political groups, public opinion, and international relations. The last-mentioned subject may be composed of three fairly distinct fields; namely, international politics, international law, and international organization. Cf. *Publication No. 426 of UNESCO, Contemporary Political Science,* Paris, 1950; see particularly p. 4.

special subject, but on the whole to a lesser extent than is the case in political science.[12] The reason seems mainly to be that relatively few historians have so far been able, or have found it necessary, to deviate basically from the traditional method of diplomatic history.

Actually, the question is not to substitute the one for the other, but rather to include both, because the two types of study supplement each other. It will be noted that international relations as outlined in part two of this volume differs somewhat from general history in that the approach adopted is more topical and less descriptive; greater emphasis is laid on contemporary affairs; and chronological or chronicle presentation, which is an essential, though not always highly esteemed method of historical research, is very much reduced. This form is considered necessary because the subject must meet two essential requirements: namely, to reduce the study of world politics to manageable proportions, and to be capable of synthesizing or coordinating the findings of the many disciplines which have a bearing upon international affairs.

It is interesting to note that there are several subjects within the broader field of history, and we speak of the historical sciences. There seems to be no reason whatever why we cannot consider international relations as one of the historical sciences.[13] Parts of this subject have for ages been major topics of historical study; what is new is the way in which the phenomena are arranged, and the points of view from which they are studied. It may in fact be argued that it forms a natural and highly needed supplement to the traditional historical study of international affairs, which has so far been primarily, if not exclusively, a recording of the main political events. There is in

---

[12] From the point of view of method there may often be little difference between history and political science. The latter sometimes relies heavily upon the findings of historical research. Cf. *Contemporary Political Science*, pp. 341—42.

[13] The IXth International Congress of Historical Sciences listed even anthropology and demography among the subjects to be dealt with. See *Rapports*, Paris, 1950.

Since international relations as a special subject is still poorly developed in Continental Europe (See Manning, *International Relations*, pp. 54—55) there was no reason to expect it on the agenda.

particular reason to stress the advantage which the study of contemporary affairs in general is likely to obtain from the elaboration of research tools and techniques for international relations; and this is not all: the dependence is mutual. A topical study of international relations which is not well founded on empirical historical study is likely to become too unreal. This fact holds good no matter whether the subject is given in special departments, as part of political science, or in any other combination.

It is generally agreed that the specialist on international relations must have acquired a broad outlook; and few academic disciplines broaden the mind more than does a wisely organized study of history;[14] it should, therefore, be a favorable point of departure. But the relative contribution of departments of history to the study of international affairs has been declining during recent years, and this trend is likely to continue.

The Need for New Views and Techniques in Research

We have tried to explain how the problems with which the statesman and the student of international affairs are confronted have been affected by the great social and political changes of our age. It has also been maintained that the techniques of research must, to some extent, be adapted to the subject matter to be dealt with. From these two contingencies, it follows that we have to ask whether we need some improvement or changes in views and techniques before we can expect to cope efficiently with the problems encountered in the study of international affairs in the second half of the twentieth century.

---

[14] "The historian is prepared, by the knowledge he has, to participate in the study of contemporary events. He brings to it a trustworthy method which he has tested by examining the events of the past, a discipline of mind acquired through a long apprenticeship in dealing with documents, and valuable practice in the criticism of diplomatic texts and evidence." — Pierre Renouvin, "The Contribution of France to the Study of International Relations," *Contemporary Political Science*, p. 568.

To avoid misunderstanding, it may be added that we do not conceive of international relations as merely the study of contemporary events, but as the study of certain aspects of social life, which of course also have their history.

It seems, in fact, that a modification of technique is necessary even for fields on which attention has been focussed for ages. This point is well illustrated by the study of the instruments and tactics of international politics. We have seen that the nature of diplomacy has changed in a way which has affected to a considerable extent the problems of research; and it is obvious that the approach and modes of analysis characteristic for the study of old-fashioned diplomatic history will not suffice for a thorough analysis of the so-called organizational weapon and subversive techniques applied in international politics today, or for obtaining a better understanding of modern information and propaganda service. The situation is somewhat similar in other fields. The extent and character of international ties and contacts have been substantially changed. The nature of state sovereignty and political independence has been modified; and the relationships between the rulers and the ruled in world politics have been considerably altered. In all these situations the research scholar must adopt views which are in conformity with reality, and elaborate tools which enable him to penetrate into the new subject matter. It is naturally beyond the scope of this brief study to provide the answer to all the questions involved in this matter; it must suffice to point out the tasks and to make some suggestions for an applicable strategy.

In the physical sciences there is a distinct chain reaction between science on the one hand and industrial progress on the other, in the sense that science promotes industry, which in turn improves the tools for further scientific research. It may suffice to mention the making of cyclotrons and research reactors in the atomic industry. In the social sciences there is not a similar chain reaction; or if it exists at all, it is at least far more difficult to discover. This may be one reason why the social sciences tend to lag behind the physical and biological sciences. But the social sciences do benefit by the general progress, also in technical culture.

When a global study of international affairs can be developed at all, not only on a philosophical, but also on an empirical basis, it is largely because of the progress made by the services and disciplines which provide data. It may be sufficient to mention the news services and the statistical publications and social reports prepared by the agencies of the United Nations. This progress is in turn mainly due to the general social and technical development all over the world, which makes collecting of data, travel, exchange of printed matters, and other forms of communication easier. It is a significant coincidence that the integration and cultural development which have made politics global have also provided the means of studying it.

However, this great extension of the field of analysis is bound to entail far-reaching methodological implications. Not even the most retentive mind can hope to master a detailed study of this comprehensive subject. It seems that the student of international relations must rather endeavor to obtain a reasonably good over-all view together with sufficient skill in using the tools and techniques for analysis of this kind of subject matter. In this way he may be able to place the phenomena into their proper social and political context, and to know where to find the data and how to examine the problems in a scholarly manner.

The student of global affairs is also confronted with difficult problems of interpretation and evaluation. We have briefly disc ussed a few of them for the purpose of illustration. To deal efficiently with this matter undoubtedly requires an open mind. Familiarity with traditional modes of thought may, under certain conditons, be an obstacle when it comes to looking at the problems in new ways;[15] and the educational molding of the mind may create mental barriers which it requires determined efforts to pass; on the whole, the culture in which the student has grown up may impose limitations which tend to reduce his ability to understand and appreciate the attitudes and behavior of people who have social systems and beliefs alien to his own.[16] If social science can cope with these kinds of methodological difficulties, it will be more able to help the

---

[15] For a somewhat more categorical view on this matter see Quincy Wright, *The Study of International Relations*, p. 80.

[16] Cf. C. A. W. Manning, *International Relations*, p. 21.

nations to realize their place and role in the world society and to learn how they can maximize their contribution to the common welfare; and it is encouraging that the task is in fact being steadily reduced. The conditions for a comparative study of foreign policy needs and aspirations are being improved as new regions are increasing their share in the common effort to describe and explain the nature of world politics.

To solve the problems of world politics is not the direct concern of the scholar. His main duty is to describe and explain the phenomena; but it seems that not even that task can be properly done merely as a national undertaking. Only by world-wide cooperation and organization is it possible to provide the needed data and to obtain the broad outlook required for the mastery of this vast and complicated subject. Even so, the task is discouragingly great. But the development of the study of world politics is itself merely an interesting aspect of the world-wide process of integration. It seems therefore predestined to make progress as global integration proceeds.

BIBLIOGRAPHY

Almond, Gabriel A. "Anthropology, Political Behavior and International Relations". *World Politics*, Vol. 2 (1949) p. 277 ff.

Arndt, C. O. and S. Everett (eds.). *Education for a World Society: Promising Practices today*. New York 1951.

Bailey, S. H. *International Studies in Great Britain*. London 1933.

— *International Studies in Modern Education*. London 1938.

Behrendt, R. F. "Der Beitrag der Soziologie zum Verständnis internationaler Probleme." *Schweizerische Zeitschrift für Volkswirtschaft und Statistik*, Vol. 91 (1955) p. 145 ff.

Bernard, L. L. and Jessie Bernard. *Sociology and the Study of International Relations*. St. Louis 1934.

Best, R. J. *Education for International Understanding*. Adelaide 1948.

Blühdorn, Rudolf. „Die wissenschaftliche Untersuchung und das Studium der zwischenstaatlichen Beziehungen". *Österreichische Zeitschrift für öffentliches Recht*, Vol. 3 (1950/51) p. 156 ff.

Bronowski, Jacob. *The Common Sense of Science*. Boston 1953.

Brookings Institution. *The International Studies Group. Report on a Conference on the Teaching of International Relations*. Washington 1950.

Carnap, Rudolf. *The Unity of Science*. London 1933.

Carnegie Endowment for International Peace. *Current Research in International Affairs*. New York 1952.

— *Institutes of International Affairs*. New York 1953.

Cohen, Morris R. and Ernest Nagel. *An Introduction to Logic and Scientific Method*. New York 1934.

Conant, James B. *On Understanding Science*. New Haven 1947.

Corbett, P. E. "Objectivity in the Study of International Relations". *World Affairs*, Vol. 4 (1950) p. 257 ff.

Council on Foreign Relations. *A Report of Twenty-Five Years, 1921— 1946.* New York 1947.

Duun, Frederick S. "The Scope of International Relations". *World Politics*, Vol. 1 (1948/49) p. 142 ff.

— "The Present Course of International Relations Research". *World Politics*, Vol. 2 (1949/50) p. 80 ff.

Duroselle, J. B. "L'étude des relations internationales. Object, méthode, perspectives". *Revue française de science politique*, Vol. 2 (1952) p. 676 ff.

"Education for the World Community". *International Social Science Bulletin*, Vol. 4 (1952) p. 147 ff.

Fifield, R. H. "The Introductory Course in International Relations". *American Political Science Review*, Vol. 42 (1948) p. 1189 ff.

Fox, William T. R. "Inter-War International Relations Research: The American Experience". *World Politics*, Vol. 2 (1949/50) p. 67 ff.

Furniss, Edgar S. jr. "The Contribution of Nicholas John Spykman to the Study of International Relations". *World Politics*, Vol. 4 (1951/52) p. 382 ff.

Gjessing, Gutorm. *Socio-Culture. Studies honouring the Centenary of Universitetets Etnografiske Museum.* Oslo 1956.

Goode, W. J. and Paul K. Hatt. *Methods in Social Research.* New York 1952.

Goodwin, Geoffrey L. (ed.) *The University Teaching of International Relations.* Oxford 1951.

Green, Leslie C. "A new Departure in the Teaching of International Relations. The University of London Diploma in International Affairs". *World Affairs*, Vol. 3 (1949) p. 310 ff.

Grosser, Alfred. "L'étude des relations internationales, spécialité américaine?" *Revue française de science politique*, Vol. 6 (1956) p. 634 ff.

Guggenheim, Paul and Pitman B. Potter. "The Science of International Relations, Law, and Organization". Geneva 1940. *Geneva Studies*, Vol. 11, no. 2.

Hempel, C. G. and Paul Oppenheim. "Studies in the Logic of Explanation". *Philosophy of Science*, Vol. 15 (1948) p. 135 ff.

Jones, S. B. "A Unified Field Theory of Political Geography." *Annals of the Association of American Geographers*, Vol. 44 (1954) p. 111 ff.

Kaufmann, Felix. *Methodology of the Social Sciences.* New York 1944.

Kirk, Grayson. "Materials for the Study of International Relations." *World Politics*, Vol. 1 (1948/49) p. 426 ff.

— *The Study of International Relations in American Colleges and Universities.* New York 1947.

Kluke, Paul. "Aufgaben und Methoden zeitgeschichtlicher Forschung." *Europa-Archiv,* 10. Jahr, (1955) p. 7429 ff.

Knorr, Klaus. "Economics and International Relations: A Problem in Teaching." *Political Science Quarterly,* Vol. 62 (1947) p. 552 ff.

Lippmann, Walter. "The Shortage in Education". *The Atlantic Monthly,* (May 1954) p. 35 ff.

Manning, C. A. W. *The University Teaching of Social Science. International Relations.* Paris 1954.

Marchant, P. D. "Theory and Practice in the Study of International Relations". *International Relations,* Vol. 1 (no. 3, 1955) p. 95 ff.

Medlicott, W. N. "The Scope and Study of International History". *International Affairs,* Vol. 31 (1955) p. 413 ff.

"Meeting on University Teaching of International Relations". *International Social Science Bulletin,* Vol. 2 (1950) p. 235 ff.

Mende, Dietrich. "Internationale Beziehungen als Forschungsgegenstand". *Europa-Archiv,* 10. Jahr, (1955) p. 8373 ff.

Menzel, Eberhard. "Aufgaben und Funktionen der wissenschaftlichen Institute auf den Gebieten des Völkerrechts, der Zeitgeschichte, der Wissenschaft von der Politik und der internationalen Beziehungen." *Europa-Archiv,* 9. Jahr, (1954) p. 6249 ff.

Ogburn, W. F. (ed.) *Technology and International Relations.* Chicago 1949.

Pool, Ithiel de Sola. *Symbols of Internationalism.* Stanford 1951.

Renouvin, Pierre. "The Contribution of France to the Study of International Relations." UNESCO. *Contemporary Political Science.* Paris 1950, p. 561 ff.

— "L'histoire contemporaine des relations internationales. Orientation de recherches." *Revue historique,* Vol. 211 (1954) p. 233 ff.

Royal Institute of International Affairs. *The future of Chatham House.* London 1946.

Schuman, Frederick L. "The study of International Relations in the United States." UNESCO. *Contemporary Political Science.* Paris 1950. p. 576 ff.

Seligman, E. R. A." What are the Social Sciences?" *Encyclopaedia of the Social Sciences.* New York 1931. Vol. 1, p. 1 ff.

Snyder, Richard C., H. W. Bruck, and Burton Sapin, *Decision-making as an Approach to the study of International Politics.* Princeton 1954.

Sprout, Harold and Margaret. *Man-Milieu Relationship Hypotheses in the Context of International Politics*. Princeton 1956.

Szczerba, K. and von Schelting. "International Relations in Soviet Sociological and Legal Doctrine". UNESCO. *Contemporary Political Science*. Paris 1950. p. 551 ff.

Taylor, Thomas Griffith (ed.) *Geography in the Twentieth Century*. London 1951.

Thompson, K. W. "Toward a Theory of International Politics". *The American Political Science Review*, Vol. 49 (1955) p. 733 ff.

Thomson, David. "British Studies in International Relations 1918—1948". UNESCO. *Contemporary Political Science*. Paris 1950. p. 582 ff.

Toynbee, Arnold J. "The study of History in the Light of Current Developments." *International Affairs*, Vol. 24 (1948) p. 555 ff.

Van Wagenen, Richard W. *Research in the International Organization Field*. Princeton 1952.

Ware, Edith E. (ed.) *The Study of International Relations in the United States*. Survey for 1934. New York 1934.

Weber, Max. *Gesammelte Aufsätze zur Wissenschaftslehre*. Tübingen 1922.

Veblen, Thorstein. *The Place of Science in Modern Civilization*. New York 1919.

Webster, Charles K. "The Study of International History." *History*, Vol. 18 (1933) p. 103 ff.

Wilson, Howard E. *Universities and World Affairs*. New York 1952.

Wolfers, Arnold. "The Pole of Power and the Pole of Indifference." *World Politics*, Vol. 4 (1951/52) p. 39 ff.

Woodward, E. L. *Study of International Relations at a University*. Oxford 1945.

Wright, Quincy. *The Study of International Relations*. New York 1955.
— *(ed.) The World Community*. Chicago 1948.

Zimmern, Alfred. *The Study of International Relations*. Oxford 1931.
— (ed.) *University Teaching of International Relations. ·A Record of the Eleventh Session of the International Studies Conference*, Prague 1938. Paris 1939.
— "Education for World Citizenship," *Problems of Peace*, 5 th series (1931).

INDEX